How Drama Activates Learning

Also available from Bloomsbury

MasterClass in Drama Education: Transforming Teaching and Learning, Michael Anderson
Drama Education with Digital Technology, Edited by Michael Anderson, David Cameron and John Carroll
Learning to Teach Drama 11-18, Andy Kempe and Helen Nicholson

How Drama Activates Learning

Contemporary Research and Practice

Edited by
Michael Anderson and Julie Dunn

BLOOMSBURY
LONDON • NEW DELHI • NEW YORK • SYDNEY

Bloomsbury Academic
An imprint of Bloomsbury Publishing Plc

50 Bedford Square   1385 Broadway
London   New York
WC1B 3DP   NY 10018
UK   USA

www.bloomsbury.com

First published 2013

British Library Cataloguing-in-Publication Data
A catalogue record for this book is available from the British Library.

ISBN: HB: 978-1-4411-3634-3
PB: 978-1-4411-8589-1
ePDF: 978-1-4411-1671-0
ePub: 978-1-4411-9416-9

Library of Congress Cataloging-in-Publication Data
How drama activates learning: contemporary research and practice/[edited by]
Michael Anderson, Julie Dunn.
pages cm
Includes bibliographical references and index.
ISBN 978-1-4411-3634-3 (hardback) – ISBN 978-1-4411-1671-0 (epdf) –
ISBN 978-1-4411-9416-9 (epub) 1. Drama in education. I. Anderson, Michael,
1969– editor of compilation. II. Dunn, Julie, 1959– editor of compilation.
PN3171.H69 2013
371.39'9–dc23
2013011748

Contents

Notes on Contributors

Michael Anderson is an associate professor and associate dean for Strategic Communications in the Faculty of Education and Social Work at The University of Sydney, Australia. His research and teaching concentrates on how arts educators begin, evolve and achieve growth in their careers and how students engage with arts and technology to learn and create in arts education. This work has evolved into a program of research and publication that engages with arts classrooms directly. His recent publications explore how aesthetic education is changing in the twenty-first century. These publications include *Masterclass in Drama Education; Transforming Teaching and Learning* (2012), *Teaching the Screen, Film Education for Generation Next* (with Miranda Jefferson), *Drama with Digital Technology* (with John Carroll and David Cameron, 2009) and *Real Players: Drama, Education and Technology* (with John Carroll and David Cameron, 2006). The research reported in these books uncovers innovative linkages between drama education and theatre for young people that could significantly improve learning outcomes for students in the arts. Michael was a drama teacher and Creative Arts Consultant with the NSW DET and holds senior positions in drama curriculum development and assessment with the NSW Board of Studies. Currently, Michael is a chief investigator in two Australian Research Council major Grants, *TheatreSpace* (2007–11) and *The Role of Arts Education in Academic Motivation, Engagement, and Achievement* (2009–11).

George Belliveau is an associate professor in the Faculty of Education at the University of British Columbia, Canada, where he teaches undergraduate and graduate courses in theatre/drama education. His research interests include drama and social justice, theatre, teacher education, drama across the curriculum, Canadian theatre and ethnotheatre. His work has been published in numerous journals.

Penny Bundy is an associate professor in the School of Education and Professional Studies at Griffith University, Australia. She has been a chief investigator on several Australian Research Council Funded Linkage Projects, including *Moving On, Sustaining Culture, TheatreSpace* and *Developing Refugee Resilience*. She was a co-winner of the 2003 American Alliance for Theatre and Education Distinguished Dissertation Award and is co-editor of the *Applied Theatre Research*.

Bruce Burton is a professor and chair of Applied Theatre at Griffith University Brisbane, Australia. His teaching across the Griffith programs has been rewarded with a Carrick Australian Award for Teaching Excellence in the Humanities and the Arts. His recent research has included the use of drama to empower school students to deal with conflict and bullying. This research was awarded two ARC Linkage Grants. The first phase of the research was part of the international *DRACON* project involving Sweden, Malaysia and Australia. The second focused specifically on *Acting against Bullying* in Australian schools. He is currently a chief investigator on two further ARC-funded projects including *TheatreSpace* and *Developing Refugee Resilience*.

Helen Cahill is an associate professor in Student Wellbeing and deputy director of the Youth Research Centre, Graduate School of Education, University of Melbourne, Australia. She leads research, development and evaluation projects in the fields of youth participation and health, and teaches in the Master in Student Wellbeing program. She has developed a number of Australian and international school and community health promotion resources addressing issues related to drugs, mental health, life skills, reproductive health and HIV prevention. Helen provides training and participatory curriculum to assist artists, teachers, parents and health professionals to use applied drama methods within well-being and empowerment programs with young people. Her current work includes a focus on youth well-being and participation in southeast Asia with a five-country trial of a participatory curriculum to assist women and girls to talk about sex and gender rights. Senior consultancies include development of a youth framework to inform Unicef's approaches to working with adolescents in emergency situations in countries in the Asia-Pacific region. Her research in the field of drama focuses on the use of applied theatre to enhance resilience in young people, and the use of poststructuralist theory to inform approaches to the use of drama for social change.

David Cameron is Deputy Director of Academic Technologies, the University of Newcastle, Australia. David's research interests are in the areas of drama, digital games, social media and mobile technology. His PhD explored the similarities between some forms of educational drama and digital game-based learning.

David has a professional and teaching background in media and communication, including radio journalism and community broadcasting.

Chan, Yuk-Lan Phoebe is a lecturer at the Hong Kong Art School, where she is the convener of the Master of Applied Theatre and Drama Education Program co-presented with Griffith University, Australia. She takes up a wide range of professional practice in Drama Education and Applied Theatre, as actress, director, workshop facilitator, course planner, researcher, teacher educator and administrator. She has recently completed a large-scale drama and language program across 50 Hong Kong primary schools, while also working closely with the Theatre-in-Education Program at Oxfam, where she is involved as an actor-teacher as well as a devisor of the work that explores issues of urban poverty with secondary students. Phoebe is widely published in the field of drama education.

Julie Dunn is an associate professor at Griffith University, Australia, where she teaches in a range of undergraduate and postgraduate courses across the fields of arts education, applied theatre and educational communication. She is convenor of the Master of Applied Theatre and Drama Education Program, also taught in Hong Kong in partnership with the Hong Kong Art School. Her research is focused on improvised and playful forms of drama and the application of these forms within school and community settings. Julie is currently a chief investigator on two major Australian Research Council-funded grants: *Playful Engagement and dementia: Assessing the efficacy of applied theatre practices* (2012–15) and *Arrivals: Developing refugee resilience and effective resettlement through drama-based interventions* (2010–13). Julie has recently taken up the role of editor of *NJ: The Journal of Drama Australia*.

Robyn Ewing is a professor of Teacher Education and the Arts and ProDean (Academic), Faculty of Education and Social Work, University of Sydney, Australia, and national president of the Australian Literacy Educators Association. She has a commitment to quality teaching and learning at all levels of education and is passionate about the transformational role that the Arts can and should play in learning. Robyn's research and writing include the use of drama and literature to enhance children's English and literacy outcomes; teacher education, especially the experiences of early career teachers and the role of mentoring in their retention in the profession; sustaining curriculum innovation and evaluation, inquiry- and case-based learning and arts-informed research methodologies. She has worked as an academic mentor at a range of Sydney schools with teachers interested in reforming their curriculum practices. Along with *TheatreSpace*, Robyn is also working in partnership with Sydney Theatre Company on '*School Drama*' a project that aims to develop the drama expertise of primary teachers. Recently, she joined the board of the Sydney Story Factory.

Michael Finneran is a senior lecturer in drama education at Mary Immaculate College, University of Limerick, Ireland, where he is also Head of the Department of Arts Education and Physical Education. He holds a PhD in drama education from the University of Warwick, UK. Michael was academic director for the *International Drama in Education Research Institute* (IDiERI), held in Limerick in July 2012. He is the conference reviews editor for *RiDE: The Journal of Applied Theatre & Performance*. Michael is also a practising theatre artist, regularly directing and designing productions in Ireland.

Josephine Fleming has a long involvement in theatre for young people as a director, writer and researcher, including two artistic directorships. She has a PhD in comparative education from the University of Sydney, Australia and her work in this field has been published internationally. Josephine worked as a lead research assistant on the TheatreSpace project and is lead and co-author on a number of forthcoming publications about this project. She is currently working with Michael Anderson and others on a large research project examining the role of arts education in academic motivation, engagement and achievement.

Kelly Freebody is a lecturer in drama curriculum at the Faculty of Education and Social Work, University of Sydney, Australia. Kelly's teaching and research interests are in the areas of drama, social justice, school-community relationships and qualitative research methods. Her PhD from The University of Melbourne, Australia, used drama pedagogy to explore the ways young people in differing socioeconomic situations understood and discussed their future prospects and pathways.

Kathleen Gallagher is Professor and Canada Research Chair in Theatre, Youth and Research in Urban Schools at the Ontario Institute for Studies in Education of the University of Toronto, Canada. Kathleen has published many books and articles on drama/theatre, urban youth, school contexts, pedagogy and gender, and travels widely giving international addresses and workshops for practitioners. Her research continues to focus on questions of engagement and artistic practice, the political meanings and pedagogical spaces of the arts in schools, as well as the methodological affordances of theatre in qualitative research. Her books include: *The Theatre of Urban: Youth and Schooling in Dangerous Times* (2007); *Drama Education in the Lives of Girls: Imagining Possibilities* (2000); *How Theatre Educates: Convergences and Counterpoints with Artists, Scholars, and Advocates* (2003) and *The Methodological Dilemma: Creative, Critical and Collaborative Approaches to Qualitative Research* (2008).

Annette Harden is an early childhood educator who currently works as a preparatory year's teacher in a small, semi-rural school in South East Queensland, Australia. She has more than 30 years of experience. Her research focuses on pedagogies at the nexus of drama, play and literacy. She is currently undertaking doctoral studies at Griffith University, Brisbane, Australia. Annette previously completed her Master of Drama Education (Honours) thesis at this same institution.

Dave Kelman is an artistic director of the Education Program of Western Edge Youth Arts in western Melbourne, Australia. He is a director, playwright, drama educator and a researcher who completed his doctorate on sociocultural meaning in young people's dramatized stories at the University of Melbourne, Australia, in 2009.

Andy Kempe is head of Initial Teacher Training and a professor of Drama Education at the University of Reading, UK. He has extensive experience of working with both trainees and serving teachers in the UK and abroad. His work with students of all ages and abilities has informed numerous articles and chapters covering a wide spectrum of issues in drama, English and arts education. His *GCSE Drama Coursebook* has been a standard text in many schools since the first edition was published 20 years ago. He has published a number of curriculum drama books and papers which explore what may be learnt when history and drama are brought together. His recent publications also include 'Watching the Words: drama and poems', in Lockwood, M. (ed.), *Bringing Poetry Alive: a guide to classroom practice*; 'Laughter in the Dark: ethical aspects of drama education', in Coventon, J. (ed.), *Drama Inspires*, and 'What dramatic literature teaches about disability', in Schonmann, S. (ed.), *Key Concepts in Theatre/Drama Education*.

Sarah Marino is a primary school teacher and drama specialist currently working in London, UK. Previously she has worked as a drama adviser and a lecturer at Auckland College of Education, New Zealand and Victoria

University, Wellington, New Zealand, where she assisted with the pre-service and professional development of teachers in the area of Drama, as well as with the implementation of the New Zealand Arts Curriculum into schools. She also assisted with the development of drama resources for the New Zealand Ministry of Education, including drama handbooks, posters and online notes. She is currently enrolled in Doctoral studies at Griffith University, Brisbane, Australia.

Carole Miller is professor emeritus in the Department of Curriculum and Instruction, University of Victoria, Canada, and she holds an honorary appointment in the Faculty of Education and Social Work, University of Sydney, Australia. The recipient of an excellence in teaching award, she is a co-author of *Learning to Teach Drama: A Case Narrative Approach* (2000) and the award-winning text, *Into the Story: Language in Action through Drama* (2004). She co-chaired the 2nd International Drama in Education Research Institute (1997), was responsible for the Academic Program for the 5th World Congress of IDEA, and served as a Reflective Keynote speaker for IDEA 2007 in Hong Kong. Carole teaches and lectures internationally, most recently at the Universities of Auckland and Canterbury. In 2011 she facilitated workshops for the New Zealand Drama Association in Christchurch and Dunedin. In Australia, she taught for the Sydney Theatre Company and the University of Sydney. Articulating the relationship of literacy and drama practice to current postmodern curricula and brain/mind research, she explores pedagogies that engender competent, confident and comfortable classroom educators in drama through real and fictional conversations of experience.

Jonothan Neelands is a national teaching fellow, professor of Drama and Theatre Education and WBS Professor of Creative Education at the University of Warwick, UK. In addition to his academic profile, he is an experienced workshop leader and a drama practitioner, with a national and international reputation for delivering high-quality professional training and development opportunities. Research interests include: the theory and practice of drama and theatre education; teaching artistry and the work of teaching artists; models of cultural and creative learning, the politics of cultural and education policy making, teaching in urban settings, the sociology of educational disadvantage and the articulation of a pro-social pedagogy of arts education.

Bethany Nelson is a faculty member at Emerson College, Boston, USA, in the area of Theatre Education. She has an M.Ed from Harvard Graduate School of

Education, USA, focused on issues of at-risk multicultural populations in urban schools, and a doctorate in education from the University of Warwick, UK. She specializes in using drama with at-risk urban populations, facilitating social skills, curriculum acquisition, and providing on-site professional development for teachers. She has conducted action research in collaboration with classroom teachers, examining the efficacy of drama in urban classrooms.

Peter O'Connor is an associate professor at The University of Auckland, New Zealand, and director of the Critical Research Unit in Applied Theatre. His work in prisons, Youth Justice Centres, Psychiatric Hospitals and schools (which he says all bear striking similarities) has been informed by a desire to create theatre in spaces where beauty is rare, social justice is invisible and stories are systemically suppressed. Peter's most recent work includes a multi arts project based on Romeo and Juliet in a Youth Justice Facility. Other recent work includes a theatre in education programme focusing on hope with 7- and 8-year olds in the most damaged areas of Christchurch following the series of earthquakes.

Cecily O'Neill is the author and editor of a number of influential books on drama including *Drama Worlds* (1996), *Words into Worlds* (1998), *Drama Structures* (1982), *Dorothy Heathcote: Collected Writing on Education and Drama* (1984) and *Drama Guidelines* (1977). A collection of her articles and papers, *Structure and Spontaneity: the Process Drama of Cecily O'Neill*, edited by Philip Taylor and Christine D. Warner was published by Trentham Books in 2006. Dr. O'Neill is an Associate Artist with the Unicorn Children's Theatre in London and Resident Dramaturg for the Plays for Young Audiences Series at New York University's historic Provincetown Playhouse. She created the programme in drama education at the Ohio State University where she was an Associate Professor, and is a visiting lecturer at New York University. She is an external examiner and visiting lecturer on post-graduate degrees at universities in Ireland, the UK, USA, Canada and Australia. The University of Winchester recently awarded her an Honorary Fellowship.

John O'Toole is a professorial fellow at the University of Melbourne, Australia, and an honorary professor at Griffith University, Australia. John taught English and then drama mainly in working-class schools for 12 years, latterly as a senior teacher in charge of curriculum, before going into teacher education, where he has spent the last 35 years exploring the possibilities of drama in schools, both as an art form and as a pedagogy. He was a co-founder of the teachers' associations Drama Queensland, Drama Australia and IDEA (the International

Drama/Theatre and Education Association). He has authored and co-authored numerous books, both scholarly and for teaching, many of which have become standard texts, besides other writings and learning resources in this area, including the forgotten monograph *Oracy, the Forgotten Basic* (Queensland Ministers' Consultative Council 1991). He has taught drama with all ages and on all continents, and is also a practising playwright in educational and community theatre. He has supervised six PhD students who have won the American Alliance for Theatre and Education distinguished dissertation award, and in 2001 this organization presented him with the Judith Kase Cooper award for Lifetime Achievement.

Erika Piazzoli has recently completed her PhD at Griffith University, Australia, in the aesthetics of process drama for additional language teaching and learning. The two case studies she discusses in the publication are part of her doctoral research project, which focuses on learner engagement and teacher artistry. Erika recently presented an invited panel keynote at the *International Drama in Education Research Institute* (IDiERI), held in Limerick, Ireland, in July 2012. She has a growing number of international publications in the field of drama for language learning, including papers in *RIDE – The Journal of Applied Theatre and Performance* (2010; 2011), the *Scenario Journal* (2012), the *Drama Research Journal* (2013), as well as *Second Language Learning Through Drama* (2012) edited by J. Winston.

Monica Prendergast is Assistant Professor of Drama/Theatre Education at the University of Victoria, BC, Canada. Her research interests include; drama/theatre curriculum and pedagogy, applied drama/theatre, arts-based and practice-based research, critical pedagogies, performance theories and poetic inquiry. She is author of *Teaching Spectatorship* (2008), co-editor of *Poetic Inquiry* (2009) and the award-winning *Applied Theatre* (2009, with Juliana Saxton). Monica is co-editor of the *Canadian Journal of Practice-Based Research in Theatre* (*CJPRT*), for which she has edited a special issue on research-based applied theatre (2010) and co-edited a special issue on Shakespeare and practice-based research (2011). Forthcoming projects include a monograph on utopian thinking in drama/theatre education, a co-authored handbook on applied drama facilitation (*Applied Drama*, 2013, with Juliana Saxton), a co-edited poetic inquiry collection and a special issue on applied theatre. Monica is also a practicing theatre artist, facilitator and reviewer.

Juliana Saxton is professor emeritus in the Department of Theatre, University of Victoria and honorary professor in the Faculty of Education and Social Work, University of Sydney, Australia. Author and co-author of a number of texts on drama/theatre in education and the seminal text, *Asking Better Questions* (with Norah Morgan, 2004), her most recent publication is *Applied Drama: A Facilitator's Handbook for Working in Community* (2013), the companion volume to *Applied Theatre: International Case Studies and Challenges for Practice* (2009). She is a recipient of the University of Victoria Alumni Teacher of Excellence, a Campton Bell Lifetime Achievement Award from American Alliance for Theatre and Education and two AATE Distinguished Book Awards (2005 and 2009). An international speaker and master teacher, in 2013 the Canadian Association of Theatre Research recognized her research and mentorship with an Honorary Membership.

Christine Sinclair is head of Drama Education at the University of Melbourne, Australia. She teaches and researches across a range of arts and drama education programs, from teacher education to community, youth arts and Shakespeare. She has been a lecturer in drama, arts education at the undergraduate and post-graduate level at a number of universities and has also coordinated postgraduate programs in professional and creative writing. She is also a freelance community artist, working as a writer and director in many community settings. She has recently directed a one-woman performance based on a personal prison memoir, *Revlon and Razor* at La Mama in Melbourne, Australia. Her PhD research was based at a primary school and centred on the creation of a whole school festival of performance for children and the wider community.

Madonna Stinson is the Deputy Head of School (Academic) in the School of Education and Professional Studies, Griffith University, where she is a member of the Applied Theatre team. She has taught drama from pre-school to tertiary level and is widely recognized for her quality practice. From 2002 to 2009, she was an assistant professor at Nanyang Technological University, Singapore, where she was the recipient of five major research grants and founding director of UNESCO/NIE Centre for Arts Research in Education. She is the director of Publications for Drama Australia. Madonna is a chief investigator on the *TheatreSpace* project and is also actively working on research projects within two primary schools in Queensland, Australia.

Christine D. Warner is an associate professor at The Ohio State University in Columbus, Ohio, USA. She is a former middle and high school teacher of Language Arts and Literature. Since 2000, Christine has been a member of the faculty within the College of Education, School of Teaching and Learning. Her research focuses on the concept of interdisciplinary inquiry, literature-based curriculum, student engagement, American Indian education, and cognitive-based instruction among elementary and middle school students, within an educational setting that is facilitated by standard and newly developed drama in education methodologies.

Joe Winston is a professor of Drama at the University of Warwick, UK. He has a background in primary and middle school education and was a head teacher for 3 years before joining the staff at Warwick in 1991. He was responsible for coordinating the Arts subjects in the BA (QTS) degree and is currently the coordinator of the MA in Drama and Theatre Education. He is joint editor of Research in Drama Education, widely recognized as the leading academic journal in its field. Well known nationally and internationally for his in-service work with teachers, he has published a wide range of books and articles both of an academic and professional nature. He has recently delivered keynote addresses at international conferences in Europe and Asia. His book '*Beauty and Education*' was published in January 2010, and was reviewed as book of the week in the *Times Higher Education Supplement* in April, 2010.

Burcu Yaman Ntelioglou is a postdoctoral fellow in the Second Language Education Program at the Ontario Institute for Studies in Education (OISE), University of Toronto, Canada. She has received a PhD in education from OISE, and a Master's in education from York University, Canada. Her research focuses on second/additional language education, applied linguistics, literacy education, applied drama/theatre, urban schooling, curriculum studies and the use of participatory ethnography and digital technologies in educational research. Her articles have been published in journals like *The Journal of Adolescent and Adult Literacy, Ethnography and Education, Research in Drama Education: The Journal of Applied Theatre and Performance,* and *Theatre Research in Canada* and she has contributed chapters to *Second Language Learning through Drama* edited by Joe Winston, and *Key Concepts in Theatre/Drama Education* edited by Shifra Schonmann.

Preface

Drama and how it operates within learning contexts is the focus of a considerable and growing body of literature. In creating this book, our goal was to capture within one volume a sense of the diversity of its approaches, participants and contexts, and to offer, through research and practice, an articulation of how it 'works'.

Originally conceptualized as 'How Drama Teaches', we soon realized that this title was problematic, privileging teaching over learning. We searched, therefore, for another term – one that would better describe the work drama does in the context of learning. The word 'activate' emerged as a contender, and a quick glance through a thesaurus soon confirmed it as a more appropriate verb, for like drama itself, the word activate seems to have a chameleon-like quality that allows it to take on a variety of meanings dependent upon its context. With synonyms including stimulate, rouse, galvanize, motivate, animate, energize, make active or more active, to accelerate a reaction in, and finally in relation to scientific work, to cause to change, to make different or to cause a transformation, the word activates seems well placed to capture our understanding of how drama influences learners and learning.

Across these pages then, descriptions of practice and research will be used to examine and attempt to understand how drama, through collaboration between the skilled practitioners who structure, facilitate and aesthetically manage it, and the participants who engage with these practitioners, and importantly each other, animates, energizes and indeed activates learners and learning.

Our section headings: activating communities, activating learners and activating curriculum reflect much of the research and discussion that has taken place in our field and offer us the chance to examine a broad sweep of work created by researchers, scholars and practitioners working in diverse contexts, geographic and social, and with children, young people, and adults using many different dramatic approaches and forms. These include young people engaged as audience members within professional theatre events all along the east coast of Australia; secondary students in Hong Kong participating in Theatre in Education performances and workshops within a non-government-organization

(NGO)-funded interactive learning centre; primary school students in New Zealand, the United Kingdom, the United States, Australia and Canada, developing their understanding of a range of curriculum-related areas through classroom drama work; young people in Massachusetts, USA exploring one of Shakespeare's great plays; newly arrived refugees and immigrants working collaboratively to devise and perform rich narratives drawn from their homelands; adults in Italy building on their language skills through process drama workshops; and even very young children creating their own rich and complex dramatic worlds through play.

The claims for what drama is able to achieve across these wide-ranging contexts vary greatly, and while the field may have, in the past, made some extravagant claims about the efficacy of drama, it seems that there is now greater caution. Nevertheless, the consensus from the authors in this book suggests that drama remains an aspirational pedagogy of hope and change. However, for practitioners to harness the power of this flexible and adaptable art, the nature of its form needs to be understood. How does drama activate learning about democracy; how does it activate learning in literacy or language; how does it create a stronger sense of community; how does it support the development of cultural identity; how does it open spaces for learner agency? The case studies that are presented in these chapters create an evidence base about these questions by both investigating and celebrating drama through praxis.

For doctoral students embarking on their studies, academics generating further research, or practitioners hoping to enhance their practice, this book will offer useful connections to an array of contemporary practice, research and policy. Our experience of working in schools and communities has suggested that such a book is needed as both a self-contained reference and a starting point for further work. In addition, we hope this book will be of interest and benefit to those whose research, theoretical backgrounds and practices lie outside of drama.

Foreword

During the last 100 years, drama in education, under a variety of names, has been alternately acknowledged, repudiated, celebrated, misunderstood, included and neglected. Recent developments towards acceptance in some places and exclusion in others follow this seemingly inevitable pattern.

Countries in Asia are beginning to embrace drama as a means of promoting creativity and activating restrictive and academic curricula. In the United Kingdom, that source of so much of the theory and practice of drama in education, the government recently proposed curricular reforms that would have removed any mention of drama at the primary level and all of the arts at the secondary level. Fortunately the negative response of the education and arts communities to these proposals meant that they were shelved. In the struggle for the recognition and more importantly the acceptance of the arts as significant factors in the success of schools and students, one step forward seems to be followed almost immediately by two steps back. In this uneven and provisional educational terrain, it is some comfort to learn that drama and the other arts have been included in a new Australian Arts Curriculum. This is welcome evidence of a degree of recognition of the power and potential of drama to activate learning.

In 2008, when he was a presidential candidate, Barack Obama championed arts education and proposed reinvesting in American arts education to reinvigorate the creativity and innovation that is associated with the study of the arts. More recently, the President's Committee on Arts and the Humanities (PCAH) reported the existence of 'a growing body of research to support positive educational outcomes associated with arts-rich schools'.[1]

This will be no surprise to anyone with a knowledge of the field. During the last three decades, research findings into the value of arts education remain positive and consistent. Study after study has shown that when the arts are given space in the curriculum, there are immediate benefits to students, schools and the wider community. There is persuasive evidence that the inclusion of the arts in education motivates and engages students in learning, stimulates curiosity and fosters creativity, facilitates collaboration, and promotes significant and relevant skills.

The research, case studies and examples of practice from around the world that are assembled in this invaluable collection certainly confirm these outcomes. Each highly relevant chapter builds on existing theory, research and practice before presenting diverse illustrations of drama operating to bring about positive change. These examples demonstrate convincingly that drama, although often the least valued of the arts in the school setting, can play a vital part in achieving a wide range of personal, educational and social objectives.

The innovative researchers, teachers and facilitators who present their research and practice in these chapters are inviting students to engage with, embody, contemplate and reflect on a range of highly significant issues. Wisely, they avoid the trap of presenting drama as a solution to all the ills of society. Instead, they seek to investigate how and why engagement in these experiences takes place. Maxine Greene, whose work has inspired a generation of teachers, believes that education through the arts is an initiation into new ways of seeing, hearing, feeling and moving.[2] This is certainly true of many of the students we encounter in this book – the refugees working on identity formation or the African Australians struggling towards integration, for example.

Drama educators face considerable challenges in the present inhospitable climate. They must find ways to engage and motivate students and, at the same time, create a stimulating environment. They must provide worthwhile learning tasks for students who are increasingly turning to digital devices instead of teachers, texts, or each other in order to process new information and express ideas. For teachers and principals who are constrained by rigid curricula, standardized testing and budget cuts, the demands may seem overwhelming. But these constraints are not recent. The poet Ted Hughes, writing in 1975, remarked on the inability of creative talent to survive schooling.[3] He saw this as a symptom of a destructive mood in society as a whole, a mood that shuts down imagination and energy, and one we may recognize today.

It is odd that business and financial leaders seem to accept the importance of subjects that promote creativity and innovation more readily than curriculum planners and educational policy makers do. They acknowledge the significance of the arts not just to schools but also to the economy and see the arts as an important catalyst for learning, discovery and achievement.

While the arts certainly do not have a monopoly on the development of creativity, the approaches used in teaching drama and the arts are highly compatible with the development of the basic skills that students need for the twenty-first century. These include the ability to engage in critical thinking and problem solving, the ability to communicate effectively, the ability to collaborate, and the practical ability to translate ideas into action. In these chapters, we observe that students, led by experienced and effective teachers and facilitators, demonstrate all of these essential skills. But we also see them going beyond mere instrumental responses to the tasks they encounter. We see them learn about who they are and how they fit into the society round them, as they gradually begin to think of themselves as people who are able to work together for tolerance and social justice.

In this book, the editors present an impressive range of research, theory and practice in a remarkable variety of contexts, and demonstrate that drama in the hands of gifted and experienced practitioners can bring about transformative learning. Above all, the impression we are left with is a hopeful one. While there are dedicated, skilled and experienced practitioners like those whose work is celebrated here, there is hope that drama will continue to make a difference in the lives of students, educators, schools and communities.

Cecily O'Neill

January 2013

Notes

1 Reinvesting in Arts Education, 2011. PCAH
2 Maxine Greene (2001), *Variations on a Blue Guitar: The Lincoln Center Institute Lectures on Aesthetic Education.* NY: Teachers College Press, p. 188.
3 Ted Hughes (1975), In *Winter Pollen.* London: Heinemann, p. 31.

Acknowledgements

Creating a book as extensive as this one does not happen easily. We would like to thank all the individuals and groups who have contributed to its development. First we especially acknowledge our contributing authors who have been so generous with the sharing of their work. Without exception they are outstanding practitioners and researchers who have engaged thoughtfully and thoroughly across the editorial process. Thanks as well to the Bloomsbury team, including Alison Baker (Senior Commissioning Editor), Claire Cooper (Production Editor) and Rosie Pattinson (Assistant Editor) who have been so helpful, supportive and professional across all stages of the publication process.

Another vote of thanks goes to our families, especially Rebecca Barrett and Greg Dunn who have so lovingly and patiently supported our efforts.

On behalf of all the authors we would also like to acknowledge the support provided by the schools, community organizations, funding bodies and universities who have so generously made available access and financial support for the various research projects detailed in this book.

Finally, our deep gratitude is extended to the children and young people whose responses within and beyond drama continually surprise and challenge us, motivating our practice and research.

Part One

Introduction

Drama and Learning: Landscapes of an Aspirational Pedagogy

Michael Anderson and Julie Dunn

Introduction

There is something striking and distinctive about the art form of drama and the way it works in drama education and applied theatre contexts. This distinctiveness springs in part from the claims it makes and the aspirations it holds in relation to learning. It aspires to be a space for activating individual learning, learning about community and learning within the curriculum. Beyond that, it claims a place not at the periphery of learning but at its very centre (Bolton 1984), as a way to make learning in other areas and for other purposes possible. In part this book is an attempt to make these aspirations more tangible; to pin down and support through examples of research and practice those areas that drama claims to be able to influence. The reader can assess whether these aspirations are justified by reading the chapters that follow and assessing the claims made within them.

This chapter attempts to prepare the reader for this assessment process by surveying the broader social, economic and educational landscapes that this paradoxical learning area inhabits. Its paradox lies in the fact that drama has its roots in the ancient art of theatre while much of the practice of contemporary drama educators has been heavily informed and influenced by the practices and thinking of individuals such as Boal, Bolton, Freire, Heathcote and others whose philosophies were developed as a result of the political, social and educational conditions present in the mid to late twentieth century. Our stance however, and we believe the stance of other contributors to this book, is that there is no dichotomy in this relationship, no concerns about hierarchies or binaries. Rather, the practices outlined here reveal that the facilitators, teachers, artists, participants and members of the audience who engage with drama do so in an eclectic manner, drawing upon multiple aspects of its nature, celebrating its rich diversity of form. In this way, drama reveals itself to be what Heathcote (2006) calls an 'ancient shapeshifter', capable of adapting and transforming itself to activate many different types of learning by engaging its participants and audiences using approaches ranging from those normally associated with theatre to those that are more improvisational and processual in nature.

In the sections below, the social and educational landscapes this aspirational and flexible art form inhabits will be explored.

The social landscape

In his 2009 inauguration speech, Barack Obama said:

> That we are in the midst of crisis is now well understood. Our nation is at war, against a far-reaching network of violence and hatred. Our economy is badly weakened, a consequence of greed and irresponsibility on the part of some, but also our collective failure to make hard choices and prepare the nation for a new age. Homes have been lost; jobs shed; businesses shuttered. Our healthcare is too costly; our schools fail too many; and each day brings further evidence that the ways we use energy strengthen our adversaries and threaten our planet (Obama 2009).

Although referring to the United States, Obama's words offer a somewhat pessimistic view that is reflective of a world beset by economic, social, political and environmental crises. It suggests that the contemporary world is somehow out of joint, where things have changed, where institutions we once depended on for certainty, have become discredited, de-stabilized or no longer exist. Sardar (2010) believes that this is a period of postnormality, suggesting that it is characterized by uncertainty, rapid change, realignment of power, upheaval and chaotic behaviour. He says:

> We live in an in-between period where old orthodoxies are dying, new ones have yet to be born, and very few things seem to make sense. Ours is a transitional age, a time without the confidence that we can return to any past we have known and with no confidence in any path to a desirable, attainable or sustainable future (p. 435).

Sardar goes on to nominate three key features of our times including complexity, chaos and contradictions. Of course, some may argue that chaos, complexity and contradictions have always been part of human experience but the combination of geopolitical power shifting from the West to the East, the power and pervasiveness of technology, the globalized implications of local actions and the tight interconnection of money, power and influence and their ability to ruin lives clearly set our times apart from those apparent late last century. Back then, there was comfort in the so-called 'normalities' of economic efficiency, the free market, good governance, religion, democracy and integrity; however, all these seem somehow less reliable in the face of what at times feels like considerable and multiple insoluble and networked threats confronting our world. Sardar (2010) concludes his article by suggesting that the only way to transition out of this period is through imagination and creativity. He argues:

> Imagination is the main tool, indeed I would suggest the only tool, which takes us from simple reasoned analysis to higher synthesis. While imagination is intangible, it creates and shapes our reality; while a mental tool, it affects our behaviour and expectations (p. 444).

This invoking of imagination as a response to chaos, complexity and contradiction suggests that the Arts, with the rich opportunities they collectively offer for the development of imagination and creativity, might be needed to provide the approaches to learning that are best suited to meet these challenges head-on. Disappointingly however, the educational landscape has, in many places, become an even more hostile space for the Arts in general and drama in particular. The following section examines this landscape.

Drama in the educational landscape: Testing times

In the last few years, we have seen the passing of several of the key pioneers of contemporary drama and applied theatre, whose innovative practice and research historically provided leadership for the field. Their influence is stamped, not only in these pages but also in the pages of the abundant scholarship and research they have inspired. At the same time, there has been a springing up of new practitioners and scholars from more diverse backgrounds, global regions and fields of learning, and to some extent this diversity is reflected in the authors who have contributed chapters to this book. There are new names and new areas of scholarship alongside those that have long established reputations in drama education and applied theatre. However, these new voices (together with the old ones) operate within a landscape that is uneven. It's a landscape marked by abundant growth in some places and concerning stunted growth in others. It is a landscape where an emphasis on 'systemic improvement' prevails on a global scale and where governments are prone to make policy decisions in haste in order to achieve 'improvements' that are not necessarily informed by quality research. As Levin (2010, p. 739) notes:

> Ever since public schools began, governments have been looking for ways to improve them. Over the last few decades many efforts have been made to address education issues through policy at various levels. Looking at these efforts around the world, one can only conclude that they have often been motivated more by untested assumptions or beliefs or by issues currently in the public mind, than by evidence of value or potential impact.

In such a culture, performativity and accountability prevail as key features. Ball (2003, p. 215) defines performativity within this context as 'a technology, a culture and a mode of regulation that employs judgments, comparisons and displays as a means of incentive, control, attrition and change – based on rewards (both material and symbolic)'. In such a culture, only those forms of knowing that can be easily measured through 'validated' or 'benchmarked' testing programs such as PISA become explicitly valued, with complex areas of human knowledge and understanding often being reduced to a series of right and wrong answers delivered through multiple choice tests. Here too, schools and indeed universities are compared to one another, not according to the support they offer children and young people as they develop their social, emotional, artistic, spiritual and cognitive selves, but rather, on websites such as *My School* (Australian Curriculum and Reporting Authority 2010) and *My University* (Australian Government 2012) where interactive graphs, charts and tables make it 'easy' for communities to rank one learning environment against another. It is also unfortunately a culture where young people, under pressure to 'succeed', crumble and where economic and social advantage and disadvantage become magnified and entrenched.

In this difficult landscape, drama has struggled to maintain its existing footing, has made limited progress in attaining new sites for development and in some cases, lost ground. In the United Kingdom, for example, where drama was once a powerhouse, there seems to have been a concerted political effort to systematically remove it from classrooms. Its exclusion from the UK national curriculum accompanied by a reduction in training places for drama teachers in universities are causes for concern. Within Australia on the other hand, drama has recently been included (along with dance, visual arts, music and media arts) in a new Australian Arts Curriculum (Australian Curriculum and Reporting Authority 2011) after a seemingly endless and at times internecine struggle with those who would seek to push it to the periphery of learning. How much support is offered to ensure this fledgling curriculum gets off the ground remains to be seen, but it is a positive sign in a global landscape that in other regions seems far more hostile.

In addition, while exciting large-scale agendas such as *Creative Partnerships* in the UK (Sharp et al. 2006) and much smaller ones like the *Yonder Project* in disadvantaged schools in Queensland (Gattenhof 2012) generated rich opportunities for children and young people to work alongside professional artists to develop artistic, social, personal and cognitive skills, funding for both of these initiatives has now dried up.

Meanwhile, although Applied Theatre continues to grow steadily in some parts of Asia and New Zealand, and isolated teams of researchers in this field have been able to attract quality research funding, artists and practitioners globally have faced real difficulties in gaining the industry and government support needed to apply the findings of this research across longer-term projects.

What does the research say?

Paradoxically, as this culture of performativity has invaded the international education landscape, compelling research extending back to *Champions of Change* (Fiske 1999), *Reviewing Education and the Arts Project* (REAP) (Hetland and Winner 2001), *Critical Links* (Deasy 2002) and the *Evaluation of School-based Arts Education Programmes in Australian Schools* (ACER 2004) highlights the critical importance of the Arts for learning. This includes Robyn Ewing's recent survey of international and national arts research entitled *The Arts and Australian Education: realising potential* (2010). This report identifies the role and effect of arts-rich programming in schools and in the broader community, while also considering the policy and practice implications of that research. Taken together, these reports provide compelling evidence of the positive role the Arts can play in enriching learning, with this now substantial body of work demonstrating why they deserve a space closer to the centre rather than the periphery of learning. Yet, with some notable exceptions, Arts disciplines across the globe struggle for curriculum space.

Ironically, in spite of this marginalization, further research funding has been provided to examine the benefits that the Arts in general and drama in particular have to offer (and some of these are projects are described in this book). For example, in the Australian context alone, drama educators have been funded to explore how drama can combat bullying and manage conflict in schools (O'Toole et al. 2005); young people's preferences in the theatre through the TheatreSpaces program (Sinclair 2011; Martin et al. 2012); how marginalized students are supported through drama and the arts (O'Brien and Donelan 2008); how drama and other art forms motivate and engage students in learning across the curriculum (Munday et al. 2012); and how drama and applied theatre can support the development of refugee resilience, particularly through the development of oral and written literacy (Dunn et al. 2012).

Of perhaps most significance internationally has been the large-scale '*Drama Improves Lisbon Key Competences in Education*' (DICE) Project (Cooper 2010). This two-year EU-funded cross-cultural (Hungary, Czech Republic, Netherlands, Norway, Palestine, Poland, Portugal, Romania, Serbia, Slovenia, Sweden and United Kingdom) project investigated the effects of educational theatre and drama on five of the eight Lisbon Key Competences. In the introduction to the project the chief investigators argue that:

> Educational theatre and drama practitioners have believed in the efficacy of their work for a long time, but until now it has rarely been measured with scientific tools. In the DICE project, several dozen educational theatre and drama practitioners from twelve countries, with the widest theoretical and professional background, have allied forces with academics (psychologists and sociologists), to measure the impact of educational theatre and drama (2010, p. 1).

Much valuable research is outlined in the final DICE report, with much of it underscoring the results of previous studies focused on the benefits of the Arts more generally (including the international Arts research discussed above). Specifically, it reveals (p. 1) that compared with peers who have not participated in any educational theatre and drama programmes, theatre and drama participants were assessed more highly by their teachers in all aspects; felt more confident in reading and understanding tasks; felt more confident in communication; were more likely to feel that they are creative; were better at problem solving; were better at coping with stress; were significantly more tolerant towards both minorities and foreigners; were more active citizens; were more empathic; and were more innovative and entrepreneurial.

These substantial claims, supported by evidence from a team of international, multidisciplinary researchers, drawing on both quantitative and qualitative data sets, provide crucial evidence base for the benefits of drama and real support for its claims as an aspirational pedagogy.

Conclusion

The challenge that inspired this book was to create a volume that identified, through research and practice, the particular features of drama – to map its coastlines, peaks and valleys to interpret and understand its potential within contemporary social and educational landscapes. In the chapters that follow, the diversity of drama as an art form will be revealed, with each set of chapter authors examining particular features that make it a potential activator of learning. Armed with the understanding these chapters offer, artists/educators working in schools and community settings may be able to expand the reach of drama into new landscapes. Fortunately, this process is already underway as applied theatre practitioners have found ways to take participatory drama and theatre into natural disaster zones, jails, hospitals, aged-care facilities and war zones, creating new spaces and places for understanding and participation. However, much work is needed to re-engage and re-activate landscapes paralysed by an over-emphasis on performativity and limited by thinking that edges towards the 'post-normal'.

References

Australian Curriculum, Assessment and Reporting Authority (ACARA) (2010), *Draft Shape of the Australian Curriculum: The Arts*. http://www.acara.edu.au/verve/_resources/Draft+Shape+Of+The+Australian+Curriculum+The+Arts-FINAL.pdf. Accessed 12 December 2012.

—(2011), *Shape of the Australian Curriculum: The Arts*. http://www.acara.edu.au/verve/_resources/Shape_of_the_Australian_Curriculum_The_Arts_-_Compressed.pdf. Accessed 2 December 2012.

—(2012a), *My School*. Retrieved from www.myschool.edu.au

Australian Government (2012), *My University*. Accessed 12 December 2012.

Ball, S. J. (2003), 'The teacher's soul and the terrors of performativity'. *Journal of Education Policy*, 18, (2), 215–28.

Bolton, G. M. (1984), *Drama as Education: An Argument for Placing Drama at the Centre of the Curriculum*. London: Longman.

Bryce, J., Mendelovits, J., Beavis, A., McQueen, J., and Adams, I. (2004), *Evaluation of School-based Arts Education Programmes in Australian Schools*. Melbourne: Australian Council for Educational Research.

Cooper, C. (2010), *Making a World of Difference: A DICE Resource for Practitioners on Educational Theatre and Drama. DICE–Drama Improves Lisbon Key Competences in Education*. DICE consortium.

Deasy, R. J. (2002), *Critical Links: Learning in the Arts and Student Academic and Social Development. Arts Education Partnership, One Massachusetts Ave., NW, Suite 700, Washington, DC 20001-1431*. Web site: http://www. aep-arts. org/

Dunn, J., Bundy, P., and Woodrow, N. (2012), 'Combining drama pedagogy with digital technologies to support the language learning needs of newly arrived refugee children: a classroom case study'. *Research in Drama Education: The Journal of Applied Theatre and Performance*, 17, (4), 477–99.

Ewing, R. (2010), 'The arts and Australian education: Realising potential', in *Australian Education Review No. 58*. Melbourne: Australian Council for Educational Research.

Fiske, E. B. (ed.) (1999), *Champions of Change: The Impact of the Arts on Learning*. Arts Education Partnership.

Freire, P. (1973), *Education for Critical Consciousness*, vol. 1. Continuum International Publishing Group.

Gattenhof, S. (2012), 'The Yonder Project: Literacy and social competency development in primary school students through co-creation of live performance'. *NJ The Journal of Drama Australia*, 36, (1), 50–61.

Heathcote, D. (2006), 'Foreword', in J. Carroll, M. Anderson and D. Cameron (eds), *Real Players? Drama, Technology and Education*. Stoke-On-Trent: Trentham, pp. ix–xix.

Hetland, L. and Winner, E. (2001), 'The arts & academic achievement: What the evidence shows'. *AEPR*, 102, (5), 3–6.

Levin, B. (2010), 'Governments and education reform: Some lessons from the last 50 years'. *Journal of Education Policy*, 25, (6), 739–47.

Martin, A. J., Anderson, M., and Adams, R. J. (2012), 'What Determines Young People's Engagement with Performing Arts Events?'. *Leisure Sciences*, 34, (4), 314–31.

Munday, C., Anderson, M., Gibson, R., Martin, A., and Sudmalis, D. (2012), *Probing the Possibilities and Potential of the Arts for Effective Student Learning*. Paper presented at the 7th International Drama in Education Research Institute, Limerick, Ireland, 10–15th July 2012.

Obama, P. B. (2009), Inaugural Address, 20 January 2009. Transcript available at http://www.nytimes.com/2009/01/20/us/politics/20text-obama.html.

O'Brien, A. and Donelan, K. (2007), 'Risky business: Engaging marginalised young people in the creative arts'. *The International Journal of the Arts in Society*, 1, (6), 15–23.

O'Toole, J. R., Burton, B. V., and Plunkett, A. (2005), *Cooling Conflict: A New Approach to Managing Bullying and Conflict in Schools*. Frenchs Forest, NSW: Pearson Longman.

Sardar, Z. (2010), 'Welcome to postnormal times'. *Futures*, 42, (5), 435–44.

Sharp, C., Pye, D., Blackmore, J., Brown, E., Eames, A., Easton, C., and Benton, T. (2006), *National Evaluation of Creative Partnerships – Final Report*. London: Creative Partnerships.

Sinclair, C. (2011), 'Why and with whom? A study of young people as theatre-goers in Australia'. *NJ – Drama Australia Journal*, 34, 71–83.

Part Two

Activating Communities

2

Drama, Community and Achievement: Together I'm Someone

Jonothan Neelands and Bethany Nelson

In the last two days, the people or the person making the choices for me was myself. . . . I would be directed to do something and would be like, "Okay, so how am I going to go about doing this?" instead of going "So what do you want me to do?"

Lily, age 16

Foucault contends that power is always in and around classrooms (Foucault 1977). Power, and the reinforcement of White, middle-class power in particular, is apparent in curriculum, the racial and class make-up of staff, faculty, and administration of schools, and in the buildings themselves (Ladson-Billings 2009; Gallagher 2007; Fine and Weis 2003). Consequently, students of colour are often denied access to power in schools, and lack a sense of agency in settings when they 'have little power over their learning, when learning has little relevance to their lives and aspirations, or when they are devalued or marginalized' (McInerney 2009, p. 24). These are familiar dynamics in the hegemonic culture of public schools in the United States, in which the achievement of students of colour and the urban poor lags far behind that of their White, middle-class counterparts (Ladson-Billings 2009; Fraser and Honneth 2003; Tatum 2003; Nieto 2002; Macedo and Bartolomé 1999).

The establishment of community in schools is a critical factor for facilitating school success for urban students of colour (Ladson-Billings 2009). Further, recent research points to the interaction of community and power for students of colour in urban settings, in which power is a consequence of classroom community and may result in improved academic outcomes (Nelson 2011).

Creating drama curriculum that brings students' knowledge and capabilities into the classroom, gives them the opportunity to explore ideas about power, and practice the skills underlying the acquisition and exercise of power in a supportive and reliable community are key to culturally relevant schooling in which students can develop a sense of agency.

Community, agency and AT/D

The fact that drama is an effective way to build community is nearly a truism in the field, and in previous research on the effects of drama on classroom community, there is compelling evidence that drama structures facilitate a sense of collaboration between teachers and students, and within the peer group (Neelands 2009a, 2009b; Nelson 2009; Gallagher 2007; Manley and O'Neill 1997). In particular, forms of Applied Theatre and Drama (AT/D) facilitate the development of community among participants (Neelands 2009a; Prentki and Preston 2009; Gallagher 2007; Cahill 2002; Nelson et al. 2001; Manley and O'Neill 1997). AT/D, defined by Nicholson (2005) as 'dramatic activity that primarily exist outside conventional mainstream theatre institutions, and which are specifically intended to benefit individuals, communities and societies' (p. 2) and characterized as 'the relationship between theatre practice, social efficacy, and community building' (p. 2), is a vehicle for building community among young people engaged in its practice. AT/D also provides the opportunity to introduce politicized curriculum which directly addresses questions of power and agency, and which, through active learning structures, encourages participants to explore and practice their application (Prendergast and Saxton 2009; Prentki and Preston 2009; Ackroyd 2000).

The project discussed below builds on work by Jonothan Neelands (2011a, 2010, 2009a), in which ensemble built through drama teaching is foundational to its effectiveness as a democratizing approach to working with complex cultural texts, Kathleen Gallagher's (2007) thesis on the effects, on urban students of colour, of various forms of drama teaching on the development of understandings of unequal power dynamics, and the work of Bethany Nelson (2009, 2011) on the role of both ensemble/community and understanding unequal power dynamics on improvement in achievement by students of colour in urban environments.

The project

This chapter reflects on the outcomes of a recent study conducted with urban students of colour in an under-resourced high school in Chelsea, Massachusetts. The primary focus of the study was a 9-week playmaking project, conducted by Bethany Nelson, considering the role of AT/D in the development of community on the class of students who participated, as well as consideration of the effects of that community on the academic performance of the students. The study included a two-day (5-hour) workshop on Hamlet, conducted by Jonothan Neelands and utilizing the 'rehearsal room' approach developed and widely utilized by the Royal Shakespeare Company (RSC), which uses a variety of drama structures and strategies for teaching Shakespeare. This chapter will consider in detail the complex interaction of community, power and academic engagement/outcomes demonstrated by the students during the Hamlet drama work.

Michael Boyd (2009), artistic director of the RSC, identifies 13 values and behaviours required for and enabled by their ensemble working style. These foster community and creativity among the diverse artists with whom they work and provide a foundation for artistic and intellectual achievement through drama. In considering the working dynamics and outcomes of the Hamlet drama work conducted with the Chelsea students, and those of the playmaking project within which it was embedded, four of these behaviours emerged as central to the success of both components. They are (as defined by Boyd): (1) Cooperation: the intense, unobstructed traffic between artists at play and the surrender of the self to a connection with others, even while making demands on ourselves; (2) Altruism: the moral imagination and the social perception to realize that the whole is greater than the sum of its parts. The stronger help the weaker, rather than choreographing the weak to make the strong look good; (3) Trust: the ability to be appallingly honest and to experiment without fear; and (4) Empathy: caring for others with a forensic curiosity that constantly seeks new ways of being together and creating together.

In this chapter, we will discuss the ways in which AT/D, both the ensemble-based rehearsal room approach of RSC and the playmaking process, fosters these values and behaviours. Both drama approaches offer a heterotopic environment that is culturally relevant for low-income students of colour in an urban environment, resulting in improved academic risk taking, creative thinking and problem solving.

Methods

The playmaking project was designed to explore the role of community in fostering the twenty-first-century learning skills of academic risk taking, creative thinking, problem solving, collaboration and communication with under-resourced urban students of colour, guided by the following research questions:

- What are the effects of using playmaking structures to facilitate students' exploration of the obstacles they face in their lives?
- What are the effects of using playmaking structures to facilitate students' identity formation as change agents in the issues that affect their lives?
- In what ways does the community established in the drama classroom affect students' engagement and facility with the material?

(In this case, playmaking refers to the use of a variety of drama/theatre techniques to develop original performance work with students which emphasizes the exploration of their ideas with the goal of developing their voices and visions of the world and bringing them to a broader audience.)

This was a qualitative study using participant ethnography as a primary form of data collection followed by participant interviews. This structure generated information-rich case studies in a social constructivist frame, with the goal of 'deeply understanding specific cases within a particular context' (Patton 2002, p. 546). Triangulation was provided by the presence of an outside ethnographer familiar with AT/D.

The 2-day workshop on Hamlet, while initially intended as a stand-alone experience unconnected to the larger study, employed AT/D structures which built on ensemble skills developed during the first half of the playmaking experience, generated surprising academic outcomes for the students, and positively affected the subsequent devising process. Consequently, it provides the opportunity for a concise and intensive consideration of the interaction of the dynamics observed throughout the project. Ethnography of the first day of the workshop was provided by the outside ethnographer; the second day was videotaped. A post-workshop discussion was conducted with the entire group, and four students of various ages were interviewed at length.

The Hamlet workshop

The workshop was conducted with a Drama 2 class of 18 students at Chelsea High School, an urban high school outside of Boston, Massachusetts, USA. The group was equally divided by gender but mixed by age (ranging from 14 to 19 years) and race/ethnicity (1 Black student, 13 Latino students from a variety of cultures and 4 White students). A third of the students had Individualized Education Plans, indicating a range of (primarily language-based) learning issues for which specific accommodations must be made.

The workshop was conducted 1 month into the 9-week playmaking project. In the first 4 weeks of the project, we had used a variety of strategies, including improvisation, tableau, scene work, movement and games to begin development of an original performance piece about the obstacles that the students face in their lives and their resources for dealing with those obstacles. The Hamlet workshop also utilized a series of games, improvisations, tableaux, and movement, first to introduce the students to the setting, plot, and characters in Hamlet and then subsequently to explore the interpersonal and political dynamics of the piece through the Shakespearean text. Discussion includes outcomes for the entire group of participants, with particular focus on three students, Bryan, Deneice and Kadiatu, who engaged in surprising ways during the experience. (Kadiatu's academic prowess allowed her to more fully engage in the community of the class; Bryan and Deneice, already integrated members of the classroom community, took increased intellectual and academic risks.)

Community and playmaking

The students in the Drama 2 class demonstrated a pronounced degree of community from the start of the project, partly as the result of 3 weeks (15 classes) of community building work with which Amy, the drama teacher, always begins the semester. In the initial observation of the class, students touched in non-sexual ways, regardless of gender. Their comfort with and physical support of one another was demonstrated repeatedly in games, improvisation and scene work. For example, during an extended exploration of obstacles, in which a student, with eyes closed, was verbally guided across a multilayer obstacle by a partner, it became a tradition to catch the blind student in a big hug when he/she made it over the obstacle safely. The students' trust in each other caused them to 'experiment without fear' and their empathy was apparent when, as a group, they carefully spotted others climbing over high obstacles. Further, they demonstrated empathy and altruism during games, voluntarily taking the role of 'It' for slower or less adept class members, or giving up their place in a group for a peer who needed a spot.

The students themselves repeatedly identified the importance of their community, and in an early exploration of obstacles they face in their lives, four of the five scenes depicted the loss of relationship with family/community members to substance abuse or death. The growth of trust among the students through their shared experiences in the playmaking structures fostered a Sense of Community (SOC), described in psychological literature as the feeling that one is part of a readily available and supportive structure characterized by belonging, connectedness, influence, and fulfillment of needs (Sarason 1986; McMillan and Chavis 1986), characteristics which closely reflect the trust, empathy, cooperation, and altruism identified by Boyd. As the SOC among the students grew, their risk taking in sharing personal stories did as well. Students cautiously introduced stories of family conflict, peer pressure to do drugs and hinted at physical abuse.

Community and Hamlet

I was proudest of the group was how well we got to know each other and how well we worked together . . . it felt good because everyone put in an effort to get through. When you came, everything started getting serious and we started thinking.

Lily, age 16

The students' SOC was equally apparent during the Hamlet workshop. In 'huggies', a grouping warm-up, boys and girls embraced with equal abandon, and the community of students made certain that every member was included. In an early exercise, four boys were charged with creating a scene in which Claudius and Gertrude are wed, and they touched, held hands, and looked lovingly at one another without embarrassment. During a 'speed through' of the plot of the play, boys and girls jumped in to play a variety of male and female roles, irrespective of gender and without any apparent self-consciousness, embodying the 'disinterested actor' that Neelands, in a line with Hannah Arendt, Amartya Sen and John Rawls among others, claims is essential to citizen identity and participation in democracy (Neelands 2011b).

This familiar community dynamic served as a foundation for the introduction of unfamiliar and challenging material and allowed the students to take risks in engaging with it. In an atmosphere of trust, empathy, cooperation and altruism, embodied by the students and supported by the workshop leader, the students were eager participants, in spite of the 'intimidating' topic and complex language. This stands in stark contrast to the students' self-reports on earlier experiences in studying Shakespeare. As one student put it:

> This summer . . . in this program you have to read a Shakespeare book and it was so hard for me to read it . . . and I'd find myself staying up until like 3:00 trying to figure out certain words and . . . when we had a quiz, or we had to act a scene out, I found myself lost.
>
> Kadiatu, 18

The entire group took risks in reading aloud and using the language of the play, and they shared talk time and leadership in the development of various pieces. For example, in creating a 'scary' interpretation of a segment of the Ghost's speech, one group with three strong leaders traded leadership of the various components of the task, cleanly and without discussion or negotiation. However, even the quietest members of the group contributed ideas which were enacted in the final presentation.

Community, power and achievement

The literature detailing the studies of power in the field of psychology tells us that power has profound effects on all aspects of human functioning and is a tool for personal growth and social transformation (Keltner et al. 2003). Power stimulates action, and communal power orientation characterizes individuals who use their power for the communal good rather than their personal good (Chen et al. 2001), which describes the community function of the students in the Drama 2 class. These constructs provide a foundation for considering the effect of community and power on the improved academic functioning of the students who participated in the Hamlet workshop relative to their performance as students in other contexts.

The work the students engaged in during the Hamlet workshop both benefited from the emerging community of the group and fostered its growth, resulting in academic engagement, risk taking, and comprehension of the play by all of the students. The students articulated sophisticated understandings of the play's themes, which were built socially through sustained dialogue and tolerance for diverse ideas and reactions. In so doing, they were rehearsing how the political participation, dialogue and social interaction associated with ensemble-based theatre making and learning becomes in Rawl's (2001) definition of democracy – 'the exercise of public reason.'

From the first day of the workshop the Chelsea students participated fully, though they were initially cautious about the Shakespearean language. Their engagement was fostered in part by the approach to the material, which initially used game structures, tableau and movement, capturing the interest of this kinesthetic group. Their facility with tableau and image work was apparent during an early task, in which they were prompted to create five tableaux, entitled Spying, Romance, Madness, A funeral which becomes a wedding and Rejection. The workshop leader's open appreciation of their work fostered increased risk-taking in subsequent pieces, as when they were asked to incorporate 'scraps' of text into the images. The students' sense of pride at having been selected to participate in the workshop and the ongoing positive feedback on their work generated escalating returns. As one student put it:

> Fernando: "Some teachers have high expectations in a negative manner. They (the workshop leaders) had high expectations for us too, but . . . gave us the high expectation that we *can*."

In return, the workshop leader sought permission to build 'earned authority' with the group by encouraging them to exercise their right to establish and negotiate rules for the engagement that were freely accepted rather than fearfully followed. This 'uncrowning of power' which is associated with the particular social dynamic required for participatory forms of drama and democracy, allowed the group to play with their own individual relationships to power, collective deliberation and knowledge.

There were three sequences of process work which particularly demonstrated the complex interaction between community, power and academic engagement for the Chelsea students in the medium of drama. First, towards the end of Day 1, the students were charged with visualizing the castle of Elsinore. Half of the group, in role as soldiers, imagined the exterior, and the other half, as servants, the interior. Each 'servant' was then paired with a 'soldier,' and they toured one another by turns through 'their' part of the castle. The student being toured was required to keep his/her eyes closed, and the commitment of both the tour guide and the toured during this experience was substantial. They described the castle, adding appropriate detail well beyond that provided in the images they'd seen, and spoke in serious tones throughout. Allowing themselves to be led with eyes closed built on trust and cooperation established in the obstacle work during the playmaking project, but the ease with which the students followed their tour guides stood in contrast to the giggly nervousness which often accompanied 'blind' exercises with this group, and their serious attention to the content of the tour was marked. Of particular note: Kadiatu, who had been generally reticent and somewhat withdrawn during the playmaking structures on which the group had been working for the previous month, was visibly engaged. She was descriptive and detailed as she toured her partner through the imaginary castle, gesturing expansively with her hands and speaking with energy and enthusiasm. Her obvious engagement and willingness to guide her partner physically stood in stark contrast to her previous behaviour.

Day 2 of the workshop was built on Day 1, and the students were able to recall both the story and the plot elements introduced on the first day and reconstruct the physical scene of the king's death and the queen's marriage. Further, they were able to extrapolate from the story and infer themes and character motivations. When asked, they identified the themes of the play as murder, love, trickery, betrayal, madness, and being spied on, and, in answer to the question of why the ghost of the dead king might come back, they chorused, 'Revenge!' The students later reflected on the dynamics of the workshop which facilitated this academic outcome.

> Monica: "Instead of just being in a classroom . . . we get to act out the words and
> *feel* them . . ."
> Abel: ". . . we actually lived it, we became part of it and that just helps overall."
> Kristie: "I just liked that we got to act it out, like, ourselves and interpret it . . .
> and I like the fact that we got into a deeper level of it."

The second component of the structure that demonstrates the interaction between community, power and academic engagement occurred in the middle of Day 2. During an extended sequence exploring Hamlet's reactions to the betrayal of his mother and uncle, his father's death, and his loss of the crown, the students demonstrated substantial engagement and insight, as well as the ability to grapple successfully with the text. The first surprise occurred when Bryan volunteered to portray Hamlet during this sequence. Bryan's literacy is 6 years below expected competencies for his grade level, and at the first meeting of the playmaking project, he placed himself on the far end of a continuum regarding unwillingness to speak in public. He explained, 'I meet people, I get scared.' Though he was an integrated member of the classroom community, he had rarely volunteered during playmaking when discussing complex topics, so his offer to portray Hamlet was unexpected. This is a good reminder that finding empathy with characters and lives that are different is more than the hug of sympathy; it's a call to action and is essential to a healthy polity.

The students then discussed where Hamlet might go to be alone and think. The suggestions were creative and built on the understandings of the castle and the time period the students had explored the previous day, as well as drawing connections to their own lives. From a range of options which included a crypt, the battlements, his room, to see a friend or to see his girlfriend, Bryan selected the crypt. The group was then charged with positioning Hamlet in a way that would communicate his emotional state. The first position, sitting with head down, arm resting on knee, invited the following interpretations, which drew on their own experiences of the emotions Hamlet was feeling and demonstrated understanding of the character:

> Jerry: "He's confused."
> Fernando: "My dad can't be dead. He's in a denial state."
> Luis: "He's anxious."
> Francisco: "If he's against the wall, to make himself feel safe. Even in
>   kindergarten, you get sent into the corner, you push back against the wall."

Kadiatu then volunteered to shape Hamlet into an alternative position and offered an insightful, complex explanation of Hamlet's thinking in this moment, integrating his anger at the murder, confusion at his mother's betrayal, sense that he should do something about it, anger at being robbed of the throne, and the fact that he had no one to turn to. In interview, Kadiatu was able to make explicit the connections between the situation in Hamlet's life and her own experiences.

> Kadiatu: ". . . stuff like that happens every day; kids find themselves getting new
>   parents after a father dies, or the mom getting married too fast because they're
>   vulnerable and don't want to be alone . . . so I finally got to understanding
>   Hamlet . . . I see this happening within my family . . ."

Kadiatu is reflecting on the 'inside-out' learning associated with playful learning. Rather than passively obeying imposed interpretations and choices of meaning, she is bringing and trusting in what she knows about the world to the old play. In so doing, she discovers what Walter Benjamin called the 'traces' of the original play that find resonances in her lived experience now.

The final component of the structure which merits separate discussion for its demonstration of the effect of cooperation, altruism, trust and empathy on academic risk-taking and skills development is a sequence in which students read aloud Hamlet's soliloquy, interpreted its meaning, and created movements which physicalized words selected from the text. This was followed by more complex physicalizations of two sections of text from the Ghost. In this sequence, every student in the group, rather than self-selected volunteers, was responsible for speaking from the text and conveying its meaning. In a group with widely divergent reading levels and facility with English, this was a challenging task. However, the students, standing in a circle, read the text without hesitation, looking up periodically for reassurance from workshop leader and peers as they struggled with unfamiliar vocabulary. Even the most challenged readers addressed the task vigorously, speaking clearly and with volume. While reading aloud can be a simple thing, for students who have English as an additional language (EAL) and for those with language-based learning disabilities, it can be a public display of incompetence which carries the potential for substantial social stigma (Tatum 2003; Alatis and Tan 2001). Further, when asked to name any words they didn't understand, the students, even the most academically successful of the group, were willing to acknowledge the vocabulary with which they were unfamiliar. Students and workshop leader then worked in concert to decode and clarify the meaning and pronunciation of the language. We were reminded of some of Jerome Bruner's propositions about playfulness and playful learners; that in play there is a reduction in the consequences of error and failure. Playful learners are less easily frustrated and treat their failures not as daunting or humiliating but as informative (1983).

When students were then asked to choose a word they liked for the next task, many selected words which had previously been unknown to them. They were charged with creating action to communicate the feeling/meaning of the word in the context of the text. This level of abstraction with language is not always accessible for EAL and language-challenged learners (Alatis and Tan 2001); however, the students produced complex and moving images. Most notable in this section was the students' emphasis on working for a high-quality outcome, and their success at doing so. For example, Deneice, who is socially integrated but academically cautious due to a language processing delay, pushed her partner, an academic and social leader, to reconsider the choice she had made and suggested a more complex and effective action. Kadiatu and Shanice, both normally reticent, committed fully to their large, open movements for 'everlasting' and 'remember', and incorporated the use of multiple levels in their images. Oskar, usually the comedian in the group, created creepy and memorable movements for 'incestuous' and 'self-slaughter' with his partner. When they repeated the gestures around the circle silently, the atmosphere created was eerie and touching by turns.

This success seemed to feed their risk taking and engagement in the last two sequences of the day. Both integrated text and movement around two speeches of the Ghost. Several moments stood out in relation to community, trust and learning. First, one student paraphrased a line from the previous soliloquy in discussing suicide as a possible option for Hamlet, referencing the 'Everlasting canon against self-slaughter' (three of these four words had been unfamiliar to him when the text was introduced). Second, Deneice risked translating a piece of text that no one else in the group would try ('make thy two eyes start from their spheres'), then later explained the story of the entire speech in her own words with clarity and insight. Finally, when assigned longer phrases from the text to physicalize through a series of gestures, several of the most cautious and quiet students, including Deneice and Kadiatu, pushed their groups to commit fully to the language and bring the emotions of the speech into their actions, resulting in effective outcomes. These were the acts of players making their own interpretative choices from the old text based in their 'exercise of public reason'. Through shared dialogue charged with the vulnerability and tolerance that characterizes pro-social playful relationships, students found their own individual values changing and growing in the processes of deliberation and decision making. In developing their shared actions in this workshop, they were also nurturing a vital, second-order identity as a citizen, as an agent, in their own worlds of social and political choice.

Conclusion

Since freshman year I've been getting straight A's, but I never really felt like I understood the plays that we read in class. But by acting it out for these last two days, it helped me get a different view on things, like my opinions did matter, and in my own way I can get to the themes that he wanted us to get, not just the way that someone told me that I should think.

Alfredo, age 18

Complicated characters will only reach you if you are trying to reach them.

Lily, age 16

The cooperation, altruism, trust and empathy demonstrated in both the ensemble-building experience of the Hamlet drama work and the community-centered playmaking experience contributed to academic outcomes that were substantially stronger than expected, based on the students' range of literary skills and analytical capabilities in other learning environments. Of particular interest is the circular nature of the interaction between community, power, and achievement through drama. The community demonstrated by the students seemed to generate a sense of power/agency fostering academic risk taking, the success of which reinforced the students' sense of agency, elevating the status of the community and increasing its strength and importance. The impact of this growth was felt in the playmaking which followed, as student community and academic effort/achievement increased noticeably for all students. The students who were most changed during the workshop, Bryan, Deneice and Kadiatu, continued to demonstrate improved academic engagement and social risk taking throughout the playmaking project.

Acts of theatre, socially made and shared as lived experience, offer a paradigm for engaging urban youth in explorations of power, agency and the distribution of economic and cultural capital. Further research is needed to explore the potential of these dynamics and their effects in different environments, including replication of this study with other urban populations, and consideration of other drama forms in generating community and achievement outcomes. Most important for these authors is further research into the value of theatre and drama for exploring unequal power dynamics and facilitating student understandings of the sociocultural obstacles they face in their lives. For the urban young in particular, drama and theatre are concrete means for gaining what Freire called the *vital knowledge* which becomes solidarity.

References

Ackroyd, J. (2000), 'Applied theatre: Problems and possibilities'. *Applied Theatre Journal*, 1: http://www.gu.edu.au/centre/atr/. Accessed 16 April 2004.

Alatis, J. and Tan, A-H. (2001), *Georgetown University Roundtable on Languages and Linguistics, 1999*. Washington, DC: Georgetown University Press.

Boyd, M. (2009), 'Building relationships'. *The Stage*, 2 April 2009.

Bruner, J. (1983), *Play, Language and Thought Peabody Journal of Education*, 60, (3), *The Legacy of Nicholas Hobbs: Research on Education and Human Development in the Public Interest: Part 1* (Spring 1983), pp. 60–9.

Cahill, H. (2002), 'Teaching for community: Empowerment through drama'. *Melbourne Studies in Education*, 43, (2), 12–25.

Chen, S., Lee-Chai, A. Y., and Bargh, J. A. (2001), 'Relationship orientation as a moderator of the effects of social power [Electronic version]'. *Journal of Personality and Social Psychology*, 80, 173–87.

Fine, M. and Weis, L. (2003), *Silenced Voices and Extraordinary Conversations… Re-imagining Schools*. New York: Teachers College Press.

Foucault, M. (1977), *Discipline and Punish: The Birth of the Prison*. New York: Pantheon.

Fraser, N. and Honneth, A. (2003), *Redistribution or Recognition: A Political-philosophical Exchange*. London: Verso.

Gallagher, K. (2007), *The Theatre of Urban: Youth and Schooling in Dangerous Times*. Toronto: University of Toronto Press.

Keltner, D., Gruenfeld, D. H., and Anderson, C. (2003), 'Power, approach, and inhibition [Electronic version]'. *Psychological Review*, 110, 265–84.

Ladson-Billings, G. (1994, 2009), *The Dreamkeepers. Successful Teachers of African American Children*. San Francisco: Jossey-Bass Publishers.

Macedo, D. and Bartolomé, L. I. (1999), *Dancing with Bigotry. Beyond the Politics of Tolerance*. New York: St. Martin's Press.

Manley, A. and O'Neill, C. (1997), *Dreamseekers. Creative Approaches to the African American Heritage*. Portsmouth: Heinemann.

McInerney, P. (2009), 'Toward a critical pedagogy of engagement for alienated youth: Insights from Freire and school-based research'. *Critical Studies in Education*, 50, (1), 23–35.

McMillan, D. W. and Chavis, D. M. (1986), 'Sense of community: A definition and theory [Electronic version]'. *Journal of Community Psychology*, 14, (1), 6–23.

Neelands, J. (2009a), 'The art of togetherness'. *NJ*, 33, (1), 9–18.

—(2009b), 'Acting together: Ensemble as a democratic process in art and life'. *Research in Drama Education: The Journal of Applied Theatre and Performance*, 14, (2), 173–89.

—(2010), 'The wheel is come full circle: Learning to play with Shakespeare', in N. Monk, C. Rutter, J. Neelands and H. Heron (eds), *Open-space Learning: A Study in Transdisciplinary Pedagogy*. London: Bloomsbury.

—(2011a), 'There is some soul of good: An action-centred approach to teaching Shakespeare in schools'. *Shakespeare Survey*, 64, 240–51.

—(2011b), 'Drama as creative learning', in J. Sefton-Green et al. (eds), *The Routledge International Handbook of Creative Learning*. London: Routledge, pp. 168–76.

Nelson, B. (2009), 'Beyond belonging: The relationship between community and power for urban students of color'. *Drama Research: International Journal of Drama in Education*, 1, 60–74.

—(2011), 'I made myself: Playmaking as a pedagogy of change with urban youth'. *Research in Drama Education Journal: The Journal of Applied Theatre*, 16, (2), 157–72.

Nelson, B., Colby, R., and McIlrath, M. (2001), '"Having their say": The effects of using role with an urban middle school class'. *Youth Theatre Journal*, 15, 59–69.

Nicholson, H. (2005), *Applied Drama: The Gift of Theatre*. New York: Palgrave Macmillan.

Nieto, S. (2002), *Language, Culture, and Teaching. Critical Perspectives for a New Century*. Mahwah: Lawrence Erlbaum Associates.

Patton, M. Q. (2002), *Qualitative Research and Evaluation Methods*, 3rd edn. London: Sage Publications Ltd.

Prendergast, M. and Saxton, J. (eds) (2009), *Applied Theatre: International Case Studies and Challenges for Practice*. Chicago: Intellect, The University of Chicago Press.

Prentki, T. and Preston, S. (eds) (2009), *The Applied Theatre Reader*. New York: Routledge.

Rawls, J. (2001), *Justice as Fairness: A Restatement*. Cambridge, MA: Harvard University Press.

Sarason, S. B. (1986), 'The emergence of a conceptual center'. *Journal of Community Psychology*, 14, (4), 405–7.

Tatum, B. D. (1997, 2003), *Why are All the Black Kids Sitting Together in the Cafeteria? And Other Conversations about Race*. New York: Basic Books.

3

Drama, Cultural Leadership and Reflective Practice: Taking the Road to Zamunda

Chris Sinclair and Dave Kelman

The authors acknowledge the important contributions to this chapter of Western Edge artists Dave Cuong Nguyen, Jane Rafe, and the Flemington Theatre Group: Damitou Edao, Mazna Komba, Maki Issa, Daniel Haile Michael, Solomon Salew, Munira Younus. Photographs by Huang Tran Nguyen.

Prologue – Travelling to Zamunda

Strong me – I am a citizen of the world
Weaker me – I am an African-Australian
Among Africans in Australia – I am African
Overseas – I am an Aussie. (Flemington Theatre Group, 2012)

Monday 2 April 2012, Flemington Community Centre

The large general purpose room is a crush of people – parents, friends, young children, grandparents, arts workers, representatives of funding bodies, interested outsiders, but mostly, people from the local community. There is only just enough room for all to find a seat or a perch on some tables at the back. The room is buzzing.

The play begins. A grandmother is remembering a traditional tale from Africa, The Cloud Princess. She begins 'Cloud People have never married those who live in earth.' (Gordon 2002)

There is a ripple of expectation as children from the local primary school appear to help with the telling – the first layers of the story begin to unfold.

Before long the play is in full swing. The actors are playing up to the larger than expected and highly excitable audience. There is much laughter and murmurs of recognition as the unusual love story of Abe, the Afro-Australian boy, and Sara, the African Princess, develops on the 'stage'. The action moves to Sara's home, the mythical place called Zamunda, where traditional values are protected and respected, most of all by Sara's father, the Chief.

> Our theatre is a mirror reflecting the community: taking the fictional stories of our community and reflecting them back, representing different sections of the community and treating them with respect. (Flemington Theatre Group 2012)

The play reaches its climax. Abe, the outsider, confronts the Chief. Abe has, surprisingly, triumphed over the many impossible tests set for him by the Chief and the people of Zamunda. Abe and Sara declare their love and the Chief must decide if he is to bless them or banish them. He does both and the play ends on the knife-edge moment of decision for the young couple – do they stay together and find a new place of belonging, or do they separate?

The grandmother concludes the tale of the Cloud Princess and the audience, thrilled, rise to their feet in applause and appreciation.

> Our theatre is meaningful and educational for our people and for the wider community. It is a social commentary. It doesn't have a closed meaning: it is open to interpretation but it can't be misleading – we don't want fabrication or stereotypical perspectives. We can show challenges and problems and we are not afraid to portray negative aspects of our community but it must always be insightful. (Flemington Theatre Group 2012)

Introduction

We begin our chapter with this brief account of a community theatre event, accompanied by a commentary from the young people who made the work. The commentary, drawn from the reflections of the young theatre makers, we believe draws attention to their artistry and the sense of community that their work engenders; and to the power a reflective process has to enrich understanding.

In part one of this chapter, we problematize notions of community, identity and pedagogy as they emerge from an artistic practice that sits at the crossroads of cultural action and education. Our exploration is grounded in theoretical understandings of culturally democratic community arts practices, and this informs our consideration of community theatre. We explore the nuanced ways

Figure 3.1 Flemington Theatre Group Zamunda Performance , Photo credit – Huang Tran Nguyen.

in which drama activates learning in and through a specific community theatre event – the making and performing of *Zamunda* by the Flemington Theatre Group. In part two, we arrive at an understanding of the critical symbiosis between artistry and pedagogy, and between action and reflection, when emerging artists set out to express, enact and enrich their individual and community identities through the creation of a theatre event for that community.

Part one

Community, community theatre and power

Brice Heath proposes that there is value in being part of a community, and that this is heightened through 'feelings of uniqueness or special qualities that set them apart from other such entities' (Brice Heath 2002, p. 142). These 'feelings of uniqueness' also draw attention to the problematic nature of 'community' as a construct. For example, communities are often both 'self-defining' and 'self-limiting' (Brice Heath 2002, p. 142), which suggests that there are rules for belonging and exclusion for those who do not 'fit'. Belonging to a community can give an individual a sense of agency and identity, especially when there are opportunities for the community to express itself and to be affirmed, which, some theorists say, is a core function of culture, or cultural expression. As Raymond Williams observes in his seminal discussion of culture: 'every human society has its own shape, its own purposes, its own meanings. Every human society expresses these, in institutions, and in arts and learning' (Williams 1989, p. 4).

Martin Mulligan states that finding the cultural spaces in which community is created or affirmed is dependent on the need the community feels to engage in such activities:

> Sometimes the experience of community is valued by enough people to ensure that they constantly create opportunities for the expression, or avowal, of community. Obviously that happens in some settings more than in others (Mulligan 2012).

The need or desire for communities to explore and express their identity brings this examination of community building and indeed community pedagogies into the domains of community arts practice and community cultural development. Barbara Myerhoff writes of the individual and collective desire to find and experience 'arenas for appearing' and maintains, like Williams, that this is an essential function of culture. According to Myerhoff, 'arenas for appearing are essential, and culture serves as both stage and mirror, providing opportunities for self and collective proclamations of being.' (Myerhoff 1980, p. 24)

For some groups, locating and managing these opportunities can be fraught. Some communities are culturally or socially marginalized and have little access to opportunities to express and explore their needs or identity either through the arts or other means. For these groups, the opportunity to engage in an act of community such as a community theatre event can be compelling and affirming, but can also raise issues of power and cultural dominance. As Mulligan reminds us community is not an unambiguous social concept and it can also manifest a 'dark side' (Mulligan 2012).

There are often unacknowledged power relations between various participants in a group situated at the borders of the community, and the artistic facilitator/s who may come from outside the community, but bring with them the authority of art-form expertise as well as organizational, practical and financial resources. The concept of cultural democracy (Watt 1991, Neelands 2010), where there is open and, notionally, equal access to the resources (material, space, skills) for expression through performance or other artistic forms, becomes an important principle in a community theatre paradigm which seeks to build and enrich community.

While questions of power, resources and artistic integrity recur as challenges to community theatre, through our research and practice we have come to believe that in the enacting of community identities through theatre, powerful learning is possible for participants, facilitators and audience members. This is the starting point for our exploration of the nexus between learning and art as it occurs in a specific community theatre practice.

The theoretical framework

Our context is a culturally and linguistically diverse community setting. Emerging theatre makers work with experienced community theatre facilitators as they seek to clarify and then communicate what it means to be first-generation refugees and migrants. Their theatre making is an avenue for exploring and expressing their identities. Our theoretical framework responds to a number of key themes (and sub-themes) which emerge from this specific context. These are:

- Activating learning through artistry.
  - Aesthetic learning.
- Agency and learning.
  - Negotiating voice and power.
- Dramaturgy as a pedagogic process.
- Critical reflection as a tool for learning through artistic practice.

Activating learning through artistry

Bennett Reimer describes works of art in the following way:

> A work of art in some cultural settings is generally conceived to be a product while in others it is more widely construed to be a process. (Reimer 1992)

In a culturally democratic model of community theatre, it is both a process and a product. It is the shaping of aesthetic elements: a purposeful manipulation of the symbolic languages of theatre to inform form and content in a collective demonstration of artistry as *process*. Then, in the moment of performance in the community setting, it is a collective demonstration of artistry as *product*.

At the heart of this engagement with artistry lies the potential for powerful learning, and, central to the artistic meaning making is an experience of the aesthetic, or, as Augusto Boal proposes, an aesthetic space. Boal's thesis is that the experience of inhabiting an aesthetic space can promote 'knowledge and discovery, cognition and recognition', liberating memory and imagination (Boal 1995, p. 20). Through the properties of the aesthetic space, art and pedagogy meet.

A number of theorists make the case for aesthetic engagement as a site for learning. Penny Bundy offers an elaboration that learning through drama is generated out of a deep 'aesthetic engagement' involving self-acceptance, self-responsibility, other-acceptance, personal surrender, attentiveness and presence (Bundy 2003, p. 2). John O'Toole (1992) makes clear that this process is intellectual as well as affective. He observes that when the 'sensuous internalisation of meaning is ... externalised and made cognitively explicit, knowledge is generated. The knowledge that emerges as dramatic meaning is neither just propositional comprehension nor sensuous apprehension, it is a fusion of both'. (O'Toole 1992, p. 98) Although very different as practitioners, Boal, Bundy and O'Toole identify the need to generate an artistic space in which participants can experience a deep immersion in the dramatic fiction while maintaining a consciousness of the dual nature of the experience, a phenomenon that Boal describes as 'metaxis' (Boal 1995).

Agency and voice

A key catalyst for learning within an 'aesthetic space' is the agency of participants. According to Boal, an aesthetic space is a space in which many voices can be heard; dissent can be tested; difference and diversity can be expressed and celebrated; or a space for silence in which the unnamable or the difficult story can be signified; where oppression can be identified and addressed (Salverson 1996, pp. 181–91). Boal describes his idealistic vision of the theatre as a site for learning in the following way:

> Theatre is powerful because we create an aesthetic space where everything is both magnified and dichotomous . . . Theatre is telescopic because it brings close what is far away and makes bigger what is small. These characteristics of the aesthetic space make it extremely powerful in analysing our situation . . . the aesthetic space allows democratic interchange, allows us to say, 'OK, that's the way things are but not the way things should be, and now I'm going to create an image of how I want the world to be'. (Boal 1995, p. 49)

Dramaturgy as an agent for artistry and pedagogy

While the search for solutions in Boal's process could be seen by some as simplistic and utopian, his model of creating an aesthetic space in which ideas can be explored 'on the floor' and considered through the lens of the dramatic fiction clarifies the presence of a powerful pedagogic tool.

The process used to generate the performance script for *Zamunda* involved the deep aesthetic engagement that characterizes process drama and the use of an aesthetic space as a forum for dialogue. These approaches were integrated into a dramaturgical process for play building that held pedagogy at its core.

Barba defines dramaturgy as the blending of writing and direction into 'the weave of the performance' (1985 p. 75). Dramaturges work inside a devising process to shape dramatic meaning. They respond, within the practice, to deepen aesthetic engagement or to heighten awareness of key moments of dramatic significance. This approach also involves 'structural thinking', an evolving understanding of 'how shape or structure affects interpretation' (Turner and Behrndt 2008, p. 164). The 'reading' of a particular performance text concerns the interplay between dramatic form and narrative to generate meaning:

> . . . a story is understood not only in terms of what happens, but in terms of the ways in which we recount it, order it, negotiate it, structure it. The 'narratives' of all these works are not merely structures of linked events, but forms that encapsulate questions, effects, emotions, stories and discourses. (Turner and Behrndt 2008, p. 29)

In a community arts context, it is also the job of the dramaturge to make the participants aware of these processes so that they become cognizant (or meta-cognizant) of the challenging process of constructing dramatic meaning for their own community. This story-building process is based on complex dialogues between participants and artistic facilitator/educators – both within the fiction and outside it – in which both agents retain and actively defend their own identities (Freire 1998, p. 246).

Reflective practice supports this dramaturgical activity and can be a catalyst for powerful learning in the community theatre context, as we learned when working with the Flemington Theatre Group. A reflective practitioner stance can be taken up by both facilitators and community participants and can serve to illuminate and expand the possibilities of the art making during and after the work. We discuss the place of critical reflection as an agent for learning in the coming section, and place it within the context of a discussion on pedagogy as an explicit function of community theatre-making practice.

Critical reflection as a tool for learning through artistic practice

> It is not just that [the facilitator] will provide care in the form of physical skills...
> Rather it is a moment in which each must decide how to meet the other and what
> to do with the moment . . . Problem solving is involved of course, but it is preceded
> by a moment of receptivity – one in which the full humanity of both parties is
> recognized – and it is followed by a return to the human other in all his or her
> fullness. (Simons 2002)

The teaching function of facilitators and artists is often implicit, rather than explicit in community theatre. However, pedagogy provides a central structural element to the collective art-making process, through which the core elements of artistry and agency are enabled. We are arguing in this discussion that processes of critical reflection embedded in the art-making activity can provide a key to developing an artistic pedagogy in community theatre.

Donald Schön's influence on reflective practice in education and in the arts is well documented. Artistic practitioners become researchers into their own practice as they reflect in action or later, on action (Schön cited in Taylor 1996, p. 28). This process involves 'mutuality, engagement with artistic materials, multiple perspectives, individual style, and transformative participation in artistic endeavours in which reflective processes are central' (Burnard 2009, p. 10). Further, Schön suggests that the artist/practitioner is no longer separating the means and the ends of a process, but regarding them 'interactively' while framing and acting upon 'a problematic situation'. Saville Kusher extends Schön's notion of interactivity as a key dynamic, proposing that 'inter-subjectivity' and mutuality are also important:

> Reflective practice is based in inter-subjectivity and mutual exploration of lives,
> especially in collaboration with young people—but always within broader contexts
> of authority and politics. (Kushner 2006, p. 14)

Drawing on Stenhouse, Kushner further builds on Schön's work to advocate for a model of reflective practice in the arts that is

- Purposeful while also connected to the art-making project as a whole;
- Collaborative, as shared endeavour rather than an individual, inward-looking process; and,
- Essentially political. (Kushner 2006)

Kushner's emphasis on collaborative enquiry, where together the group seeks to understand and make meaning of their collective practice and the broader sociopolitical intent of what is being made and how it is being communicated, is a most useful way of understanding the Flemington Theatre Group as reflective practitioners: they are learning through and about their art while embracing the greater shared project of pursuing expressions of identity and cultural belonging.

In part two of this chapter, we examine the artistic and learning practices of the Flemington Theatre Group (FTG) and explore some of the ways in which emerging theatre makers, through reflection on their own art making and performance, acquire a language and conceptual tools to begin to become cultural leaders in their own community.

Part two

The Flemington Theatre Group – becoming community

> The interactions within a group of people who choose to see themselves as a community continually alter the nature of that community, so that it is always in a state of 'becoming'. (Watt 1991, p. 61)

This exemplar is an account of a community of young theatre makers who find themselves in a state of 'becoming': becoming artists; becoming cultural leaders

Figure 3.2 Flemington Theatre Group Zamunda Performance image 2, Photo credit – Huang Tran Nguyen.

in their community; becoming adults in the space between a traditional world and a contemporary world; and becoming researchers and collaborators. At the heart of this story are the parallel processes of drama and critical reflection, as experienced by young artists negotiating the complex intersections of culture, identity and collaborative art making while they are engaged in making and performing a play for and about their own community.

In 2011, we initiated a participatory research project to run in tandem with a theatre-making project undertaken by the Flemington Theatre Group, a group of emerging artists mainly from Horn of Africa refugee backgrounds in the Western suburbs of Melbourne. As researchers and community artists ourselves, we wondered how an engagement with a reflective process framed as reflective practitioner enquiry might support and enrich the creative work these young people were involved in, and whether it might contribute to the development of cultural leadership by young people within their community.

Context

The FTG is a company of 12 young people aged between 17 and 23, living in the Flemington Commission Flats and surrounding suburbs, and predominantly from Horn of Africa refugee backgrounds. The group is a major initiative of Western Edge Youth Arts, an organization which collaborates with young people under the age of 26 from diverse cultures and backgrounds.

Many of the FTG members have grown up with Western Edge, starting as participants in various school and after-school projects. Over the years, a self-determining performing group has emerged. They have committed to using theatre to express and interrogate cultural identity with the continued support and mentorship of Western Edge and two community artists in particular, Dave Kelman and Dave Cuong Nguyen.

FTG sees themselves, and are seen by many, as community leaders in Flemington. They aim to be role models for other young people while representing the concerns of the older generation, creating spaces for community and generating cross-generational dialogue through their art making. Their commitment to making theatre by and for their own marginalized refugee community is central to their work and they see themselves as representing the experience and values of that community through their art.

In 2011–12, the company agreed to take part in a participatory research project in partnership with Western Edge and the Melbourne Graduate

School of Education at the University of Melbourne. There were several notable outcomes of the group's engagement with this project. The company formulated a Manifesto. This provided an articulation of their own understanding of their artistic practice and their goals and intentions as a group. They then presented the Manifesto and accompanying research findings at an Arts Education Colloquium at the University of Melbourne, attended by academics; community arts stakeholders, including artists, young people and policy makers; and their friends and supporters. This event emerged as a living representation of the learning which took place during and after the *Zamunda* project.

Research meets practice – the evolution of reflective practitioners

The central aim of this project was for experienced practitioner researchers to provide a framework through which the skills and insights generated in reflective practitioner research could be used by emerging artists to inform their developing practice. The reflective processes were guided by two trusted mentors, Kelman and Nguyen, during the workshops and rehearsals, and in interviews and two focus group sessions set aside for review and reflection, facilitated and recorded by Jane Rafe, a research assistant and community artist well known to the group. Workshops and group interviews produced robust and challenging discussions, with individuals questioning decisions and the direction of the group and the play.

The acquisition of a confident language of practice to emerge from the developing research–artistry paradigm relates powerfully to several ongoing concerns for this group of young community artists (and possibly for many groups in the community arts sector). These are the issues of power, agency and marginalization. The introduction of a participatory research methodology centred on reflective practice unexpectedly provided tools for the emerging artists not only to address questions around their art-making processes, purposes and responsibilities, but their relationships with artistic facilitators, with their own community and with the broader community.

Agency and learning – negotiating voice and power

For the Flemington Theatre Group, the issue of the power relations between young artist and facilitator as 'outsider' was negotiated and renegotiated repeatedly, through the discussions about the script, about what it meant to be African, and what it meant to be African in Australia, and about how these meanings should be written and represented in the performance text. The role of reflective practice ultimately became pivotal in these ongoing and challenging artistic transactions.

The young artists voiced their experiences of marginalization as a central tension in their quest for identity as a theatre group and as Afro-Australian individuals. They were mindful that the large-scale theatre event was not part of everyday life in their community. By generating this kind of performance, they were positioning themselves at the heart of the community, but also, somewhat paradoxically, at its margins, as they tested the behaviours expected of young Africans living in a migrant community context.

The large turnout of people who would not normally attend a theatrical performance, and the importance the FTG attributed to the community context in which their work occurred, suggests that there was a need for the Horn of Africa community in Flemington to affirm their identity through a performance event. However, this event became both interrogation and affirmation, in the way that Bhabha suggests, when he says, 'all forms of culture are continually in a process of hybridity' (Bhabha 1994, p. 211).

This perspective is particularly pertinent for newly arrived refugee communities (such as the Horn of Africa community in Flemington) where the differences in experience and cultural understanding between generations are often very wide. Engaging with the complex and shifting cultural context of Afro-Australian cultural identity could be seen to place this project in a cultural 'third space', defined by Bhabha as a space where 'new structures of authority and new political initiatives' displace the histories which constitutes the space in the first instance (Bhabha 1994, p. 211). The young people occupied a 'third space' where aesthetic and cultural concerns could be freely expressed through the crafting of the play and the enactment of Afro-Australian identities. Two members of the FTG, Solomon and Mazna, express their understanding of how this cultural tension was explored in the work:

It's saying the essence of who we are as African Australians is first we're Africans, I mean we have to recognise where we came from and always draw back to our roots, to create different relationships and pathways into society for us to survive, that's what the Chief is saying in the play. (Soloman Salew)

Creating the piece was a struggle because we were trying to decipher who we were – deciphering our identity within Australian society. (Mazna Komba)

Storytelling as cultural agency

> Our process is story and meaning over form. (Flemington Theatre Group 2012)

As this bold statement from their Manifesto indicates, the process of play building for the FTG was predicated on a fundamental commitment to story. In the making of *Zamunda*, there was a complex interweaving of fiction, folk tale, meta-narrative, and personal experience. As noted earlier, the group had a keen awareness of their community audience for *Zamunda* and a sense of telling their stories back to them, as well as telling their own. Maki Issa explains:

> We are strict on how you tell a story – how correct it is. Every line has its own debate. In FTG you can't make bullshit and get away with it. We make the script page by page, each page is a revelation. (Maki Issa)

In the process of constructing *Zamunda*, there was a deliberate, yet evolving need to juxtapose the personal with the cultural, the 'real' story with the 'authentic' story, to embrace the hybridity that Bhabha refers to. And, in this pursuit of complexity in narrative structure and style, the group sought to actively resist the temptation to spin the 'victim narrative' (Nagle 2007; Jeffers 2010) that they saw as characteristic of much community theatre. As a member of a refugee community, as well as a member of the Flemington Theatre Group, Maki articulates what was at stake when finding the balance between a truthful representation and his version of the 'victim narrative':

> We work with fictional stories. It's different to autobiographical stories – refugee victim narratives. I don't want you to cry for me. I don't want you to feel it, I just want you to know it. It's more healing. It takes out the element of guilt and replaces it with developed consciousness. (Maki Issa)

Another member of the FTG, Solomon suggests that the nexus between the personal and the cultural is fundamental to the artistic practice of the group and to their drive to explore issues of identity:

> Some of the material in the play is based on our stories, they are our reality. These actual stories work together with the cultural stories to represent the community but at the same time we are the community and we are representing ourselves by telling them our own stories. (Solomon Salew)

What Solomon refers to as 'cultural stories' are the folkloric underpinnings of *Zamunda* and the multiple ways in which they have been adapted to address the cultural context of the African Diaspora in inner Melbourne. He is describing a cultural balancing act between stories that reflect the group's experience as young Africans with complex shifting identities and stories that represent deeper cultural values that resonate for the whole community. The project became a process of exploring what those values were and how they related to young Africans growing up in Australia.

Artistic Pedagogy – dramaturgy in action

In the making of *Zamunda*, dramaturgy involved a multifaceted process that shaped dramatic form and narrative meaning, while developing a performance text specific to the context.

For the group, the dramaturgical role of artistic facilitators Kelman and Nguyen, shapers of the performance text, was recognized as critical to the group's capacity to deliver a successful outcome, but without compromising their own efficacy and agency as final arbiters of content and intent. Munira Younus observed:

> Sometimes, the Daves say, 'ok what do you think, how do you guys think we should do this?' And the group puts out all of their ideas and the Daves mold it. It all comes from what everyone thinks, how everyone feels, how they think it should be done, and they, mold it. (Munira Younus)

Through the project there was a tangible exchange of skills. The 'Two Daves' provided dramaturgical skills in narrative construction, performance building, character construction and communication. The young artists provided nuanced introductions for the facilitators and others, to the cultures from which they came, and, to the issues which confronted them daily and the moral/political statements they wished to make about those issues through theatre. The young people also brought aptitude and facility with dialogue, constructions and interpretations of cultural and social meanings, in and beyond the theatre, to the play-making processes. These provided critical moments of artistic pedagogy which enabled the group to engage their community at a deep level:

> In Zamunda, we represented their perception of their culture. There is a togetherness generated by this process: for that moment, most of our minds are on the same level – through us showing our story, which is their story. This puts us in a position to communicate, educate, share, generate empathy and voice concerns. (Soloman Salew)

Flemington Theatre Group – building community

The collaboration between FTG and Western Edge is ongoing, and for all the participants the work is at times difficult and confronting. The exchange between the two key groups, the facilitating artists and the young emerging artists, is evolving. Many of the young people have worked with Western Edge since their early years of high school, now almost 8 years. Over this time, trust and a recognizable way of working 'on the floor' have accrued but it remains a complex and challenging cultural transaction in which artistic statements are constantly analysed and challenged.

In the making of *Zamunda*, the FTG sought to make their art relevant and culturally significant to themselves and their community. In our view, they were able to do this because they were engaged in a process of critical reflection while making their performance. Their process echoed Kushner's model of reflective practice in that it was purposeful (and connected to the artistic practice), collaborative, and essentially political (Kushner 2006). At every stage of the process, the emerging artists questioned what they were creating and what its impact might be on their community. In addition, through the introduction of a methodological framework, they also developed a meta-cognitive awareness of the processes they were engaged in. This led to a challenging and sophisticated practice that not only effectively engaged its cultural context but also allowed the young people to develop further as art makers and emerging leaders in their own community.

For the FTG, it was in the making of the artistic work, and the reflection that ensued, that these young theatre makers experienced the most profound learning. Their discoveries were grounded in the artistic and cultural problem-solving required for the creation of a culturally sensitive performance event where the goals transcended the immediate and personal, and pointed to a bigger picture of belonging and becoming. Their reflection in- and on- action was not an end in itself, but was part of the larger purpose, of contributing to their community in its state of becoming.

> A person's understanding of who they are and where they belong is at the core of their wellbeing. I believe exploring culture through an imaginative arts process allows them to discover and understand new perspectives and facets of 'identity'. The 'Arts' within Community Development . . . has a huge role in promoting social and cultural awareness within people's environments. (Mazna Komba)

References

Barba, E. (1985), 'The nature of dramaturgy: Describing actions at work'. *New Theatre Quarterly*, 1, (1), 75–8.

Bhabha, H. (1994), *The Location of Culture*. New York and London: Routledge.

Boal, A. (1995), *The Rainbow of Desire: The Boal Method of Theatre and Therapy*, trans. A. Jackson. New York: Routledge.

Brice Heath, S. (2002), 'Working with community', in G. Dees, J. Emerson and P. Economy (eds), *Strategic Tools for Social Entrepreneurs*. New York: John Wiley, pp. 141–60.

Bundy, P. (2003), 'Creating opportunities for aesthetic engagement: Reflections from a drama classroom'. *Applied Theatre Researcher*, 4, (2), 1443–726.

Burnard, P. (2006), 'Rethinking the imperatives for reflective practices in arts education', in P. Burnard and S. Hennessy (eds), *Reflective Practice in Arts Education*. Dordrecht: Springer, pp. 3–12.

Flemington Theatre Group (2012), *The Flemington Manifesto*, presented at *Arts Education Colloquium*. University of Melbourne, May 2012.

Freire, P. (1998), 'Pedagogy of hope', in A. M. Freire and D. Macedo (eds), *The Paulo Freire Reader*. New York: Continuum, pp. 237–52.

Gordon, M. (ed.) (2002), *Nelson Mandela's Favorite African Folktales*. New York: Norton, pp. 87–92.

Jeffers, A. (2010), 'The rough edges: Community, art and history'. *Research in Drama Education: The Journal of Applied Theatre and Performance*, 15, (1), 29–37.

Kushner, S. (2006), 'Adolescents and cultures of reflection: More than meets the eye', in P. Burnard and S. Hennessy (eds), *Reflective Practice in Arts Education*. Dordrecht: Springer, pp. 13–22.

Mulligan, M. (2012), 'Working with the idea of community'. *Paper presentation. The Turn to Community in Arts Symposium*. Footscray Community Arts Centre, June 2012.

Myerhoff, B. (1980), 'Telling one's story', in *Center Magazine*, 8 March, 22–40.

Nagle, E. (2007), 'An aesthetic of neighborliness: Possibilities for integrating community-based practices into documentary theatre'. *Theatre Topics*, 17, (2), 153–68.

Neelands, J. (2010), 'Mirror, dynamo or lens? Drama, children and social change', in P. O'Connor (ed.), *Creating Democratic Citizenship through Drama Education*. Stoke on Trent: Trentham Books.

O' Toole, J. (1992), *The Process of Drama: Negotiating Art and Meaning*. Routledge: London.

Reimer, B. (1992), 'What Knowledge is of Most Worth in the Arts?', in B. Reimer and R. A. Smith (eds), *The Arts, Education and Aesthetic Knowing*. Chicago: University of Chicago Press.

Salverson, J. (1996), 'Performing emergency: Witnessing, popular theatre, and the lie of the literal'. *Theatre Topics*, 6 (2), 181–91.

Simons, J. (2002), 'Drama and the learner', in K. Donelan and H. Cahill (eds), *Drama and Learning: Melbourne Studies in Education*, 43, (2), 1–11.

Taylor, P. (1996), 'Doing reflective practitioner research in arts education', in P. Taylor (ed.), *Researching Drama and Arts Education: Paradigms and Possibilities*. London: Falmer Press, pp. 25–58.

Turner, C. and Behrndt, S. (2008), *Dramaturgy and Performance*. New York: Palgrave Macmillan.

Watt, D. (1991), 'Interrogating "Community": Social welfare v. cultural democracy', in V. Binns (ed.), *Community and the Arts: History, Theory, Practice*. Sydney: Pluto Press, pp. 55–66.

Williams, R. (1989), 'Culture is ordinary' (1958), in R. Gable (ed.), *Resources of Hope: Culture, Democracy, Socialism*. London: Verso.

4

Drama and Social Justice: Power, Participation and Possibility

Kelly Freebody and Michael Finneran

Introduction

This chapter is, above all, hopeful. The subject matter is serious – social justice, inequitable social relationships, power structures, and a global schooling system which is, at best, not always helpful, and at worst, deliberately unjust (Connell 1993). The intent of this chapter is to explore possibilities for doing better. Specifically, it is concerned with drama pedagogy and its potential for teaching for and about social justice.

Social justice in this discussion is understood in a relatively straightforward manner: for us it represents an aspiration to bring equality and fairness to bear in any area of society and community where a conspicuous or indeed hidden inequity exists. As such, the aspiration to teach social justice should be understood as being fundamentally emancipatory in intent; premised upon the belief that improvements can be brought about in the lives of the people with whom we work and teach. This is not an entirely straightforward assertion, however, as it embodies the Habermassian ideas that self-emancipation through reflection is possible and indeed the primary means by which human beings acquire knowledge (Habermas 1972).

In adopting this perspective, we seek to move beyond assumed understandings of drama for empowerment or drama for development, to explore the complex concept of social justice education and the potential synergies this area has with the work of drama education. There can be a tendency in drama education to, at times, assume that drama can provide a powerful and universal educational resource to deal with all the ills of the world. As practitioners, we certainly believe in the possibility that drama can shine a light where none other can illuminate. However, we believe it is also incumbent upon us to interrogate where, how and why that engagement might occur.

With this caveat in place, this chapter will introduce four key ideas about how drama operates within social justice contexts: the development of critical consciousness (or *conscientizacao*) (Freire 1970); the reflective opportunities available when one is positioned in both the real and imagined worlds simultaneously (often understood as *metaxis*)(Boal 1979); the importance placed on dialogue in both drama work and in critical pedagogy more broadly; and the centrality of reflection in all drama pedagogy, but particularly drama work focused on a deepening understanding of the social world. To explore these ideas, material drawn from a diverse range of contexts will be introduced and discussed. While it may differ in context, practice, place and purpose, all of this work is connected by the centrality of these four ideas and the explicit or implicit development of a social justice agenda.

The key terms

Prior to discussing the theoretical and historical perspectives connecting drama and social justice, we want to outline a few of the key terms and ideas that inform our way of thinking. First, when we use the term 'drama pedagogy' we are referring to 'drama as a practice and as a process for learning rather than as a body of texts for passive reception' (Winston 1998 p. 75). These practices and processes include process drama, applied theatre, educational drama and theatre in education.

Secondly, while acknowledging a large overlap and somewhat artificially created dichotomy between drama *for* social justice and drama *about* social justice, we would like to make a distinction between these areas. In the former, we refer to drama that has a practical, emancipatory intent; work that explicitly seeks to contribute to the process of making participants or audience more aware of oppression and to make the social world more just, with a view to helping them escape that oppression. In the latter, we refer to drama that explores issues of social justice in order to broaden the participants' awareness of sociocultural issues, to learn about social justice, or to develop a deeper understanding of how participants view social issues and the impact that these issues have on the lives of the participants.

Finally, this chapter engages with the philosophy of praxis – the interconnected and symbiotic nature of theory derived from practice and practice derived from theory (Freire 1970). For this reason, the discussion will shift between research, theory and practice in drama education work and social justice principles or outcomes. We hope that the synergies between these interconnected aspects of drama work will ensure that this chapter is relevant to drama educators working in a variety of contexts, seeking deeper knowledge of the unique contribution drama can make to the young people's social development.

Theoretical and historical connections – social justice and drama pedagogy

The connecting ideas in this chapter – critical consciousness, *metaxis*, dialogue and reflection – are foundations in both drama education and critical pedagogy. Indeed, a strong philosophical and historical connection exists between critical education perspectives and the traditional stance of drama education. Philosophically, both are concerned with action and active participation. Critical pedagogy places the students in powerful positions and asks them to consider ways to change and influence aspects of society they find unjust, while drama education often requires students to enact agency and imagine possible futures for the characters they are working with/as. Historically, the work of Paulo Freire (1970) and Augusto Boal (1979) has provided a strong link between applied drama, social justice and education. Freire is seen by many educational philosophers and practitioners as 'the inaugural philosopher of critical pedagogy' (McLaren 2000, p. 1). His work challenged educators to move beyond the role of mere technicians in a banking system of education and work towards their role as 'scholars, community researchers, moral agents, philosophers, cultural workers and political insurgents' (Kincheloe 2008, p. 70). According to Freire, learning should not be separate from personal and political growth and should encourage change. Central to Freire's work was the notion of *conscientizacao*, a term referring to the need to learn to perceive social, political, economic contradictions and fight against oppressive elements of society (Freire 1970). Freire criticized pedagogy in which the teacher discusses reality as if it were static and unconnected to the world of the student, viewing this type of pedagogy as a prevalent exercise in domination that indoctrinates students to 'adapt to the world of oppression' (1970, p. 78). To combat this, Freire posited that teachers and students should view reality as a constantly evolving process, rather than as a static entity. Through this we can understand reality as an active entity, explore how it came to be, and most potently, how it may be changed: that is, 'students can begin to imagine ways that research the future from the dictates of the past' (Kincheloe 2008, p. 72).

In examining critical pedagogy for social justice, Smyth (2011) looks at developing the triumvirate of teachers as intellectuals, students as activists, and communities that are politically connected and engaged. At the heart of his conceptual discussion lie ideas such as hope, responsibility, imagined futures, and teachers and students as social actors: all themes which run to the very heart of much drama education (Neelands 2009a, 2009b). Most striking perhaps is the shared concern around dialogue and dialogic teaching. Freire (1970) sees open and critically informed dialogue as the means through which political and social inequality and oppression can be subverted and changed. He promotes a move away from 'verbalism', 'idle chatter' or talk which is entirely action-oriented (activism), and instead emphasizes that '(d)ialogue is the encounter between men, mediated by the world, in order to name the world' (1970, p. 69). The promotion of dialogic teaching is one of the central planks of a critical pedagogy: seeking to create situations whereby as teachers we foster 'conversation with a focus and a purpose' (Peterson 2009, p. 313).

There are many ways in which and many reasons for which drama educators have aligned themselves with theories of critical pedagogy in general, and Freirean notions of dialogic education and *conscientizacao* more specifically. In spite of there being a variety of different definitions and practices in drama education, Grady (2003) identifies three common theoretical and practical underpinnings of work in our field:

1. A belief in the effectiveness of dramatic, aesthetic and artistic engagement;
2. A belief in the productiveness of active participation; and
3. A belief in the importance of reflection.

These three values of drama education align strongly with more general understandings of teaching for critical consciousness and social justice. Dramatic engagement requires participants to accept the fiction and view the constructed reality as a process in which they must be active to construct, shape and change. It also allows participants to experience *metaxis* – the simultaneous belonging to both a real and an imagined world (Boal 1979), potentially leading to more layered and detailed understanding of both worlds (Grady 2003). Similarly important is the notion of active imagination; Edminston (2000) argues that in drama we can adopt positions that are in addition to those in our everyday lives and can therefore imagine how we might act in such positions. When exploring how drama education aligns with ethical education, he refers to the process of shifting positions (or roles) in drama work in order to experience and explore the consequences of our actions on others. This potentially gives us 'a vision of how the world could be different and what our lives would be like if we acted in different ways' (Edminston 2000, p. 67). Similarly, reflecting on both the fictional and the real leads to a deeper understanding of the topic at hand, allowing participants to engage in 'reflection and action upon the world in order to transform it' (Grady 2003, p. 73).

Drama *for* social justice

Many drama educators have traditionally had a sharpened social outlook (O'Toole et al. 2009, p. 109). This is undoubtedly due in some part to the socially efficacious origins of the dramatic form of tragedy in the city state of Athens, and also because of the essentially social nature of the art form (Neelands 2011), and indeed the emergence of drama as an educational concern during the latter part of the twentieth century, a time of global social change. This change orientation has very often been an implicit tension in the field, and the debate about learning in and through drama is a well-charted one (Anderson 2012; Fleming 2011). O'Toole et al. (2009) note that the social change and values agenda is most visible in drama education in the exploration of moral education and cultural difference – the critical concepts of societal values and otherness.

The practice of the Brazilian playwright and activist, Augusto Boal (1931–2009), is among the most visible and frequently cited in this tradition of socially emancipatory theatre. With his *Theatre of the Oppressed* work (2000), Boal entered poor Brazilian communities and addressed issues which were oppressing members of the community through the medium of theatre techniques. By following the theatrical intent of Brecht and the emancipatory philosophy of Freire, Boal established an innovative platform for addressing social justice through dramatic form, though its legacy and efficacy as a vehicle for true change is legitimately questioned by some (Österlind 2008). Boal latterly attempted to use theatre as the basis for democratic legislation, utilizing similar community-based work to inform his newly acquired status as a member of parliament (Boal 1998). His belief was in the power of the theatrical form to bring people to 'act' politically as well as socially, and thus ultimately involve them in the process of their own emancipation:

> The politics of the oppressed is essentially the poetics of liberation: the spectator no longer delegates power to the characters either to think or to act in his place. The spectator frees himself; he thinks and acts for himself! Theater is action! (Boal 1979, p. 156)

Boal's work remains an inspiration to many and is carried on through individuals and organizations such as the 'International Theatre of the Oppressed Organisation' and 'Pedagogy and Theatre of the Oppressed', though the explicitly political function, the very public nature and perceived scale of the work remain a challenge to some.

A similarly explicit social vision is also to be clearly seen in more contemporary work in drama and theatre education. Kathleen Gallagher's innovative volume on *Theatre of the Urban* examines drama as a vehicle for exploring concepts such as freedom, control, ethnicity and particularly sexuality and gender in contemporary school systems. Gallagher's research is premised differently from that of Boal's in that while it recognizes the fundamental inequity of the world, it has a different assessment of how dramatic form can bring about social justice. In her work, Gallagher 'takes difference (and sometimes conflict)' as the starting point for drama 'rather than its challenge' (2007, p. 88). Framing classrooms, as 'locations of possibility', her critical ethnography looks at the possibility of drama leading to learning through the creation of embodied and experiential knowledge, something the dramatic form is fundamentally very good at. The major difference, however, lies in the fact that Gallagher is content to acknowledge that she cannot know definitively 'whether [the] work with the youth of our study will lead to tangible social change, a goal privileged in our methodologies' (2007, p. 173). The commitment to social justice as an end result is no less, however, and the work asserts that increasing the democratic distribution of power through classroom cultures will take time in its realization while also understanding it presents a problem for 'dialectical examination rather than quantifiable analysis' (2007, p. 174). This belief that working to change social understandings and classroom culture through dialogue-based reflection, though taking time and being difficult to 'measure', leads to more democratic and aware citizens, is a belief shared by many drama practitioners (e.g. O'Connor 2008; Neelands 2009a) and offers an enduring link between drama and social justice.

Another pertinent example of drama for social justice work is that of *Everyday Theatre*. Dealing with issues of domestic abuse and violence in schools throughout the country, the *Everyday Theatre* project is carried out by the *Applied Theatre Consultants* in New Zealand and is framed around the idea of the participating children being players in an interactive video game. Starting with a 25-minute dramatic presentation by the visiting theatre company, the journey through the games levels is guided by a *gamesmaster* who helps the children to utilize dramatic conventions in order to unlock levels and progress through the game. In a similar vein to Gallagher's work, the social justice intent is framed around awareness and the possibility of dialogic learning within a safe and structured environment. The hope is that the participants will 'develop their knowledge and understanding of issues which may ultimately contribute to their wellbeing and safety' (O'Connor et al. 2006, p. 244). Aitken's (2009) detailed analysis of aspects of the work centres around its role in developing *conscientizacao*. Already discussed in this chapter, the drama work orients to social justice principles through the development of critical consciousness in the participants. Aitken's discussion throws some interesting light on drama for social justice in that it is not as straightforward or immediate as some might suggest it to be, but instead is a layered and involved journey, even in the case of a long-term, highly researched and government-funded project such as *Everyday Theatre*. Aitken concludes that:

> . . . Everyday Theatre proposes a form of agency for children in abusive situations based on becoming aware of their operational 'restrictions and enablements' and asserting their right to alter the narratives of their lives.(Aitken 2009, p. 525)

These three examples of drama for social justice, though different in their contexts and purpose, share elements that appear to be common across much drama for/about social justice: the development of *conscientizacao*, a centrality of active participation, dialogue and reflection, and a thoughtful engagement in *metaxis* whereby participants are provided distance from both the real and imagined worlds in order to examine their place in both. What they also undoubtedly shared is a commitment to bring about social change with a view to equity. Our perception is that this change comes through dialogue leading to the possibility of reflective self-emancipation.

Drama *about* social justice

The discussion so far in this chapter has attempted to highlight the centrality of reflection and dialogue in drama work. When working with drama about social justice, time for reflection ensures that participants are given the opportunity to connect the learning with their own lives in positive and thoughtful ways. Drama educators claim that the work in a drama classroom has the capacity to act as a mirror to participants' worlds and to give those participants a vision of humanity and a sense of the possibilities facing them in the community in which they live (O'Neill 1995). Within this claim, drama's purpose is seen to serve as a mirror – not necessarily to provide flattering reflections but to be used 'as a means of seeing ourselves more clearly and allowing us to begin to correct whatever is amiss' (O'Neill 1995, p. 152). This notion is elaborated on by O'Connor (2003) who suggests that drama pedagogy seeks ambiguity rather than clarity, and therefore adopts the term 'refraction' as a more appropriate description of the opportunities for students to understand themselves within a wider context. Participants working in role have the potential to actively engage in such reflection/refraction. While role-playing, participants in a drama remain themselves, but are at the same time given distance from their expressions through the fictional context. Through this students are not necessarily reacting outside of themselves or what they know, but are rather experiencing *metaxis* by behaving as themselves, but also in ways that are appropriate to the role and context of the drama (O'Toole 1992; Boal 1979).

Like all classrooms, the drama classroom is a space in which students learn specific theatrical knowledge and skills. To achieve this skill-building, students spend much of their time engaging with the issues of the drama: creating roles, forging imagined and real relationships and exploring fictional contexts. This makes it an ideal space for young people to come to understand the world in which they live, explore what others think about it, and develop their own perspectives and opinions. The drama classroom, therefore, is a space that is concerned with the human condition. Drama educators argue that when participating in drama, students explore social boundaries, not just by crossing them, but by dismantling and rebuilding them in an attempt to see how they work (e.g. O'Connor 2008; O'Neill and Lambert 1982). This crossing of boundaries and movement between fictional worlds can be harnessed effectively by the drama teacher to explore specific issues relating to social justice. The following section explores two brief examples of drama work taken from a high-school drama classroom (Freebody 2010). In the first example, students are discussing the relationships between having money and being happy. By engaging with this topic, students are formulating and expressing their views about what makes a happy life and whether it is possible to be poor and happy. In the second example, students are working in role as teachers and a parent of a student who has suddenly started behaving badly in school. In this situation, the participants explore their social expectations of *good mothering* in order to establish how to help the student. Both of these examples illustrate the manner in which social issues and social justice often pervades many aspects of classroom drama work, without necessarily being the explicit focus. Students learn about social issues and social justice through each other's opinions and experiences, expressed through the safety of responding to fictional roles and scenarios.

Example 1 – 'just coping': Exploring the relationship between happiness and money

The following extract from an out-of-role classroom discussion about a character's situation has been drawn from a process drama about careers and life choices. The discussion provides some insight into the ways in which young people participating in drama, in this case as part of a reflective discussion, are given opportunities to develop their understandings and opinions about the social world. Out-of-role talk such as the segment below allows participants to explore and negotiate who and what the drama work is about. The intentions of stakeholders both within (the characters) and outside of (author, actors, directors) can be collected, discussed and used in future in-role drama work. The students are trying to decide whether the character should follow her dream and risk losing her inheritance, or follow her parents' desired path for her and live a financially comfortable life. Directly prior to the segment below, the teacher (Nick) had expressed the opinion that money isn't everything and that people should strive to be happy rather than rich.

> Call: well you kind of do need money to be happy I reckon
> Nick: what do you mean by that (.) cause that's a very interesting point
> Call: cause if you're not (.) if you don't have any money then you're poor and you
>   live in a you'll like//
> Ann: //you live in a bin
> Call: yeah

Ant: well not exactly if you if you//

Nick: //you're talking about (.) you're talking about an extreme though aren't you

Ant: no but//

Nick: //extreme poverty

Ant: sir, not exactly if you if you if you

Nick: just hold on a moment Anton (3) ((chatter)) sorry it's very important I'm
   miked there's mikes all over

Ant: yep cool yep

Nick: just got to wait (.) and Kate please hold that thought yeah just for a second
   Anton

Ant: um like (.) if you're not rich but you're not poor but you're kind of like
   not well off so you're just kind of like just coping (.) it (.) um it puts a lot
   of stress on the family as your parents have to like pay a lot of bills and um
   like they're always stressing about how they're going to get the money to
   keep the phone on or electricity or like so and so (1) in order to (.) have
   no debts and not have to stress about (.) needing to pay bills um I think
   like having money would make you happy as you don't have to stress about
   those things

This excerpt demonstrates the ways in which students can draw upon issues
of social class as implicit resources when discussing the role money plays in a
happy life. The teacher introduced the notion that happiness and money are
separate things, with happiness being important and money not as important.
The students then disagree with the teacher by initially connecting the two so
strongly that not having money could be seen as a definition of unhappiness.
This definition eventually becomes a more subtle connection between money
and happiness – that not having much money (or 'just coping') can lead to
stress. This stress is then placed in a cause–effect relationship with happiness.
Within this excerpt, the students demonstrated a nuanced understanding of
how a lack of money can affect one's life – their living conditions, their family
life and their ability to be happy. Although there are potential interpretations
that can be made about the students' own lives outside of the drama classroom,
it is also the case that these discussions do more than simply illuminate the
students' views regarding a topic. These views are negotiated within the class,
often (although not always) striving towards a consensus that the students, as
a group, can take into the in-role phases of the lessons. As a result, students
often not only express, but also argue for their views, using examples and
explanations to ensure that the other participants can understand their
perspective.

Example 2 – 'the bad mother': Exploring social understandings and expectations of role

When working in role, young people are also given opportunities to refine and argue for their views. By taking on a character, participants demonstrate their understandings of the role, situation and context. Therefore an exploration of how students interact with each other in role can illuminate ways in which students understand social roles and relationships. Not only do students make decisions about how to present their allocated role, they also experience *metaxis* by reacting to each other in ways that are role-appropriate (how would a *teacher* talk to a *mother*), while at the same time expressing their own opinions about a chosen character (what do I think of this *mother*).

The example below takes place with the students (and *teacher*) in role as *teachers* who are having a meeting about a student who has started to behave badly in school. Throughout the course of the meeting, we have discovered that she is currently fighting with her *mother* because she wants to be a chef while her *mother* is insistent that she go to university and study medicine. This excerpt comes towards the end of the meeting. Initially, before the *mother* was called in, the *teachers* had discussed how disappointed they were in the student because of her lack of effort. Once introduced to the meeting, the *mother* had displayed a lack of care and empathy for her daughter, claiming she just wanted her to be wealthy. After this, the *teachers* shifted their blame away from the student and her lack of effort towards the *mother* and her lack of care for her daughter.

> Nick: . . . would it be possible if this is ok with you if she worked closely with the
>   food technology teachers in preparation for the next day (.)
> Ann: (it would be ok)
> Nick: sorry
> Ann: it would be ok with me but that's if she gets her head out of her bum
> Nick: right and if and if she completes the work her homework at home
> Ann: yep
> Liam: and also and also um I believe that she should start cooking meals at home
>   and you should sit down and eat it ((laughter)) (3)
> Son: yeah you'll boost her confidence as well (.) honestly you can be (.) what I've
>   seen of you you've been really a (bitch to her) (2)
> Liam: with the upmost respect
> Son: you honestly don't look like you care about her (.) and that might be the
>   reason for all this misbehaving trouble//

Call: //yeah =
Son: = she's caused us (1)

In this excerpt, and the meeting more generally, the student called Ann disrupted the generally accepted role of *mother-as-caring* by being disengaged. This disengagement is evident through her mumbling responses, one word answers, and defensive attitude. Also interesting is the how the students in role took turns, notably without the *teacher*'s allocation of turn-taking, to accuse Ann of failing to adhere to the generally accepted traits of a *good mother* – failing to support, care for, or build confidence in, her daughter. The laughter at Liam's suggestion that Ann eat Jacinta's meals, followed by the next five turns, in which Sonia expressed her belief that Ann is a *bitch* to Jacinta; Liam's utterance that they have the 'upmost respect', which at this interactional point that would suggest sarcasm; and the accusation of not caring about Jacinta and therefore being the result of all the trouble that Jacinta has cause them as staff, all demonstrate that the students as *staff* have turned the blame for Jacinta's situation onto her *mother*.

Thus we see, as discussed above, that while working in role the participants demonstrated their sociological understandings of particular characters and, using those understandings, managed to negotiate mutually productive, sociologically interpretable characters. Through this, students build their understanding of the social world, notions of justice, blame and responsibility. This demonstrates the ways in which action and content within the drama – in this case the *teacher*'s meeting with the *mother* to help Jacinta – are 'identical with the members' procedures for making those settings "account-able"' (Garfinkel 1967, p. 1). In other words, through learning how to act in this particular situation, students are simultaneously learning how to be theatrical actors and 'actors in and for the real world' (O'Connor 2010, p. xxiii).

Issues, tensions and concerns

While engaging in discussions about the centrality of reflection in our work, we thought it important to next turn the microscope onto ourselves to critique the practical and philosophical 'system' that is drama education practice. In any given field there are a variety of assumptions. In community work, these revolve around ideas of agency, student voice, and dialogue. In addition, there are potential difficulties associated with *teachers* unproblematically encouraging students to speak with 'authentic voice' while at the same time ensuring the safety and trust of the entire group. As Elsworth suggests, the marginalized or disadvantaged do not necessarily 'speak of the oppressive formations that condition their lives in the spirit of "sharing". Rather, the speech of oppositional groups is a "talking back", a "defiant speech" that is constructed within communities of resistance and is a condition of survival' (1989, p. 310). This defiance does not necessarily align with romantic notions of dialogue as mutually trusting and sharing, and can be a practical issue for teachers and students attempting to create spaces that encourage personal expression. Having problematized this, however, it is important to acknowledge that Freire's philosophy of critical pedagogy encouraged dialogue that was *BOTH* respectful and critical. Therefore, although teachers should honour all students and their experiences, they should not simply take them as they are but challenge and encourage them to move beyond their current understanding of a situation (Kicheloe 2008, p. 73).

There are also issues concerning stereotype and understanding of the complexity of different perspectives in drama work. When students explore ethical behaviour from a variety of positions, perspectives and roles, as Winston (1998) and Edminston (2000) argue they can, they are necessarily drawing on the potentially limited knowledge they have about those social roles, likewise, when students are asked to explore a cultural event or particular action. As Edminston acknowledges, 'we always imagine what *might* have happened and the images of representations of those events are always incomplete' (2000, p. 69). In fact, the immediacy and spontaneity of participant involvement in the dramatic action sometimes results in a necessarily simplified response. Further, it is important to ask to what extent can it be assumed that students will take the identity and political position from which they can act as change agents? Definitions of agency acknowledge that agentive behaviour can be used to both shift and entrench the status quo (Emirbayer and Miscbe 1998). Therefore, student action in drama work, particularly when there is limited understanding of the sociocultural context, can sometimes fail to achieve a greater awareness of the issue in question. For applied drama work to move from simplified to complex and critical, taking on a role should be a process of discovery. As participants learn more about a situation, explore and discover their characters, their representations should gradually become more complex (O'Neill 1995). The hypothesis is that it is through their representation of roles that participants in drama demonstrate their deeper understanding and learning. However, this places enormous importance on both the students' and the facilitators' ability to use their own roles to disrupt stereotypes as they emerge in the dramatic context. As a result, an important caution for drama practitioners is that they need to be aware that role-play 'may work eventually to confirm students in the restricted range of roles most readily available to them in the world' (O'Neill 1995, p. 78).

Issues of emancipation and agency have also been sign-posted in this chapter. These are contested intellectual ideas that run across fields of academic endeavour and discourse. They are intrinsically tied up with ideas of power and politics, the abuse of which of course run to the very heart of any understanding of justice or injustice. But, it is important that these ideas are afforded the complexity they deserve. We may not fully understand the full extent of drama's potential to bring about changes in people's lives. However, we can be assured that singular understandings of how change comes about, particularly in complex and emotive issues typical of social justice, only do damage to the project immediately at hand, and by implication, the standing of drama as an educational concern.

Conclusion

This chapter has endeavoured to introduce the key theoretical and practical ways in which the field of drama education holds a range of possibilities in educating for social justice. While acknowledging this is a large field of study with contested ideas, we have focused on the connection with Frierian ideas of *conscientizacao* and Boalian understandings of *metaxis* in drama work. These provide a strong theoretical link with the contemporary and emergent field of critical pedagogy, within which we argue the work of many drama facilitators fits. It is our belief that these ideas – the development of critical consciousness and the ability for participants to engage in both the real and fictional world simultaneously – provide drama with a unique ability to encourage active participation, dialogue and reflection. Our aim was to provide a few examples from this large field, in order to illustrate these theoretical claims about drama for/about social justice.

The potential for drama to teach social justice is, we believe, great. However, it is dependent on a number of distinct choices on the part of the practitioner. These decisions involve practical considerations about the scale of the change being sought and the manner in which it may be most effectively be brought about. Moreover, they involve reflection and recognition on the part of the practitioner on their own worldview, regarding both emancipation and the possibility of striving for freedom and improvement around social justice. We also urge practitioners to consider the implications that all of this has for the dramatic form, and the ever-present potential for a disservice to be done to it. Despite the inherently social nature of drama, along with its versatility, the nature and form of the work remains vitally important.

Like most teaching, dialogue is the heart of any drama work that it is motivated in terms of social justice. While there are issues and tensions in this work, and it may be difficult to assert that any emancipation is actually as a result of a drama intervention, there are countless excellent examples of drama for/about social justice taking place in classrooms and community spaces across the world. The possibility of emancipation or achieving improved situations of social justice seems to lie in the space and opportunity afforded by the safe and imaginary world of drama, and the reflective space between the fictional world and the real world. It is in these spaces that participants create their own worlds, interrogate the real world, and imagine a range of possible, hopefully hopeful, futures.

References

Aitken, V. (2009), 'Conversations with status and power: How Everyday Theatre offers 'spaces of agency' to participants'. *RiDE: The Journal of Applied Theatre and Performance*, 14, (4), 523–47.

Anderson, M. (2012), *Masterclass in Drama Education*. London: Continuum.

Boal, A. (1979), *Theater of the Oppressed*. London: Pluto Press.

—(1998), *Legislative Theatre: Using Performance to Make Politics*. London: Routledge.

Connell, R. (1993), *Schools and Social Justice*. Sydney: Pluto Press.

Edminston, B. (2000), 'Drama as Ethical Education'. *Research in Drama Education: The Journal of Applied Theatre and Performance*, 5, (1), 63–84.

Ellsworth, E. (1989), 'Why doesn't this feel empowering? Working through the repressive myths of critical pedagogy'. *Harvard Educational Review* 59, 297–324.

Emirbayer, M. and Miscbe, A. (1998), 'What is agency?'. *The American Journal of Sociology*, 103, (4), 962–1023.

Fleming, M. (2011), 'Learning *in* and *through* the arts', in J. Sefton-Green, P. Thompson, K. Jones and L. Bresler (eds), *The Routledge International Handbook of Creative Learning*. Abingdon, OX: Routledge, pp. 177–86.

Freebody, K. (2010), 'Exploring teacher–student interactions and moral reasoning practices in drama classrooms'. *Research in Drama Education: The Journal of Applied Theatre and Performance*, 15, (2), 209–25.

Freire, P. (1970), *Pedagogy of the Oppressed*. Harmondsworth: Penguin.

Gallagher, K. (2007), *The Theatre of Urban: Youth and Schooling in Dangerous Times*. Toronto: University of Toronto Press.

Garfinkel, H. (1967), *Studies in Ethnomethodology*. Cambridge: Polity Press.

Grady, S. (2003), 'Accidental Marxists?: The challenge of critical and feminist pedagogies for the practice of applied drama'. *Youth Theatre Journal*, 17, (1), 65–81.

Habermas, J. (1972), *Knowledge and Human Interests*, 2nd edn. London: Heinemann.

International Theatre of the Oppressed Organisation. Retrieved 20 October 2012, from http://www.theatreoftheoppressed.org

Kincheloe, J. (2008), *Critical Pedagogy*. New York: Peter Lang Publishing Inc.

McLaren, P. (2000), 'Paulo Freire's pedagogy of possibility', in S. Steiner, H. Krank, P. McLaren and R. Bahruth (eds), *Freirean Pedagogy, Praxis and Possibilities: Projects for the New Millennium*. New York and London: Falmer Press, pp. 1–22.

Neelands, J. (2009a), 'Acting together: Ensemble as a democratic process in art and life'. *RiDE: The Journal of Applied Theatre and Performance*, 14, (2), 173–89.

—(2009b), 'The Art of togetherness: Reflecting on some essential and pedagogic qualities of drama curricula'. *NJ*, 33, (1), 9–18.

—(2011), 'Drama as creative learning', in J. Sefton-Green, P. Thompson, K. Jones and L. Bresler (eds), *The Routledge International Handbook of Creative Learning*. Abingdon, OX: Routledge, pp. 168–76.

O'Connor, P. (2003), *Reflection and Refraction: The Dimpled Mirror of Process Drama*, unpublished thesis, Griffith University.

—(2008), 'Drama for inclusion: A pedagogy of hope', in M. Anderson, J. Hughes and J. Manuel (eds), *Drama and English Teaching: Imagination, Action and Engagement*. South Melbourne: Oxford University Press.

—(ed.) (2010), *Creating Democratic Citizenship through Drama Education: The Writings of Jonothan Neelands*. Stoke On Trent: Trentham Books.

O'Connor, P., O'Connor, B., and Welsh-Morris, M. (2006), 'Making the everyday extraordinary: A theatre in education project to prevent child abuse, neglect and family violence'. *RiDE: The Journal of Applied Theatre and Performance*, 11, (2), 235–45.

O'Neill, C. (1995), *Drama Worlds: A Framework for Process Drama*. Portsmouth, NH: Heinemann.

O'Neill, C. and Lambert, A. (1982), *Drama Structures: A Practical Handbook for Teachers*. London: Hutchinson.

O'Toole, J. (1992), *The Process of Drama: Negotiating Art and Meaning*. London: Routledge.

O'Toole, J., Stinson, M., and Moore, T. (2009), *Drama and Curriculum: A Giant at the Door*. Dordrecht: Springer.

Österlind, E. (2008), 'Acting out of habits – can Theatre of the Oppressed promote change? Boal's theatre methods in relation to Bourdieu's concept of habitus'. *RiDE: The Journal of Applied Theatre and Performance*, 13, (1), 71–82.

Pedagogy and Theatre of the Oppressed. Retrieved 20 October 2012, from http://www.ptoweb.org/

Peterson, R. E. (2009), 'How to read the world and change it: Critical pedagogy in the intermediate grades', in A. Darder, M. P. Baltodano and R. D. Torres (eds), *The Critical Pedagogy Reader*, 2nd edn. New York: Routledge, pp. 304–23.

Winston, J. (1998), *Drama, Narrative and Moral Education: Exploring Traditional Tales in the Primary Years*. London: Falmer Press.

Smyth, J. (2011), *Critical Pedagogy for Social Justice*. New York: Continuum.

5

Drama, Conflict and Bullying:
Working with Adolescent Refugees

Bruce Burton

Introduction

The power of Drama to assist young people to deal with conflict in their lives has been the subject of extensive literature and research, ever since Augusto Boal's work using theatre to empower dispossessed and disadvantaged communities was documented and reported in Theatre of the Oppressed (1979). Since then, key projects such as the *International DRACON* program (1996–99) its offshoot, *Cooling Conflicts* (2000–02) and the *Acting against Bullying* Program (2003–13) have been devoted to a deeper exploration of the possibilities drama offers, and to identify how learning in this area is activated.

Based on these works and others, there appears to be strong evidence that drama in the classroom has the power to address complex issues of cultural difference, conflict and bullying among students of all ages, and this was confirmed by the case study reported in this chapter.

The case study, involving action research as the key methodology, was part of *The Arrivals* project (2010–13), an Australian Research Council-funded research grant aimed at investigating the use of drama to assist newly arrived refugees to deal with conflict, develop resilience, and reinforce their sense of identity. The industry partner in the research was Multi-Link, a government-funded organization responsible for assisting refugees to re-settle in Australia.

The participants were newly arrived adolescent refugees aged between 14 and 17 years. All were members of a designated additional languages unit at Riverside State High School, a large Brisbane secondary school in a very low socioeconomic area with a large refugee population.

Key literature

Drama and conflict

A major claim for the power of drama education to effect behavioural change, especially in adolescents in schools, is the contention that it provides learners with opportunities to experience 'reality' from different perspectives – creating the distance that is needed for young people to see themselves as others and to be able to appreciate different points of view (Fleming 1998).

> Acting behaviour is an act of fiction-making involving Identification through action, the conscious manipulation of time and space and capacity for generalisation (Bolton 1998, p. 258)

Bolton and Heathcote (1998) insist that adolescents behave in certain ways based on their personal beliefs and their cultural belief systems, and classroom drama enables them to explore and change both beliefs and behaviour. Indeed, Neelands (2009) argues that through drama young people can be led to imagine and look for new ways of living together rather than against each other; to find a shared understanding and to create new models of pluralist community.

By using drama to specifically investigate and address issues in their lives, students can enact realistic events and characters that can be manipulated and reflected upon, and can deal with issues of conflict and bullying in a safe, fictional context (Burton 1991). In this way, the participants are both actors and audience, able to experience fictional roles and situations, while perceiving and reflecting on the meaning of these experiences at the same time (O'Neill 1995; Boal 1996; Bolton 1998).

Other international research has indicated that secondary school students themselves prefer the use of drama strategies when learning about real-world problems such as bullying in comparison with other forms of instruction (Crothers et al. 2005).

The Acting Against Bullying programme was developed following 15 years of action research into the use of drama to address conflict and bullying in schools. It began as the international *DRACON* research project with partners in Sweden, Malaysia and Australia (Lofgren and Malm 2005) and explored conflict within schools (Burton 2008). The project, using a combination of improvisation, process drama, forum theatre and peer teaching, evolved into an effective whole school program that impacted positively on conflict and bullying in both secondary and primary schools. This is particularly significant because bullying remains the most serious behavioural problem encountered in schools worldwide (Burton 2012) and a report commissioned by the Australian Government in 2009 found that up to half of all students are bullied during their schooling (McDougall and Chilcott 2009).

The key drama strategy in the *Acting Against Bullying* programme is Enhanced Forum Theatre, which developed and refined Boal's (1979, 1996) original participatory form of Theatre of the Oppressed. Enhanced Forum Theatre involves the creation of a realistic play in three scenes, rather than the single-scene structure of Boal's version (O'Toole et al. 2005). The students are encouraged to improvise each of the three scenes of their Enhanced Forum Theatre plays to represent a specific stage in the escalation of the bullying they are exploring, and to incorporate the three parties involved in bullying (the bully, the bullied and the bystander).

The use of specific drama strategies is combined with older students teaching younger ones. This peer teaching component has proved to be a crucial factor in the success of the *DRACON, Cooling Conflicts and Acting Against Bullying* projects, and this is unsurprising given the numerous studies over a number of years that have found that having students teach, individually tutor or academically mentor each other can be an extremely effective tool for improving learning in the classroom (Billson and Tiberius 1991; Rubin and Herbert 1998; Boud et al. 2001; Gordon 2005).

Furthermore, research on the use of peer teaching and drama together to re-engage negative leaders in secondary schools in the United Kingdom (Morrison 2004; Morrison et al. 2006) demonstrates that it has the power to transform the behaviours and attitudes of negative leaders in schools. Not only do these students re-engage in the schooling process, but their peer teaching experiences appear to re-orient them towards positive leadership roles.

The combination of drama strategies and peer teaching was applied successfully in schools in Sweden and Australia to address a range of conflict situations, and over 100 schools in NSW implemented the programme (O'Toole et al. 2005) as part of the *Cooling Conflicts* project (Lofgren and Malm 2005). In the next phase of the research in Australia, bullying was targeted as the specific issue to be addressed using the same strategies. Extensive data was collected across a range of high schools and primary schools. The data clearly and consistently indicated that the combination of forum theatre and peer teaching enabled students of all ages to deal more effectively with bullying (Burton and O'Toole 2009). Further iterations of the programme have confirmed the power for this combination to transform the attitudes and behaviours of school students in relation to conflict and bullying (Burton 2012).

The refugee experience

Recent reviews of literature about the re-settlement of young refugees have identified the importance of the school in the process, with Taylor (2008, p. 58) stating that: "Studies have highlighted the crucial role that schools could play on facilitating the transition from refugees to participating citizens." A number of studies of refugee re-settlement in different countries confirm this research, and Rossiter discovered that for refugee youth at risk:

"One of the most critical factors in a successful transition to Canadian society is education". This is confirmed by Matthews (2008, p. 39) who argues that "A broad range of interventions including the development of safe and nurturing educational environments . . . are key to best practice."

However, the extensive literature on the refugee experience makes it clear that the preparation young people are given for settlement in Australia and elsewhere is most often inadequate. For example, Ferjoa and Vickers (2010, p. 150) note that:

Existing research has found that 4 terms of attendance at Intensive English Centres in standard high schools is insufficient to prepare many refugee students for a successful transition to mainstream classrooms. This transition is difficult for students in terms of their learning and acculturation needs, as well as for many of their teachers.

The 32 students involved in *The Arrivals* project reported in this chapter had in fact been in the intensive language unit at Riverside High School for just two terms when the project started.

The use of arts-based interventions to assist refugees has been trialed in a number of countries. The Hope Project in Canada (Yohani 2008) used visual art, photography and crafts with groups of young children and adolescents. There has been a range of Theatre in Education programs where actors perform plays about the refugee experience for groups of adolescent immigrants and refugees in both the United Kingdom and Canada.

Liebmann (2004, p. 275) found that storytelling by both adolescents and adult refugees could be a powerful tool:

I have seen people transformed as their self-esteem grows through better communication skills. I have witnessed a similar transformation in people as they acquire storytelling skills. Learning to tell a story is a very affirming process and confidence grows once people have overcome their initial fears of speaking on public.

The step from telling stories to improvise and perform them, with all the positive outcomes that Drama can provide, would seem to be a small one. However, the potential of classroom drama to contribute to the successful transition from adolescent refugee to citizen has been largely neglected, both in the research and in schools.

The research project: Arrivals

In line with contemporary research and practice, this chapter explores an Australian case study of the use of improvisation, process drama and forum theatre with a group of adolescent refugees from a diverse range of cultural backgrounds and life experiences. The majority of the 32 students in the case study at Riverside State High School were from African nations, but many other cultures were also represented, including seven students from Burma plus individuals from Thailand, Cambodia and China. A number of the students were from war zones, including child soldiers from The Sudan, while others had been members of a persecuted minority in their homelands, and some had lived in refugee camps overseas for a number of years before arriving in Australia.

The director of the school language unit, the classroom drama teacher and the supervisors and counsellors responsible for the refugee students requested that the drama work offered as part of the research project should include the application of the *Acting Against Bullying* programme. They were aware that many of the young people in the language unit had experienced significant conflict situations since their arrival in Australia, or been the targets of bullies, from both within the school community and beyond it.

All the responsible adults associated with the refugee students believed that they needed greater competence in handling conflict and bullying and in forming positive social relationships if they were to develop the self-esteem and sense of identity that would enable them to operate effectively in the mainstream of the school when they were moved out of the language unit at the end of the year.

The aim of *The Arrivals* project was therefore to enhance the present and future developments of the adolescents in the language unit, using drama to give them a voice within conflict and bullying situations, both now and in the future. At the same time, the drama forms being used were adapted by the participants according to their needs, their cultures, experiences and languages.

The project did not attempt to revisit their experiences before they came to Australia. This is not only because of the ethical problems related to re-traumatization. There is also increasing evidence that the experiences of young people after their arrival in Australia are actually more important in their psychological development and adjustment than their previous experiences in refugee camps and war zones. Other studies have concluded that integrating refugee adolescents into the society they have joined, while valuing the cultures they bring with them, is the most beneficial approach (Berry et al. 2006, p. 328). Recent literature on the adjustment of adolescent refugees at risk strongly supports this approach (Ferjoa and Vickers 2010).

The case study involved a sequence of one and a half hour drama workshops delivered by the research team each week for 5 months across the second half of the school year. The research team comprised five research assistants who were final year Griffith University students (participating as part of their required work integrated learning practicum) and three more experienced Applied Theatre researchers. All took detailed observation notes, as did the classroom teacher, and the workshops were filmed. This data strongly reinforced the literature and research in the field about enhancing the transition of newly arrived refugee adolescents through positive school experiences. There were also a number of other effective outcomes in relation to language, cross-cultural relationships, self-esteem and identity. The power of drama to enhance language learning and identity formation has been addressed in other chapters of this book. Here the focus will be on the role drama played in helping these young people to both understand and teach others about cultural conflict and bullying behaviour.

The learning experiences

The project involved three phases of action:

Phase One: *Learning about conflict and bullying – and about drama*

This phase began with assisting the students to understand the nature of conflict and bullying and achieve a basic level of competence in classroom drama. Most of the students had arrived in Australia in the past 12 months and had been at the school for just 6 months. None had studied drama as a subject before and they only had limited experience in improvisation and performance of dialogue. Furthermore, almost half of the 32 students had only begun to learn English in the 6 months before the project began. The seven Burmese girls and the Thai and Cambodian boys in particular struggled to understand even simple instructions and were very reluctant to answer questions, or indeed, speak at all in the first few workshops conducted for the research. While the African students were much more fluent in English, for some of them it was still their third spoken language after Swahili and French.

The overt teaching about conflict and bullying was therefore done in groups, with each group led by one of the young researchers, who described the nature of the problem to their groups, and told stories about their own experiences and knowledge of conflict. They helped the refugee students to identify some key features such as the deliberate misuse of power, the ongoing and escalating nature of both bullying and conflict, and the harm caused. They encouraged their groups to talk about, and enact, their experiences of conflict and bullying since coming to Australia.

The workshops in this phase focused on a range of drama activities and exercises, including freeze frames, mime, spontaneous improvisation and dramatic storytelling. Initially the students chose to work in their ethnic groups, facilitated by the researchers and research assistants. When asked to share some of their improvisations in the early workshops, a number of the students were reluctant to do so, and the performances were very brief, sometimes only a matter of seconds in length. To engage the students initially and encourage them to take on roles and become involved in fictional situations, a number of classroom drama games and activities were used, and students were encouraged to share games and enacted stories from their own cultural backgrounds with the whole class.

Specific drama concepts and techniques proved particularly successful for the students who had no background in Drama, not only in developing drama skills but in enhancing conceptual understanding of the effectiveness in exploring human issues (Nicholson 2006). The use of transformation as developed by Grotowski and Brook (Burton 2011, pp. 194–200) was explicitly taught in one session, with the students transforming chairs, rostra blocks, lengths of material and their own bodies to create the settings, costumes, characters and creatures for a range of dramas. When asked what she had enjoyed the most in the project one student with very little English enthusiastically replied by identifying storytelling and transformation.

> Interviewer: What did you most like?
> Burmese Student: Oh ya. When we did the thingy, the talking about the daily life of a person, and the activity, the transformation of things.

A genuine level of engagement and enjoyment quickly developed, and as the students became more confident, cross-cultural groups were structured placing the articulate African students in groups with the less fluent Asian students. In informal interviews conducted at the end of the first four weeks, all the students except one approved the workshops and their desire for them to continue. The one exception was a Chinese boy who joined the project in the third week and who spoke no English. When the group was offered the opportunity to do visual art instead of drama, this boy was the only one who took up the offer.

Phase Two: *Exploring conflict and bullying through improvisation and enhanced forum theatre*

By the 5th week of the project, the students were freely and enthusiastically engaging in a range of drama exercises, activities and improvisations. These dramas explored a range of conflict and bullying scenarios, focused on identifying how conflicts start and escalate, and can be de-escalated, and how the actions of the bully, the bystander and the person being bullied contributes to bullying – and to its effective management. As they performed their rehearsed improvisations, the students became increasingly more verbal and more expressive. The classroom teacher observed:

> Initially they found it very difficult to improvise, but now they actually have to be stopped because the improvisations run on and on.

The use of enacted stories, told both by the students and by the researchers, formed the heart of the improvisations dramatizing conflict and bullying. Storytelling was the technique Liebmann (2004) found most useful in her arts approaches to conflict, and it was particularly effective with the Burmese refugee students when the storytelling was followed by enactment. Working in small groups, the girls told stories of their lives, both before and during their time in Australia. From these stories fictional scenarios were created of bullying situations the girls were interested in exploring. These scenarios were turned into group performances that were shared with the rest of the class.

Ka Mai: When I was in primary school, like year 6, and like I got my photo taken, and then I was like holding my photo on my hand and an old girl came and she took my photo, and then she ripped the plastic bag and my photo flew away. I never told my teachers.

This was one of the very few cases where a participant went back to their childhood experiences to illustrate their understanding of bullying. It was acted out by a group of the Burmese girls, much of it in their own language, with great enthusiasm and embellishment, and directed by Ka Mai, but not performed by her. This approach, where a refugee who really wanted their story enacted became the director of the performance, was used consistently throughout the project, providing distance and safety (Hunter 2008). After the improvisation that dramatized this story, Ka Mai went on to say that she thought the whole school should do the *Acting Against Bullying* programme, and she articulated her own learning from the experience:

Interviewer: What would you do now?
Ka Mai: I would say to her. I would say: "Stop doing that to people. How will you feel if people do that to you? So . . . like, they will not bully other people, and they will not hurt other peoples' feelings."

The last part of this phase was devoted to Enhanced Forum Theatre. The research team prepared and performed a play in three scenes about a serious bullying situation involving cultural issues. The first scene presented the latent stage of the conflict, scene two developed the emerging stage, and the final scene showed the manifest stage when the bullying was at its most serious. The play was performed thrice as part of the Enhanced Forum Theatre structure. The refugee students watched the first performance through, then hot – seated and thought – tracked the characters during the second performance. Many of the questions asked in these process drama interventions demonstrated clear understanding of the nature and impact of bullying and conflict.

During the third performance of the play, members of the audience were able to intervene to take on the role of any of the characters and to try and de-escalate the situation. This was accepted by a number of the students with great enthusiasm, and some of the interventions were successful in reducing the severity of the bullying, at least temporarily. All the interventions clearly demonstrated at least some authentic learning and a genuine desire to find strategies to manage the problem.

Phase Three: *Peer teaching a year eight class*

In the final phase of the research, in the last month of the project, the refugee students took responsibility for sharing their knowledge and expertise about bullying and conflict through peer teaching another class (Goodlad and Hirst 1998). This involved not only teaching of the bullying concepts and the use of improvised drama but also the preparation and staging of forum theatre performances. Before the refugee students took on the role of peer teachers, the research team worked with them in groups to help them develop their peer teaching about bullying and conflict, and to create their own enhanced forum theatre pieces to perform. In this phase the students were much more willing to work across cultural divides and across gender boundaries than they had been in earlier phases of the research.

The overt teaching in the first of these sessions was extremely difficult in terms of communication and cultural interaction, particularly because they were working with a standard year eight class, not the ESL class originally chosen. Even with the assistance of the research team and the classroom teachers, the refugee students initially had serious problems making themselves understood. They struggled to explain the bullying concepts, and they completed the formal teaching they had planned within 20–30 minutes of the hour-long class. However, in the second session of peer teaching a day later, one group of peer teachers initiated a number of drama activities about bullying – both demonstrating them and setting up improvisations for their peer learners, and the year eight students became engaged and enthusiastic. The other peer teaching groups quickly adopted this strategy with success.

In the following sessions, small groups of refugee students acting as peer teachers performed the forum theatre pieces they had previously developed with the help of the research team for their groups of peer learners. These forum theatre pieces were effective in demonstrating different bullying scenarios, and in engaging the Year eight audience. There were several significant interventions by the peer learners in each group and all involved genuine attempts to resolve the bullying.

As Kana and Aitken (2007) found, using the safety and distance of drama allows students to take on leadership roles and to articulate issues of social justice. The refugee students in *The Arrivals* project were able to perform their forum plays effectively for the year eight class and to lead reflective discussions on the issues and consequences of bullying.

The final workshop saw the refugee students assisting the peer learners to prepare their own peer teaching. This was far less successful because the refugee students did not have the pedagogical skills or the language to teach this component of the *Acting Against Bullying* programme effectively. More time and more training were necessary, and in a future iteration of the research this workshop would be eliminated unless sufficient time could be devoted to providing the refugee students with effective teaching strategies and class management techniques.

Discussion

In terms of learning about bullying and conflict, a number of the students spoke at unusual length and with some passion, attempting to overcome the language barrier to fully convey their learning in the summative interviews. One of the Thai girls, Dila, who had initially been very quiet and passive, but then emerged as a really confident and assertive leader, observed in her summative interview:

> Dila: It's good we get to know how we can stop bullying. And drama is how we can stop bullying, and we act a bully, and everyone gets to know why we bully everyone. And what the bully feels. What the victim feels and what the bystander feels.

Here she clearly articulates her understanding of how drama can stimulate empathy, and also her knowledge about the nature of bullying and conflict. This observation about her learning through drama is remarkable for a student for whom English was her third language.

Mahmoud, an African boy who had been experiencing ongoing serious bullying by a gang of older African boys when *The Arrivals* project began, actually used the drama activities to explore ways of dealing with this bullying, and with the support of the school, was able to manage it so effectively that the bullying ceased altogether.

> Mahmoud: I have more ideas about bullying, and then how to solve bullying. Then what are the different kinds of bullying. You can learn that someone can hurt someone's' feeling and then what type of bully there is, and how bully

take . . . um . . . Bully topic. Make me know what is a solution, and then it gets bigger, just as the three stages of bully which is latent, emerging and also manifest. Ya.

Recommendations for further research

The outcomes of the *Acting Against Bullying* research with this group of recently arrived refugees offer clear confirmation of the results of extensive, previous studies that established that this particular combination of drama and peer teaching works to empower students to deal with bullying and conflict irrespective of the educational background, ethnicity, culture or the language level of the participant group. As with all previous implementations of the programme, the use of drama allowed the newly arrived refugee participants to draw on their own experiences of bullying and conflict to create scenarios that allowed them to explore these experiences from a number of perspectives and in a safe space where conflict could be distanced and fictionalized. Kai Mai and Mahmoud were able to control the representation of past or present bullying encounters as the directors of the performances, allowing them to experiment with strategies of dealing with them they could apply in future – as Mahmoud in fact did.

The range of drama activities also allowed all the students to create and enact completely fictional scenarios, providing a range of reflective opportunities both in the action of the drama and outside it. The summative interviews confirmed that these forms of reflection had occurred, and all the students were emphatic that they had acquired valuable information and skills which they believe had empowered them, not only to deal with conflict uses, but in their school experiences more generally.

At the same time, *The Arrivals* research provided further evidence of the requirement to adapt drama-based programmes to the needs of each participant group. In this case, the differing English language levels of the students and their lack of experience with classroom drama meant that a number of strategies had to be implemented. These included some overt teaching of improvisation and enactment skills such as the use of transformation, and also encouraging groups of students to perform in their own languages. These modifications to the programme allowed the students to feel more confident in their use of drama and enhanced their confidence and self-esteem in regards to performance.

References

Berry, J. W., Phinney, J. S., Sam, D. l., and Vedder, P. (2006), 'Immigrant youth: Acculturation, identity, and adaptation'. *Applied Psychology: An International Review*, 55, (3), 303–32.

Billson, J. and Tiberius, R. (1991), 'Effective social arrangements for teaching and learning'. *New Directions for Teaching and Learning*, 45, (3), 87–109.

Boal, A. (1979), *The Theatre of the Oppressed*. London: Pluto.

—(1996), 'Politics, education and change', in J. O'Toole and K. Donelan (eds), *Drama Culture and Empowerment: The IDEA Dialogues*. Brisbane: IDEA Publications.

Bolton, G. (1998), *Acting in Classroom Drama: A Critical Analysis*. Stoke-on-Trent: Trentham.

Bolton, G. and Heathcote, D. (1998), 'Teaching culture through drama', in M. Byram and M. Fleming (eds), *Language Learning in Intercultural Perspective*. Cambridge: Cambridge University Press.

Boud, D., Cohen, R., and Simpson, J. (2001), *Peer Learning in Higher Education*. London: Kogan Page.

Burton, B. (1991), *The Act of Learning: The Drama-Theatre Continuum in the Classroom*. Melbourne: Longman Cheshire.

—(2008), 'Acting against Bullying in schools', in A. O'Brien and K. Donelan (eds), *The Arts and Youth at Risk: Global and Local Challenges*. Cambridge Scholars Publishing, Newcastle upon Tyne, UK, pp. 139–55.

—(2011), *Living Drama*, 4th edn. Melbourne Pearson Education.

—(2012), 'Peer teaching as a strategy schools for conflict management and student re-engagement'. *Australian Educational Researcher*, 39, 1.

Burton, B. and O'Toole, J. (2009), 'Power in their Hands: The outcomes of the Acting Against Bullying Research Project'. *Applied Theatre Researcher*, 10, 1–15.

Crothers, L. M., Field, J. E., and Kolbert, J. B. (2005), 'Navigating power, control and being nice: Aggression in adolescent girls' friendships'. *Journal of Counselling and Development*, 83, 349–54.

Fleming, M. (1998), 'Cultural awareness and dramatic art forms', in M. Byram and M. Fleming (eds), *Language Learning in Intercultural Perspective*. Cambridge: Cambridge University Press.

Ferjoa, T. and Vickers M. (2010), 'Supporting refugee students in school education in Greater Western Sydney'. *Critical Studies in Education*, 51, (2), 149–62.

Goodlad, S. and Hirst, B. (eds) (1998), *Mentoring and Tutoring by Students*. London: Kogan Page.

Gordon, E. E. (2005), *Peer Tutoring: A teacher's Resource Guide*. Lanham Maryland: Scarecrow Education.

Hunter, M. (2008), 'Cultivation the art of safe space'. *RIDE*, 13, (1), 5–21.

Kana, P. and Aitkin, V. (2007), 'She didn't ask about my grandmother: Using process drama to explore issues of cultural exclusion and educational leadership'. *Journal of Educational Administration*, 45, (6), 697–710.

Liebmann, M. (2004), *Arts Approaches to Conflict*. UK: Jessica Kingsley.

Lofgren, H. and Malm, B. (2005), *Bridging The fields of Drama and Conflict Management: Empowering Students to Handle Conflicts through School – Based Programmes*. Studia Psychologica et Paedagogica Series Altera CLXX Malmo University Sweden, School of Teacher Education.

McDougall, B. and Chilcott, T. (2009), *Bullying is Out of Control in Schools. The Courier Mail June 1 2009*. Brisbane : Associated Newspapers.

Matthews, J. (2008), 'Schooling and settlement: Refugee education in Australia'. *International Studies of Sociology in Education*, 18, (1), 31–45.

Morrison, M. (2004), 'Risk and responsibility: The potential of peer teaching to address negative leadership'. *Improving Schools*, 7, (3), 217–26.

Morrison, M., Burton, B., and O'Toole, J. (2006), 'Re-engagement through Peer teaching drama – Insights into reflective practice', in P. Barnard and S. Hennessy (eds), *Reflective Practices in Arts Education*. Netherlands: Springer.

Neelands, J. (2009), 'Acting together: Ensemble as a democratic process in art and life'. *Research in Drama Education: The Journal of Applied Theatre and Performance*, 14, (2), 173–89.

Nicholson, H. (2006), *Applied Drama: The Gift of Theatre*. UK: Palgrave Macmillan.

O'Neill, C. (1995), *Drama World: A Framework for Process Drama*. Portsmouth, NH: Heinemann.

O'Toole, J., Burton, B., and Plunkett, A. (2005), *Cooling Conflicts: A New Approach to Conflict and Bullying in Schools*. Sydney: Pearson Education.

Rubin, J. and Herbert, M. (1998), 'Peer teaching – Model for active learning'. *College Teaching*, 48, (1), 26–30.

Taylor, S. (2008), 'Schooling and the settlement of refugee young people in Queensland. The challenges are massive'. *Social Alternatives*, 27, (3), 58–65.

Yohani, S. (2008), 'Creating an ecology of hope: Arts-based interventions with Refugee children'. *Child and Adolescent Social Work Journal*, 25, 309–23.

6

Drama and Global Citizenship Education: Planting Seeds of Social Conscience and Change

Chan, Yuk-Lan Phoebe

Post-performance workshop. Oxfam's Interactive Education Centre.

The students are having a discussion on how they would arrange six objects spatially to represent the relationship between the characters in the Theatre-in-Education performance they have just watched.

'I think the child labour is at the bottom as she is powerless.'

'The factory owner and the salesperson should go next. They also have little say on what happens to them.'

'The boss of the multinational corporation is at the top; he is in control of everything.'

'But isn't the government official having the most crucial role? His policies govern how business is done.'

There was a short debate at this point, until another student decided to place the cap, the object representing the consumer, on top of everything. 'I think the consumer has the utmost power. If he doesn't buy any goods from the enterprise, there will be no business.'

'I don't agree,' another student said. Then she took the cap away, put it at a far corner of the room and turned it away from all the other objects. 'I think the

Figure 6.1 *Fifty Square Feet* – a Theatre-in-Education program on local poverty at Oxfam's Interactive Education Centre.

consumer has no idea about what is happening. He is ignorant. As consumers we have not paid attention to the fact that what happens in the other side of the world is closely related to us.'

The above vignette gives a glimpse of students' learning experience at Oxfam's Interactive Education Centre (IEC) in Hong Kong. The Centre was established out of the concern about inspiring young people to think about their roles and responsibilities as citizens in the globalized world. Oxfam identified drama as an effective teaching approach for Global Citizenship Education (GCE), as both drama and GCE stress participatory and empowering learning processes that build connectedness, develop critical thinking and enable learners to take actions. For the past 11 years, I have been collaborating with Oxfam in designing and conducting drama programs at IEC. This collaboration recently gave rise to a pilot project named *Drama and Liberal Studies: A Crossover* (abbreviated as *Crossover* in the remainder of this chapter), aimed at exploring the impact of an extended drama-GCE program in a Hong Kong school. In this chapter I will draw upon personal reflections of my experiences at Oxfam's Interactive Education Centre and students' voices in the *Crossover* project to conceptualize the role of drama in GCE.

Educating for critical global citizenship

In the past decades, GCE has become a focal point of educational discourse within the formal school sector and non-governmental organization (NGO) sector. The fast-changing world brings about the need for equipping young people with the capacity for addressing the large and globally interconnected issues facing our society – social, political, economic and environmental issues like poverty, climate change, racism, war and conflicts . . . to name a few. At the heart of GCE is a concern about finding relevant and meaningful pedagogical approaches that enhance students' global perspectives and commitment to engaging with global civic society.

GCE has been widely discussed within different domains of education including: global education (Hicks 2003); citizenship education (Demaine 2002); multicultural education (Banks 2004); human rights education (Gaudelli and Fernekes 2004); and environmental education (McNaughton 2004). However, there is little consensus in terms of achieving a definition of GCE. It remains a contested concept that involves ongoing debates about politics, identity, equality, rights and pedagogy (Davies 2006; Demaine 2002). The definition of GCE in contemporary literature 'spans from a vague sense of belonging to a global community to more specific ways of individual and collective involvement in global politics' (Rapoport 2010, p. 180).

Shultz (2007) asserts that differences in theoretical standpoints and assumptions about citizenship have led to vastly different, and even contradictory, approaches to GCE, and reminds global citizenship educators to be conscious of the underlying assumptions that inform their practice. As a facilitator of Oxfam's GCE initiatives, I employ Oxfam's definition of GCE in my work and as such its key assumptions underpin my thinking. It offers a critical view of this term by emphasizing that global citizenship:

> . . . goes beyond simply knowing that we are citizens of the globe to an acknowledgement of our responsibilities both to each other and to the Earth itself. Global Citizenship is about understanding the need to tackle injustice and inequality, and having the desire and ability to work actively to do so. (Oxfam 1997)

This 'critical' view contrasts with other 'soft' approaches to GCE (Andreotti 2006), for as Andreotti asserts, in order to understand global issues, a complex web of cultural and material local/global contexts needs to be scrutinized with a lens that addresses unequal power relationships in the society and the structural causes of social and economic inequalities. GCE, in this perspective, is far more than just bringing about international awareness or celebrating cultural diversity, but essentially deals with justice, human rights and responsibilities.

This view of GCE also forces educators to consider how global citizenship curricula need to be conceived with consideration of theoretical, philosophical and ethical positions on social development. In addition, it urges educators to adopt pedagogical approaches that are 'based on human rights and a concern for social justice which encourages critical thinking and responsible participation' (Osler and Vincent 2002, p. 2). Also, enabling young people to act upon their responsibilities to humanity becomes essential in nurturing 'agents of change rather than passive observers of world events' (Lim 2008, p. 1074).

The importance of action and participation is a key focus in GCE literature (e.g. Brooks and Holford 2009; Clougherty 2009; Nugent 2006) and is central to Oxfam's belief that GCE should aim at enabling people to 'act in such a way that the world may become more just and sustainable' (Oxfam Hong Kong 2012, p. 8). Griffiths (1998), in outlining the 'shared agenda' that characterizes various international NGOs, looks to global citizenship as based on civic duty and action:

> . . . the global citizen [is] not merely aware of her [sic] rights but able and desirous to act upon them; of an autonomous and inquiring critical disposition; but her decisions and actions tempered by an ethical concern for social justice and the dignity of humankind; therefore able, through her actions, to control and enhance the 'trajectory of the self' through life while contributing to the commonweal, the public welfare, with a sense of civic duty to replenish society. (Griffiths 1998, cited in Davies 2006, p. 8)

Davies (2006) asserts that Oxfam's critical, action-oriented definition of GCE challenges existing pedagogical philosophies that are tied to content knowledge and passing of examinations' (p. 7) and calls for participatory approaches to learning to be adopted. Clougherty (2009), in discussing the role of service learning in GCE, asserts that to enhance learners' ability to effect change, not only knowledge is required but skills and the willingness to participate in community action bear an important role. Knowledge, skills and values are widely regarded as the chief goals of GCE (Clougherty 2009; Davies 2006; Hunter 2004), and for Oxfam, they refer to:

1. *Understanding (knowledge)* – the background to global issues, including concepts of diversity, interdependence, world development (from different

perspectives), causes of poverty and social injustice, their repercussions and solutions, as well as knowledge about oneself, one's identify and one's worldview;

2. *Ability (skills)* – critical thinking, self-reflection, conflict resolution, listening to others and expressing oneself, empathetic understanding, collaboration, problem solving and turning ideas into action;

3. *Belief and willingness (values)* – empathy, humility, thankfulness, commitment to social justice, respect for others' values and autonomy, respect for diversity and interdependence, as well as belief in everyone having the capacity to change the world for the better or for worse. (Oxfam Hong Kong 2012, p. 5)

Davies (2006) suggests that these elements are integrally linked and best learned through experience so that students can see how the components work with one another holistically.

The above discussions of GCE all point to pedagogical approaches that are experiential and democratic in nature, foster critical thinking, empower learners and explore a wide range of values. Clearly GCE and drama education share much common ground.

Drama and Global Citizenship Education

My collaborations with Oxfam across the years have caused me to reflect deeply upon the role of drama in GCE. A search for literature that directly addresses drama for GCE does not offer fruitful returns, but there are of course abundant resources that position drama as a learning medium for social and ethical issues (Johnson and O'Neill 1984; Wilhelm and Edmiston 1998), drama for citizenship and human rights (Winston 2012), drama for exploring justice (Bond 2000), and drama as a pedagogy democratizing classrooms and radicalizing teaching (O'Connor 2010). Above all, the notion of 'theatre for social change' is now widely discussed in the growing field of applied theatre (Ackroyd 2000; Nicholson 2005; Thomson 2003), where drama is regarded as 'a way of conceptualizing and interpreting theatrical and cultural practices that are motivated by the desire to make a difference to the lives of others' (Nicholson 2005, p. 16).

McNaughton's (2004, 2006, 2010) empirical research in the field of sustainable development is by far the closest in terms of its philosophy to my work and experiences at Oxfam. In her work, she identifies the role of drama as:

- engaging students with learning;
- engendering sympathy and empathy;
- exploring values;
- providing a meaningful context for research about environmental issues; and
- developing skills for effective learning and in communicating, collaborating and expressing ideas and opinions.

She attributes these roles to certain pedagogical features of drama education such as a positive classroom climate fostered by democratic teaching, an emphasis on metacognition and the construction of learning, and an approach where story and the art-form are well-utilized.

Crossover: Drama and GCE in practice

In order to explore the role of drama in GCE, this chapter will now examine the findings of a project conducted for the Oxfam IEC. It was generated in response to research (Yuen et al. 2007) aimed at evaluating the effectiveness of IEC's programs (including its drama initiatives). This report found that the centre's programs were successful in arousing interest and attention towards global issues, and the impact on students' values and attitudes towards GCE issues was evident. However, the report revealed that the one-off nature of the IEC programs made behavioural changes difficult to attain.

In response to this report and these concerns, *Crossover* was designed as a pilot project to address these shortcomings by allowing students to have ongoing engagement with GCE issues over a more extended period. The program adopted multiple drama interventions and integrated drama and GCE into the existing school learning environment to examine whether behavioural changes would more likely occur when a more supportive environment and sustained intervention was available. Throughout the project, the students were asked to share narratives on the changes that had occurred (if any) across the entire range of the project, and decide on why such changes were significant to them.

The project comprised three phases:

Phase 1: Theatre-in-Education performances and workshops (12 hours)

Students attended two participatory Theatre-in-Education (TIE) performances at IEC, exploring how inequality in the society impacts on the lives of people in poverty both locally and globally. Pre- and post-performance multi-arts workshops were then held to deepen understanding of the related themes.

Phase 2: Community Research (6 hours)

Students took part in a community research project employing an inquiry approach that stressed sensory feelings and artistic methods to collect data on their communities. Data were collated to develop various forms of artistic presentations for sharing in class and for use in Phase 3 of the project.

Phase 3: Devised Theatre (18 hours)

Nine interested students participated in a devised theatre project, making use of materials collected by the whole class in Phase 2 to create a short play that conveyed global citizenship messages. Other students in the class and students in other classes attended as audience.

The project took place in a Form Four class with 33 female students (about 16–17 years old). The students were described by their teacher as 'typical adolescents in Hong Kong' who are not particularly interested in studying social issues. Interviews conducted at the beginning of the project revealed that although the students had already taken some form of action in response to social issues prior to commencing the project, the majority of them regarded acting upon social issues as 'adults' business' that bears no relation to them. Many of them expressed a sense of powerlessness in making a difference in the society.

From reading the transcripts of these interviews, I found that these young people were not as indifferent as their teacher had described, but rather, that they were selective about the social issues they paid attention to. Connectedness and feelings played an important role in this process – when the social issues were directly related to them (e.g. the government's proposed policy of compulsory drug test in schools) or when they had strong feelings about those issues (e.g. natural disasters in Mainland China), they were more ready to discuss them and take action in response to them. The forms of action they take are typical of what I come across with Hong Kong students – they tend to be soft in nature, like donating money for charity, sharing views or spreading messages in person or online. Many interviewees saw more critical actions like demonstrations and protests, taking a stand in signing petitions or advocating ideas in online platforms, as being 'unnecessarily radical'.

These themes of connectedness, strong personal feelings and soft approach to action would continue to be apparent in students' narratives throughout the project. For example, after the first phase of *Crossover,* which consisted of two TIE programs about local and global poverty, the students noted that they had gained deeper empathic understanding of poor people's situations and that these understandings had brought about change in attitudinal terms. For example, one student explains:

> . . . like the cleaning workers or shopkeepers . . . In the past I used to think that they are of lower class, and I somehow looked down on them. Now I begin to respect them . . . I've realized that there are many stories behind their hardships, which I didn't know before . . . Yet these people work very hard to try improving their families' situations. I feel more strongly for them, respect them more, and am more motivated to help them.

The students explained that their empathic understanding arose from the impact of the live TIE performance, in which feelings were more immediate and the mood more intense compared with watching TV documentaries or reading newspaper in ordinary classrooms. Coupled with the role-taking activities in the pre and post-performance workshops, they found that these drama experiences elicited 'concrete images and genuine experiences', brought 'something afar closer to me', made them 'believe that poverty does exist in our society' and enhanced 'critical thinking as it gets me to consider the issue in multi-angles when I step into different roles'.

By contrast, the students' responses to the community research project in the second phase of the program were a lot less enthusiastic. When asked to complete an investigation into everyday encounters within their immediate communities and collect materials for a multi-arts presentation (drama, video or installation), the students found the task uninteresting and of little relevance to their studies. They explained that since it was close to exam time, they were concerned about the time demands of accomplishing these projects. However, from the research team's observations, the students' disengagement appeared to also relate to the form of the intervention and the topic chosen. These research and presentation tasks, though artistic in nature, had much weaker dramatic impact than the TIE works they encountered in the first phase of the program. Furthermore, researching on their personal experiences was seen as 'too trivial' in comparison with larger societal issues. Although the task was set in an attempt to help students see how the society is connected to them in their everyday lives, it was not as effective in bringing about emotional responses as the more controversial, but personally relevant topics like compulsory drug testing of students might have done.

In the final phase of the program, interested students participated in the devising of a short play to convey GCE messages to peers. The play was presented for their own classmates as well as others in the same grade level. In this phase, a stark difference was noticed between the response of the audience group and the devising group.

While the audience group for these performances did not show significant changes in their attitudes when compared to those generated by their TIE experiences, data relating to the nine students who participated as devisers and actors in the play revealed that by embodying the characters within a performance, they developed much stronger feelings and a deeper understanding of other people in the society. The characters became very real to them as they were based on research of real people's cases. The students had to consider detailed information in order to create believable and coherent characters, and this process changed 'dead information into live, vivid knowledge', as one student put it. This resulted in stronger concern and connectedness with other people in the society, as evidenced by two student comments:

> I used to think that those things like minimum wage protection are unrelated to me. I didn't find any reason for paying attention to low-wage workers. After this performance I found that . . . their lives are really deprived, and I am more interested in studying the news related to them (a student who played the role of a dish washer in a restaurant).
>
> Now, when I see minibus or taxi drivers on the street, I would pay more attention to them . . . I don't know why but I would observe their facial expressions . . . Looking at them I feel that I am somehow related to them (a student who played the role of a minibus driver who also drives taxi at night to make ends meet).

The devised theatre project also developed strong ownership to the project and a sense of agency. The students regarded their work as being highly successful in educating their peers and believed that the audience would have made deep reflections on the themes of their play. Importantly however, interviews with students in the audience group showed that they did not find the performance particularly enlightening in comparison with the TIE works they participated in during the earlier phase of the project.

These results suggest that participation in an action-learning project, in the form of a devised theatre performance, played a significant role in helping this smaller group of students internalize learning, build stronger connection with the society and gain agency. These outcomes were brought about through not only the affective embodiment of the others, but also the emancipatory nature of the drama pedagogy. For example, a student shared that she had become more outspoken as the project always encouraged her to express her own opinions because views were openly accepted. Another student shared how drama helped her see 'possibilities of change':

> I am learning how to change things that you don't like to see happening . . . Who am I? What do I want? What ability do I possess to make a difference? . . . Drama helped me pay more attention to details . . . those small things that the characters did . . . I saw alternatives, choices . . . I realized that there are indeed possibilities for change at many levels . . . The impact of what we do may not be obvious, but I do see possibilities . . .

The students' response to the three phases of the program indicates that drama is able to arouse empathy and concerns, build connectedness to the society and give young people agency to make small changes in their lives. The difference between those who took part in the action learning project and those who didn't also indicates the more positive impact of sustained engagement and opportunity for taking initiative and ownership in the learning process. The lessons learned from Phase 2 of the program are worth considering in future projects, including topics to be addressed and forms of drama interventions that appeal to young people.

How did the drama work support these students?

The findings in *Crossover*, together with more than 10 years' work in Oxfam's IEC, help me in developing an understanding of how drama supports GCE. This understanding is encapsulated in a recent book published by Oxfam, in which I shared a documentary account of a facilitator development course and listed five characteristics of drama that I believe are pertinent to Oxfam's goals for GCE (Chan 2012, p. 18). Here I would like to take the discussion further by accounting for the theoretical and pedagogical assumptions behind the five themes:

1. **In drama, participants identify with roles and situations and embody other people's experiences to develop emphatic understandings.**
   At the heart of drama is 'the idea that it can take people beyond themselves and into the worlds of others . . . and this chimes particularly well with a vision of social citizenship as a collective and communitarian undertaking' (Nicholson 2005, p. 24). By embodying situations of the others, participants in drama actively engage in moral imagination that challenges

the self-centred perspective (Winston 2012). In so doing, and as they step
out of the drama to reflect upon their experiences, a kind of empathy that
is both cognitive and affective could be produced. The interplay between
cognitive and affective factors in empathy is essential in bringing about
altruistic and moral behaviours (Hoffman 2000).

2. **Drama provides authentic contexts for exploring complex ideas,
   adopting multiple perspectives and tackling controversial issues safely.**
   Exploring global issues puts learners in touch with a range of topics that are
   complex and often abstract or conceptual. Drama, by placing these topics
   within fictional, human contexts, helps visualize ideas and abstract concepts
   for understanding to be developed and values to be explored. With suitable
   framing of roles and scenes, drama can provide learners with a range of
   perspectives to examine an issue so that alternative views are considered. The
   pedagogy of drama also allows learners to temporarily suspend reality without
   binding consequences, providing a safe arena in which the very controversial
   issues defining contemporary democracy can be explored in depth.

3. **Drama is a reflection of the human world in which there is no absolute
   'right' or 'wrong'. It enables dialogues between different voices and
   perspectives, between self and role, and between teachers and learners to
   develop dialectic discourses, critical thinking and self-reflection.**
   GCE has the most successful impact when it is set within a learning
   environment which 'resist the lure of absolutism' and 'enable comfort
   with uncertainty and fluidity' (Davies 2006, p. 18). Drama does not aim
   to transmit a particular ideology but provides us a place to 'see anew,
   understand ourselves more fully, expand our thinking and understand how
   that thinking has been shaped by our social positions'(Gallagher 2000,
   p. 82). Through role taking, participants in drama not only can develop
   dialogues between oneself and the others, but may also discover 'a more
   complex range of selfs or multiple subjectivities' (O'Connor 2010, p. 123)
   upon which critical self-reflections can be based. Further reflections can
   also occur when dialogues are formed between the fictional and the real
   world, through the 'dual effect' (Vygotsky 1976) in drama. At its best, the
   pedagogical process in drama is also dialogic in itself, in which teachers
   and learners are engaged equally, communicate in a collaborative manner
   and 'so gaining a progressive control over social processes' (Jackson 2005, p.
   113). Such kind of dialogic pedagogies fosters empowerment and liberation
   for the citizens of a democracy.

4. **Drama adopts experiential pedagogy that develops the habit of responding to matters through action, and brings about an acknowledgement of the power of actions.**

   Rooted in Dewey's pragmatic educational philosophy, the praxis of drama education is grounded in the primacy of experience. Experiential learning in drama stresses active engagement and the body as a learning vehicle. The holistic body-mind experiences in drama is likened to those in Eastern cultural practices, and developing the possibilities of the body becomes an essential process in unraveling habitual bodily patterns that has been shaped socioculturally (Hwang 2009). In the Boalian sense, the body becomes the site of rehearsing for ways of dealing with oppressions and power struggles in real life, and 'theatre [becomes] rehearsal for revolution' (Boal 1979, p. 122)

5. **Drama is a group art. The process of drama entails listening, expression, respect, collaboration, problem solving and interdependent relationship among its participants.**

   Drama pedagogy is characterized by its collaborative processes requiring participation skills in a communal art event. It empowers students to strive for greater individual and collective achievement and at the same time celebrating their own contributions and creativity. Neelands (O'Connor 2010), in arguing for a 'theatre of direct democracy', asserts that this process must involve learners in:

   > . . . a participatory theatre which is made by all who engage with it. A theatre in which the roles of social and artistic actor are fluid and transposable. A theatre which negotiates different perspectives of the world and different possibilities for changing it. A theatre which is more like a hologram or a kaleidoscope than a finely focused and well lit mirror. (p. 148)

But . . . have we made a (big) difference?

The discussion above offers a very positive view of drama as an effective pedagogy for GCE. However, one aspect of the data in *Crossover* troubles me and causes me to wonder about the degree it has helped tackle the structural causes of social injustice at the core of Oxfam's GCE. As noted above, the drama approaches used in the project clearly helped students build affective connectedness to those social issues which they regard as pertinent. For some students, this affective connection was useful in strengthening the motivation behind their social actions, such as donating money. For example, one student notes:

> I would save up some money for donation. I used to do that too, but the thinking is now different. In the past I only took it casually and thought 'Let's try to help people when I can.' Now I feel more strongly about their helplessness and wish to help them from the bottom of my heart.

However, responses from a considerable number of students in the non-devising group reveal that the deepened empathic understanding of poor people's lives actually brought them to consider their own situations more than that of others. For example, students suggested that they now realize that earning money is difficult, that it is important to treasure what they possess or that they should spend less money and study hard to earn more in the future in order to avoid becoming poor. In this group of students, the project seemed to turn them inwards, causing them to consider taking actions only to improve their own situations rather than conditions in the society at large.

As our program did not just aim at arousing empathy, but also discussed with students the role inequality plays in global citizenship issues, these comments reveal that these students are not always ready to act upon changing inequality. Instead, what was generated was a desire to change people's individual circumstances to cope with the structural problems. For the students who are willing to offer help to the deprived, it is achieved by donating money to improve their financial situations. For some other students, it is about ensuring that they avoided being poor – a mindset that potentially reinforces the rich and poor divide and is therefore not useful in addressing the structural causes of injustice.

Among other social and development issues, those related to inequality are the ones young people in Hong Kong are often least ready to engage with (Centre for Youth Research and Practice 2008). One reason may be that the complexity of these issues can easily trigger a sense of helplessness when one comes to understand them more deeply. At the same time, the 'plural atmosphere' (Oldfield 1990) in the students' upbringing may be another factor influencing their readiness to become moral social agents, while their previous exposure to discourses about social injustice in the society, in the media and in their most immediate family contexts may have limited their ability to respond. When they step out of the drama classroom into this plural atmosphere, how much of the impact of programs like these remains? Importantly too, how does the impact stand up against the grand narratives of social development that privilege economic growth over justice?

It is perhaps unrealistic to expect our students to gain agency for fighting against inequality in one day – or even in 6 months (the duration of our program). What the project shows, nevertheless, is how drama was able to plant small seeds of 'I care' and 'I am capable of doing something'. Whether personal relevance could later turn into moral and social obligation is something we cannot foresee and for this reason, Balfour's (2009) reminder is a useful one. He believes that a more realistic view of drama work is to see it as 'a theatre of little change' which resists the 'bait of social change' and acknowledges instead that our practice is 'not always linear, rational and conclusive in its outcomes, but is more often messy, incomplete, complex and tentative' (p. 375).

Acknowledgement

I would like to thank all the young people in this study for their participation and candid sharing, their teacher and their school for the tremendous support in the program. Special thanks to Julie Dunn for her valuable advice on the design and implementation of project, and Liu Pui-Fong, Lam Yin Krissy, Poon Wing-Shuen Iris, Law Yuk-Lan Paris and So Yuk-Yan for participating as co-researchers.

References

Ackroyd, J. (2000), 'Applied theatre: Problems and possiblities'. *Applied Theatre Researcher*, 1, Article 1.

Andreotti, V. (2006), 'Soft versus critical global citizenship education'. *Policy and Practice: A Development Education Review*, 3, 40–51.

Balfour, M. (2009), 'The politics of intention: Looking for a theatre of little changes'. *Research in Drama Education: The Journal of Applied Theatre and Performance*, 14, (3), 347–59.

Banks, J. A. (2004), 'Teaching for social justice diversity, and citizenship in a global world'. *The Educational Forum*, 68, (4), 295–305.

Boal, A. (1979), *Theatre of the Oppressed*, trans. A. Charles and M.-O. L. McBride. London: Pluto Press.

Bond, E. (2000), *The Hidden Plot: Notes on Theatre and the State*. London: Methuen.

Brooks, R. M. and Holford, J. A. K. (2009), 'Citizenship, learning and education: Themes and issues'. *Citizenship Studies*, 13, (2), 85–103.

Centre for Youth Research and Practice (2008), *Research on Youth Engagement in Social and Development Issues*. Hong Kong: Hong Kong Baptist University.

Chan, Y. L. P. (2012), *Exploring Poverty through Drama: The Use of Drama in Global Citizenship Education*. Hong Kong: Oxfam. (Chinese publication: 陳玉蘭 (2012), 《戲中探貧窮 ：以戲劇手法進行世界公民教育》, 香港 ：樂施會。)

Clougherty, C. H. (2009), *A Critical Evaluation of the Nobis project – A Creative Process Approach to Service Learning and Global Citizenship Education*. Unpublished PhD thesis, The University of Birmingham.

Davies, L. (2006), 'Global citizenship: Abstraction or framework for action?' *Education Review*, 58, (1), 5–25.

Demaine, J. (2002), 'Globalisation and citizenship education'. *International Studies in Sociology of Education*, 12, (2), 117–28.

Gallagher, K. (2000), *Drama Education in the Lives of Girls*. Toronto: University of Toronto Press.

Gaudelli, W. and Fernekes, W. (2004), 'Teaching about global human rights for global citizenship'. *The Social Studies*, 95, (1), 16–26.

Hicks, D. (2003), 'Thirty years of global education: A reminder of key principles and precedents'. *Educational Review*, 55, (3), 265–75.

Hoffman, M. L. (2000), *Empathy and Counselling: Explorations in Theory and Research*. New York: Springer-Verlag.

Hunter, W. (2004), *Knowledge, Skills, Attitudes, and Experiences Necessary to Become Globally Competent*. Unpublished PhD thesis, Lehigh University, Pennsylvania.

Hwang, H. Y. (2009), 'Between artistic instrumentalism in applied drama and the notion of cultivation in Eastern theory and practice of art', in C. Y. J. Shu and Y. L. P. Chan (eds), *Planting Trees of Drama with Global Vision in Local Knowledge: IDEA 2007 Dialogues*. Hong Kong: Hong Kong Drama/Theatre and Education Forum, pp. 205–21.

Jackson, A. (2005), 'The dialogic and the aesthetic: Some reflections on theatre as a learning medium'. *The Journal of Aesthetic Education*, 39, (4), 104–18.

Johnson, L. and O'Neill, C. (eds) (1984), *Dorothy Heathcote: Collected Writings on Education and Drama*. Evanston, IL: Northwestern University Press.

Lim, C. P. (2008), 'Global citizenship education, school curriculum and games: Learning mathematics, English and science as a global citizen'. *Computers & Education*, 51, (3), 1073–93.

McNaughton, M. J. (2004), 'Educational drama in the teaching of education for sustainability'. *Environmental Education Research*, 10, (2), 139–55.

—(2006), 'Learning from participants' responses in educational drama in the teaching of Education for Sustainable Development'. *Research in Drama Education: The Journal of Applied Theatre and Performance*, 11, (1), 19–41.

—(2010), 'Educational drama in education for sustainable development: Ecopedagogy in action'. *Pedagogy, Culture & Society*, 18, (3), 289–308.

Nicholson, H. (2005), *Applied Drama: The Gift of Theatre*. Basingstoke: Palgrave Macmillian.

Nugent, R. (2006), 'Civic, social and political education: Active learning, participation and engagement?' *Irish Educational Studies*, 25, (2), 207–29.

O'Connor, P. (ed.) (2010), *Creating Democratic Citizenship through Drama Education: The Writings of Jonothan Neelands*. Stoke on Trent: Trentham Books.

Oldfield, A. (1990), 'Citizenship: An unnatural practice?' *Political Quarterly*, 61, 177–87.

Osler, A. and Vincent, K. (2002), *Citizenship and the Challenge of Global Education*. London: Trentham.

Oxfam (1997), What is Global Citizenship? Retrieved 12 August 2012, from http://www.oxfam.org.uk/education/gc/what_and_why/what/

Oxfam Hong Kong (2012), *Global Citizenship Education School Guide: Concepts, Practice, Experience*. Hong Kong: Oxfam.

Rapoport, A. (2010), 'We cannot teach what we don't know: Indiana teachers talk about global citizenship education'. *Education, Citizenship and Social Justice*, 5, (3), 179–90.

Shultz, L. (2007), 'Educating for global citizenship: Conflicting agendas and understandings'. *Alberta Journal of Educational Research*, 53, (3), 248–58.

Thomson, J. (2003), *Applied Theatre: Bewilderment and Beyond*. Bern: Peter Lang.

Vygotsky, L. S. (1976), 'Play and its role in the mental development of the child', in J. S. Bruner, A. Jolly and K. Sylva (eds), *Play: It's Role in Development and Evolution*. New York: Basic Books, pp. 537–54.

Wilhelm, J. D. and Edmiston, B. (1998), *Imaging to Learn: Inquiry, Ethics, and Integration through Drama*. Portsmouth, NH: Heinemann.

Winston, J. (2012), 'Citizenship, human rights and applied drama'. *Research in Drama Education: The Journal of Applied Theatre and Performance*, 12, (3), 269–74.

Yuen, Y. M. C., Yeung, S. Y. S., Leung, Y. W., and Lam, T. S. J. (2007), *Report on the Evaluation Study on the Oxfam Hong Kong's Interactive Education Centre*. Hong Kong: Centre for Citizenship Education, The Hong Kong Institute of Education.

7

Drama, Listening, Risk and Difference: On the Pedagogical Importance of (not) Knowing the Other

Kathleen Gallagher and Burcu Yaman Ntelioglou

Introduction

Cultural geographer Doreen Massey (2006) writes about the myth of the shrinking world, an idea that is perpetuated by the powerful, she argues, and one that presents us with the illusion that we know the world and each other much better than we do. This impulse can dangerously mask difference, material conditions and power relations, while limiting opportunities for recognizing spaces of conflict and potential growth. It becomes difficult, she further argues, for alternatives to be developed and easy for tentative attempts at alternative ways of doing things to be defeated.

A specific, highly multicultural, urban drama class is the space at the centre of this chapter. Contrary to ubiquitous notions of drama as a space of empathic learning, or of classroom communities as unproblematic and homogeneous entities, this chapter articulates a perspective on drama as a space where unfamiliarity is important, where rigorous listening is prized and where simply knowing one another becomes complicated by deeper understandings of one's own investments and positionings in a broader social structure. In such a space, how drama teaches us about one another is rather an opportunity for the as-yet uninitiated conversation.

Summary of the research project:
Context, methodology and purpose

The study from which this chapter is drawn is an international multi-sited 5-year ethnographic project aimed at better understanding the complexities of artistic, social and academic engagement for high-school students in socioeconomically marginalized schools in Toronto, Canada; Boston, USA; Lucknow, India; and Taipei, Taiwan. Researchers in all four sites engaged in ethnographic work in each school, working collaboratively with classroom teachers, students, and visiting artists who contributed to the drama curriculum. The curricular expectations, and the way drama was positioned in the larger school, remained different in each site, as was the kind of drama pedagogy experienced by the students in the particular classrooms. Further on-line surveys across sites and 'live' surveys completed in each classroom, following what the teachers deemed particularly engaging lessons, gave us a sense of how drama students were responding to the pedagogies and the artistic work they encountered. The theatre-making from each site was also shared with other international researchers via digital video uploading to blog sites. On-line collaborative questions and analysis of the digital performance data engaged the researchers across sites in a sustained dialogue about the differences and similarities we noted in the classroom cultures, the student (dis)engagement, the drama pedagogies and the theatre-making practices.

In this chapter, we put forward for consideration some analyses of qualitative data from one of our Toronto sites, Middleview Technical High School (pseudonym), and examine the drama classroom as an alternative space where we come to know one another; a space that teaches us about one another through experiences of conflict and processes of rupture.

The golden rule: Listen to each other
(aka 'Respect the Pumpkin')

The compulsion in education generally, and for teachers in particular, to manage the environment is powerful. Despite democratic principles and utopic dreams of community, a teacher is often, despite even her/his own professional desires, thrust into the position of autocrat. There have to be rules; ergo, there have to be guardians of rules. Rules make us behave better, it is believed. But what if

Figure 7.1 The Doors Project Rules.

the rule to 'listen to each other' is taken at its word? What if listening is not a simple performance of compliance but a serious activity in a classroom? And what, therefore, happens when we hear things we don't like? when we hear views that disturb us, or challenge us, or call into question the things we hold dearest? or interrupt our easy judgements about who our classmates are?

We recall here Doreen Massey's caution about the myth of the shrinking world in reference to the drama class that we observed in the first year of the project. In this drama class a rather expansive sense of the world rather than a familiar and 'shrinking' one was fostered. As with any metropolis, however, there would need to be rules of governance. The students signed 'The Doors Project Rules' (pictured above), a set of guidelines to outline the terms of engagement for the collaborative project they were about to begin together. Contemplating the importance of 'safe space' in drama classrooms where creativity is the modus operandi, Nicholson (2006) writes:

> Transforming highly regulated spaces into creative performance and workshop spaces is not just an interesting artistic challenge. It involves reconstructing how space is conceived, temporarily overlaying its codes with alternative spatial practices . . . If spaces for drama are to become 'seedbeds of cultural creativity', they will enable participants to experiment with the production and reproduction of space collaboratively, recognizing that its meanings can be complexly symbolized and layered. (Nicholson 2006, p. 129)

'The Doors Project' was a collective creation built from monologues written by the students that were inspired by the idea of a door as a metaphor, a door as a threshold, something that opens or closes in our lives. The teacher, Ms S, and the students decided together to agree upon a written set of rules because of some tensions among students and policing of one another's behaviours that had previously been happening in the classroom. These uncomfortable events, prior to the drama project, the 'baggage' students brought to class, had complicated this rather more easy notion of listening to one another. Still, one of the rules Ms S and the students included in the list was 'respect the pumpkin', that is, 'listen to each other'.

Ms S had brought a small pumpkin to class, which stood in as the symbol for listening. When someone held the pumpkin, all others in the room were obliged to respectfully listen to the words of the student holding the pumpkin so that the usual cacophony of the room did not reign. Students had been complaining that they were not being heard, that they were always being interrupted. Ms S thought she would make more tangible the act of listening by symbolizing it, by using the pumpkin to clearly demarcate who held the power at any given moment so that the more complicated social relations in the room would not interfere with her basic plea for students to listen respectfully to one another.

A review of key literature: Listening in education

In *The Other Side of Language: A Philosophy of Listening*, Gemma Corradi Fiumara (1990) writes: 'Among the widespread meanings of the Greek term logos there do not appear to be recognizable references to the notion and capacity of listening; in the tradition of western thought we are thus faced with a system of knowledge that tends to ignore listening processes' (p. 1). A number of scholars in education have pointed to the importance of listening for democratic and critical dialogue in school contexts (Boler 2004; Garrison 2004; Zúñiga et al. 2002; Zúñiga et al. 2012). Boler (2004) writes 'one of the few places we may be able to exorcise some of the roots of inequality of speech is in the classroom, as painful and messy as this process may be.' She maintains that it is important to give space for students to be heard, especially those voices usually silenced in society. She further argues that, 'until all voices are recognized equally, we must operate within a context of historicized ethics which consciously privileges the insurrectionary and dissenting voices, sometimes at the minor cost of silencing

those voices that have been permitted dominant status for the past century'
(p. 13) Garrison (2004) too writes: 'I endorse the emphasis on open-mindedness
and listening as an antidote to violence', however cautioning that 'they too
can conceal violence' (p. 101). Listening, in his view then, is powerful but also
potentially complicit in power imbalances.

In *Democratic Dialogue in Education,* Burbules (2004) writes that there are
many kinds of listening and many reasons to listen: 'listening to learn, listening
as an expression of empathy or concern; listening as an act of obligation to others,
growing out of respect; listening as an active process of perspective talking;
listening as a passive receipt of information; and so on.' Burbules claims that 'the
educational benefits of listening, and of encouraging listening in the classroom,
depends on what kind of listening is going on' (p. xxv). He warns educators that
creating a discursive space in which some class members can speak does not
automatically mean that others will listen to them; or if they do, whether it will
be of the sort desired. This observation suggests that there is a way to listen that
encourages others to speak. In the following section, we describe a classroom
context where we were witness to the kind of engaged listening that Burbules is
clearly calling for.

In the drama education/applied theatre literature, particular theorizations
or studies of listening are not in evidence. Given the importance of listening
in theatre-making of all kinds, it is surprising that listening as a key idea has
not emerged more strongly in the literature. It is of course implicit in most
studies of drama, that is, that processes of role-playing, ensemble work, acting or
community development through theatre rely heavily on listening as a central
skill. Examining listening, speaking and more general skills of communication
honed in drama classrooms, Andy Kempe (2003) argued that teachers ought to
pay more attention to the ways in which drama increases such skills because they
help students to develop social capital. Although focusing more on speech in his
research, Kempe nonetheless concludes that drama 'can play a significant role in
helping young people accrue social capital by enhancing their understanding
of and ability to engage effectively in live oral discourse' (p. 77). Sarah Jane
Dickenson (2006) as a writer of plays for young people, reflected on her attempts
to use linguistic devices to encourage young performers to listen better in order
to develop greater performance skills by helping them understand that 'effective
communication requires connectivity' (p. 100). Yassa (1999) examined the role
of creative drama in developing social interaction skills, examining such things

as democracy, communication, respect, empathy, flexibility and tolerance. Yassa's data validated the widespread assertion that 'drama education enhances the development of social skills' (p. 38). She concluded that by being able to regulate their emotions (e.g. anger), students became more willing to listen to, and discuss things, with others.

In drama research which focuses on community building, listening also surfaces as a noteworthy skill. Community development drama practitioner Vicki Doësebs (1998) writes about the challenges of trying to conduct a project 'on building capacity in rural communities in KwaZulu-Natal, for the National Government's Reconstruction and Development Programme' (p. 167). Doësebs touches upon the importance of listening in her project as participants explored what it meant to 'listen to one another's fear, hatred, pain, anger and hope' through drama in a village that had been affected by political violence and crime (p. 172). Similarly Lorenzo Garcia (1998), in his work, asks the question 'what does it mean to create "community" in a theatre production that seeks to display and explore cultural "difference" and identity?' (p. 156). Focusing on the themes of inclusion, collaboration and voice, Garcia asserts that 'the creation of community is . . . advanced by a willingness to recognise individual identity and the interconnectedness among group members' and that 'finding common ground is associated with preserving a compact of affirmation, solidarity and critique' (p. 155). Garcia argues that it is important for the performers (in this case, university students) to find ways to share histories, life experiences, cultures, hopes and fears for the future. (p. 164). Both Garcia and Doësebs conclude that healthy community building in drama asks participants to draw on their life experiences, as well as to listen to, and learn about, those of others.

As evident in our class list above, one could easily fathom that most students designing 'rules of conduct' for collaborative artistic projects in drama classrooms would put 'listening to each other' at the top of their list. Students know very well how important it is to hear and be heard when engaged in collective theatre-making projects. Or, to put it as Neelands (2009) does when quoting former artistic director Michael Boyd of the Royal Shakespeare Company, pondering whether ensemble can 'act in some sense as a . . . better version of the real world on an achievable scale which celebrates the virtues of collaboration' (p. 184). Listening to others, and being heard in turn by them, is a fundamental feature of such a better world.

Key findings and discussion

Listening was a vital part of our teacher, Ms S's philosophy. She is an experienced teacher who has taught drama in this technical high school for 13 years. She has training in both theatre and education. In her conversations with us, she said that teaching high-school students is very gratifying for her because teenagers are 'questioning everything'; she enjoys teaching them because she shares their curiosity. She explained, 'I don't think I've ever stopped really questioning everything. I find teenagers most connected to that way of being.' Ms S often referred to her desire to connect with broader issues and stories in life; to connect with students, their personal and cultural narratives and to create a community in her drama classroom.

Ms S described her drama pedagogy as risky, a pedagogy that invites students and teachers to speak openly and to listen to one another. For her, listening was a basic tenet, but it was also one of the most radical things we can do in a classroom. She explains that the kind of listening she was aiming to cultivate in her classroom goes beyond familiar and rote kinds of listening exercises 'where you do an exercise of active listening, you know, look at someone in the eye, nod when they're speaking, you know smile sometimes . . .' In this drama class, students were engaged in an important kind of listening, where they were asked to listen carefully to each other's experiences in order to make something of those experiences, to creatively and critically work with the narratives to produce a devised piece called 'The Doors Project' inspired from their collective personal narratives.

Through the development of the creative project, we witnessed a teacher who regularly abandoned the façade of control for a very different kind of engagement, one that demanded that students hear one another and remain attentive listeners even through all the ways in which the diverse views, experiences, cultural knowledges and artistic ideas shared may have created dissonance for them or made them feel uncomfortable. She did not paper over 'difference' but asked instead that students find a respectful way to hear the very things that may make others in the room less knowable to them. It is from this chaos wherein moments of understanding and creation became perceptible. Ms S, herself, in a spring 2011 interview reflects:

> Those conversational moments for me are the- those are the key aesthetic experiences for me in the drama classroom. Beyond the plays and the, you know,

it's the sharing of the space and it's the listening and responding to each other and
each other's experiences.

One student, Erica, revealed in an interview that it is not just listening, but
listening without judgement that is important to her as a student. In her
individual interview, she noted repeatedly how important it was for her to be
listened to without judgement. She referred to the notion of 'not being judged' on
five separate occasions throughout the 30-minute interview. She explained that
it was very significant for her to be able to share her personal narrative in which
she described her reactions to the ubiquitous discourses of homophobia she
experiences in and out of school contexts. Her narrative was written in response
to the concept of 'heaven's door'. In it, she troubled the notion that 'heaven's door
is closed to gays and lesbians'. She explained that sharing this concern was very
significant for her and that she felt extremely grateful for the opportunity to
reflect on this in her drama class. Erica said that at the beginning of the project,
when she first shared her narrative with her classmates, she worried that it was
risky to share something so personal. However, because of the overall support
she felt she received from her classmates, despite some tensions that clearly
existed among some students, she reported that their support, their ability to
hear her, compelled her to take the risk and perform her monologue for the
whole school:

> I was actually, like, really grateful, I guess I could say. A lot of kids my age don't
> handle the whole homosexual thing very well and so to have my whole class
> behind me and supporting me and stuff like that was actually – like it helped me
> a lot. Like the way I felt about myself and the way people looked at me. To know
> that my whole class was behind me no matter what and they didn't judge me or
> anything was really great . . . like I've had my family and stuff like that but when
> it comes to a whole classroom, that's never happened before really . . . it was just
> nice to have the support and that they actually wanted my piece to be in the Doors
> performance. So I was like, 'that's pretty cool.' (Erica, Individual Interview, 3 June
> 2009).

In *The Government of Self and Others*, which includes Foucault's Lectures at the
Collège de France, he discusses the importance of the notion of parre–sia. He
explains that 'one of the original meanings of the Greek word parre–sia is to "say
everything"; but in fact it is much more frequently translated as free-spokenness
(franc-parler), free speech, etcetera' (p. 43). He stressed, however, that parre-sia
also requires a relationship to the other, explaining:

. . . one cannot attend to oneself, take care of oneself, without a relationship to
another person. And the role of this other is precisely to tell the truth, to tell the
whole truth, or at any rate to tell all the truth that is necessary, and to tell it in a
certain form which is precisely parre–sia, which once again is translated as free-
spokenness (franc-parler). (p. 43)

Ms S's pedagogy invited students to care for themselves through attending to
the social relations in the room, to care for themselves through others. This
speaking, this franc-parler, takes courage. The outcome cannot be predicted. But
what is gained, as Erica describes above, is the possibility of seeing people anew,
releasing others from the prescriptive roles we assume they will take.

Erica, and other students whose voices we include below, illustrate that
this kind of frank speech, the sharing of the personal and engaged listening,
was possible because of the unique space created in the drama class. In their
interviews, they discuss the significance of interaction and communication with
other students that they 'would have never spoken to' otherwise. In fact, Erica
recounts to us:

I guess you shouldn't judge a book by its cover. That's kind of like common sense
but a lot of us don't use it sometimes. And I think that class was a really good
example because coming into that class I was like, 'oh this is going to be horrible'
like, the people that I see. (Erica, Individual Interview, 3 June 2009)

But the space made it possible to listen with fresh ears. And when you listen
in this way, you discover that you may not know others as well as you thought
you might have. It does not mean you have a politically or culturally consistent
community. On the contrary, you have the possibility to see others and yourself
as socially positioned, as holding dissonant views perhaps, but as still able to
talk across those differences. Fabian remarks, 'Even if you don't like them you
still – you have a better bond with them':

Fabian: The thing about Drama class is you feel like you have a tighter bond with
people in your Drama class then you do in any of your other classes. I don't know
why it is but when you're in that Drama class you feel almost like, I don't know
how to say it, but when you're in your Math class there are kids you don't talk to
during the whole class but Drama class you talk to everyone. Even if you don't like
them you still – you have a better bond with them -even if you don't like them.
Yeah, you're acting with – you're interacting a lot more too in this class, more than
any other class. That's what I like about Drama. (Fabian, Focus Group Interview,
Middleview, 24 November 2008)

What Fabian is describing here is something like what Hannah Arendt describes as 'thinking without a banister' (1979). To incite thinking without a bannister is to call for a way of proceeding without reliance on previously conceived critical categories, to instead be inspired by one's engagement with a phenomenon or an idea. This seemed to be what was happening for many students in the classroom. They felt released from adherence to rigid categories, understanding others only through the constricting prism of perceived social categories.

This was also a world that seemed detached from other norms and practices of high school. It was a space that demanded its own rules of play. There seemed to be a tacit understanding that students could share in ways that would not otherwise occur and they could count on their peers to respect the drama room as a space of sharing thoughts that should not spill over into the rest of the school:

> Chrysanthemum: And it's nice because – and it's also like, we kind of have this code where we could talk about something but it's not something for you to go tell the world about. It's like you have this –
> Fabian: What you say or repeat in the Drama room stays there . . . You know, if Chrysanthemum tells me something that's going on, if she just wants to talk to me in Drama class, there's no way I should go and tell any other person unless you told me to, so it makes you feel a little more open. So all the people who are in your Drama class you can open up to them knowing that they won't tell your lives. (Focus Group Interview with Chrysanthemum, Erica, Bertham, and Fabian, Middleview, 24 November 2008)

For this group, at least, the drama room was a space in which there was a kind of agreement that each was free to hear and see in ways that were less bounded by social norms and stigmas that reigned all powerful in school. 'Representative thinking' (1978), in Arendt's terms, is a way of populating one's imagination with a multiple cast of characters. Jonothan Neelands (2009) describes the space that working as an ensemble creates in the drama classroom. He writes:

> The demands of living and learning together in drama require, in any case, a form of constitutional learning based on the negotiation and continual re-negotiation of the 'laws' in the learning group. Students cannot be coerced into role-playing or other forms of artistic acting for instance; they must enter into it willingly and this presupposes a pedagogy of choice based consciously or

unconsciously on the principles of the ekklesia and the temporary 'uncrowning' and distribution of the power of the teacher in favour of a more democratic and demanding autonomy. (p. 184)

However, this space of negotiation and re-negotiation in the context of ensemble work does not assume easy decision-making or lack of risk. In fact, on the contrary, as Gallagher (2007) has elsewhere suggested, risk-taking and conflict can be collectively and creatively explored. If the goal in the drama classroom is to create a space for 'participatory democracy' as Neelands (2009) hopes, risk-taking and exploring conflict is indispensable. Drama scholar Mary Ann Hunter (2008) also asserts that:

> particularly in applied performance settings with peace-building at the core, heightened participant risk may be apparent: the risk of expressing open emotion to 'the other'; the risk of 'the other' belittling such emotion; the risk of prolonging conflict by addressing it inappropriately; even the risk of resolving conflict and thereby losing the right (and perceived status) to be indignant. (p. 16)

Students in Ms S's class recognize that hers is a risky pedagogy. They perceive the risk of vulnerability when personal stories are shared with others in the classroom. The teacher herself discussed the challenges and merits of 'risky' pedagogy in the interviews we had with her. She recognizes that the price for this kind of attention to personal experiences can be high, for there are many lost opportunities too, many moments in which students struggle to be heard or highjack the creative endeavour because it makes them feel too vulnerable.

Never a zero-sum game, making something of our differences, engaging in representative thinking, and keeping alive the conflict that makes us mysteries to one another and fuels our artistic imaginations are important pedagogical features of a strong drama classroom. Of representative thinking, Arendt (1977) writes:

> The more people's standpoints I have present in my mind while I am pondering a given issue, and the better I can imagine how I would think and feel if I were in their place, the stronger will be my capacity for representative thinking and the more valid my final conclusions, my opinion. (p. 241)

In Ms S's case, the pay-off was that students came to respect the space as one where they could engage in 'representative thinking', taking in other views, and they could release themselves to some extent from the constraining categories of understanding that make it impossible, most of the time in school, to, in Arendt's terms, 'think without a bannister'.

Instead of trying to avoid conflict and contain uncertainty, Ms S recognizes the value of taking the risk and fostering classroom conversations about difficult issues. She also understands the responsibility required in populating one's mind, as Arendt describes it, with the stories and views of others:

> Well, a lot of the work that I do does allow for opportunity for students to tell their own stories and I'm interested in that kind of work because I think I'm just drawn to people's stories artistically in general. I think you find your own voice. I think also it helps to build community in the classroom, you know, because it's hard to be um . . . to be negative or demeaning towards someone whose story you know- so there's kind of an ethical level. BUT having said that, I wouldn't ever do that with every class because in some classes the dynamic is so uh . . . tense, let's say that it's just not safe enough to enter into that kind of sharing. So, I don't do it all the time and I do believe in the safety of metaphor idea- and the idea that you, you know, drama really allows students to escape their reality a lot of times by being other people- not just to escape, but to connect to their experiences through the safety of being a character. So, I wrestle myself with how much reality I'm doing with students and how safe is it? And so if I'm doing that, I'm not doing that the whole year, like we're also spending time being characters, and being other people . . . I'm always judging – does this feel safe? Does this feel, you know, and always when it comes to performance, giving them the veto power to say no I do not want to tell my story in front of an audience, you know, or even the kinds of classrooms- like you would never enforce that as part of your curriculum. It's always entered into voluntarily. (Ms S, Teacher interview, Middleview, 3 February 2011)

Not only is there inherent risk, as Ms S clearly understands, but there is also the important revelation that we may not know others as well as we think we do. That small discovery alone liberates the listener and the speaker.

> Chrysanthemum: We would have those discussions and they would go on for way longer than we expected just because I guess everyone was so comfortable to say what they felt and you know, when one person was saying one thing – for me personally, I didn't want to say a lot because, you know, you want to hear what everybody else is saying but when someone like – a person in our class who is quiet started talking that showed me that we could all have this long conversation. I remember it because it was one of the beginning points of our class becoming like a community. (Focus Group Interview with Chrysanthemum, Erica, Bertham, Fabian, Middleview, 24 November 2008)

Conclusion

Garrison (2004) writes about an inherent tension in socially committed classrooms. In line with Ms S's pedagogy, Garrison (2004) argues that instead of attempting to construct safe spaces in their classrooms, it would be better if teachers sought to grow in relationship with their students by rendering themselves vulnerable and at risk without necessarily requiring their students to do the same. Garrison addresses the impossibility of knowing the other despite efforts of speaking openly and cultivating engaged listening. He (2004) writes:

> We must resist the notion we may ever know, recognize, or realize 'the other' with absolute certainty, nor can we complete the quest for certainty backwards by proving the other is unknowable, unrecognizable, or unrealizable. We must learn to live creatively with the paradox. Passionate ambivalence in the pursuit of social amelioration calls for a cautious compassion that exercises moral imagination and perception in the attempt to concede the unique singularity of 'the other' by refusing to reduce otherness and difference to the sameness of our self-identity. (p. 89)

What was important for the students in Ms S's classroom was having the chance to be heard, without the feeling of being judged. Erica did not assume that others knew her just because they listened to her story. But she felt that they listened without judgement, without assuming sameness. Even as students spoke about feeling 'like a family' in the drama classroom, they did so in the face of the differences consistently acknowledged in the room. Erica again, 'You might not like what your sister is doing but, you know, you cope.' Social and artistic dissonance fuelled the space in ways we greatly admired as researchers observing the social and artistic dynamics of a diverse group of young people in a vibrant urban classroom.

In *Inclusion and Democracy*, Young (2000) suggests that it is important to understand how social difference is a potential resource for democratic communication. Young references Arendt's definition of public, explaining, 'For Arendt the public is not a place of conversation among those who share language, assumptions and ways of looking at issues . . . The public consists of multiple histories and perspectives relatively unfamiliar to one another, connected yet distant and irreducible to one another' (p. 111).

Recommendations for further research

It is almost a cliché of multicultural classrooms in the twenty-first century to propose that they celebrate difference and welcome diversity. But what does this mean pedagogically? What does a drama classroom look like that resists the assimilation of social, cultural and artistic differences? It is a place of risk, we have learned, and a place where differences and disagreements sit alongside fleeting moments of solidarity. This is a classroom where students and teacher agree to hear stories that may unsettle norms, and to listen attentively. Future research in drama/applied theatre could make much more of the frequent disruptions in creative processes, the 'artistic differences' that surface; they are a barometer of the social health of a classroom.

Listening well, argues cultural theorist Richard Sennett (2012), 'is an interpretive activity which works best by focusing on the specifics of what one hears, as when we seek to fathom from those particulars what another person has taken for granted but not said' (p. 24). The study of listening in theatre-making processes will loom large in our own future research. Does listening in the drama classroom simply reinforce our image of the other, or does it make possible new categories for pondering those things, and people, we thought we already knew?

References

Arendt, H. (1977), *Between Past and Future*. New York: Penguin.

—(1978), *The Life of the Mind. Vol.1*, ed. Mary McCarthy. New York: Harcourt Brace Jovanovich.

—(1979), *Hannah Arendt: The Recovery of the Public World*, ed. Melvyn Hill. New York: St. Martin's Press.

Burbules, N. (2004), 'Introduction', in M. Boler (ed.), *Democratic Dialogue in Education: Troubling Speech, Disturbing Silence*. New York: Peter Lang Publishing, Inc.

Boler, M. (2004), *Democratic Dialogue in Education: Troubling Speech, Disturbing Silence*. New York: Peter Lang Publishing, Inc.

Dickenson, S. J. (2006), 'Listening better to look better: The manipulation of linguistic devices and listening skills in the writing of Booters, a play for young people.' *Research in Drama Education*, 11, (1), 99–105.

Doësebs, V. (1998), 'Lay down your arms: Drama as an efficacious remedy in South Africa'. *Research in Drama Education: The Journal of Applied Theatre and Performance*, 3, (2), 167–79.

Fiumara, G. C. (1990), *The Other Side of Language: A Philosophy of Listening*. London: Routledge.

Gallagher, K. (2007), *The Theatre of Urban: Youth and Schooling in Dangerous Times*. Toronto, Buffalo, London: University of Toronto Press.

Garcia, L. (1998), 'Creating community in a university production of Bocon'. *Research in Drama Education*, 3, (2), 155–66.

Garrison, J. (2004), 'Ameliorating violence in dialogues across differences: The role of Eros and Lógos', in M. Boler (ed.), *Democratic Dialogue in Education: Troubling Speech, Disturbing Silence*. New York: Peter Lang Publishing, Inc, pp. 89–103.

Hunter, M. A. (2008), 'Cultivating the art of safe space'. *Research in Drama Education: The Journal of Applied Theatre and Performance*, 13, (1), 5–21.

Kempe, A. (2003), 'The role of drama in the teaching of speaking and listening as the basis for social capital'. *Research in Drama Education*, 8, (1), 65–78.

Massey, D. (2006), *Is the World Really Shrinking?* Retrieved from http://www.open2.net/freethinking/oulecture_2006.html

Neelands, J. (2009), 'Acting together: Ensemble as a democratic process in art and life'. *Research in Drama Education: The Journal of Applied Theatre and Performance*, 14, (2), 173–89.

Nicholson, H. (2006), *Applied Drama: The Gift of Theatre*. Basingstoke and New York: Palgrave Macmillan.

Sennett, R. (2012), *Together: The Rituals, Pleasures and Politics of Cooperation*. New Haven, CT: Yale University Press.

Yassa, N. (1999), 'High school involvement in creative drama'. *Research in Drama Education*, 4, (1), 37–49.

Young, I. (2000), 'Social difference as political resource', in *Inclusion and Democracy*. Oxford: Oxford University Press, pp. 81–120.

Zúñiga, X., Nagda, B., and Sevig, T. D. (2002), 'Intergroup dialogue: An educational model for cultivating engagement across differences'. *Equity & Excellence in Education*, 35, (1), 7–17.

Zúñiga, X., Mildred, J., Varghese, R., DeJong, K., and Keehn, M. (2012). 'Engaged listening in race/ethnicity and gender intergroup dialogue courses'. *Equity & Excellence in Education*, 45, (1), 80–99.

Part Three

Activating Learners

8

Drama, Creating and Imagining:
Rendering the World Newly Strange

Juliana Saxton and Carole Miller

During the early 1990s, Dorothy Heathcote had been working closely with The Dukes TIE Company. Warwick Dobson (2012) remembers ' . . . we were considering the possibility of creating a programme based on the story of Prometheus. One of the company members asked [Dorothy] where she would begin if she were going to create a drama centred on the Greek myth; she thought for a moment, and then replied, "I'd start with a fire in a fish and chip shop"' (p. 11). There is no further information on where this extraordinary idea might have gone but it illustrates the 'out of the box' thinking that Heathcote demonstrated so admirably and so consistently. It is the kind of remark that makes you sit up and take notice and made her practice so astonishing. Such thinking is what is required in order to develop learners who can see the world through new and multiple perspectives.

In 2011, The President's Committee on the Arts and the Humanities reported:

> The field of neuroscience in particular is beginning to unpack the complex ways that certain types of arts experiences affect cognitive development—research that will have major implications for the field of education, including helping to shape arts experiences for maximum benefit to students (p. 32).

In this chapter, we examine the demands of creating and imagining that arise as a means to illuminate the ways in which the mind/brain operates most effectively for learning in drama. We use a text which meets Bruner's (1986) criteria that, 'stories of literary merit . . . are about events in a "real world" but they render that world newly strange' (p. 24). We draw on the work of a number of recognized researchers (Eagleman 2011; Damasio 2010; Siegel 2007; Rizzolatti and Craighero 2005; Cozolino 2002) who demonstrate, through fMRI, how the brain lights up when participants engage in specific activities. We acknowledge that research on the relationship between the brain, cognition and the arts is evolving, contingent and contested. And while we appreciate that there is a great deal that still awaits clarification, we think we have enough on which to begin to build our understanding of why drama is an important learning medium. This research examines drama and mind/brain compatibility through three lenses: invariant representations – a brain disposition that appears to have a variety of names: conditional language; and metaphor. We then illustrate these concepts in terms of their coherence with effective practice.

Invariant representations

Invariant representations' describes the predisposition of the human brain to lay previous knowledge and feelings over incoming experience and rob us of the ability to see things freshly.
                              Jeff Hawkins and Sandra Blakeslee 2004, pp. 52–3

To begin, we build on the kind of creative thinking that Heathcote demonstrates in Dobson's story in which she sees the potential of an idea 'without the burden of an old label' as she herself put it in 1978 (p. 21). The reason for this labelling is that in order to survive the explosion of information, thoughts and feelings that we are receiving at almost every moment, the brain has developed the ability to act as a very responsible and efficient secretary, sorting, filing and organizing so that we can recognize something quickly, assess its significance and take action (should action be necessary). Daniel Eagleman (2011) refers to this as 'cognitive control'; Daniel Kahneman (2011) calls it 'fast thinking' with variants such as 'cognitive biases', 'cognitive illusions'. Perhaps the most effective example of that capacity is the way in which we recognize a face – often from very little detail. Like so many things in life, this extraordinary survival ability to classify, store and retrieve in an instant is, as Heathcote called it, a 'treasure/burden'. To survive is a given but to have our brain frame what we see in the same way each time diminishes our ability to move beyond the predictable. To question, imagine, create and innovate are dispositions that are, paradoxically, equally imperative to survival!

Familiar devices such as role, metaphor, tableau, narration, reflection and so on (Eriksson 2009) interrupt, disturb or push against 'invariant representations'. Such strategies enable participants – among other things – to see their experiences from multiple perspectives in order to discover new views and reconsider habitual responses. The responsibility of the facilitator cannot be underestimated; it is his/her responsibility to generate the curiosity and desire to know. Curiosity engages multiple areas of the brain, including memory storage; it is the 'wick of the candle of learning' (Kang et al. 2009, p. 963). When this is engendered, 'imagination and creative output challenge [participants] to see beyond that which can be seen and imagine the world as if it were otherwise' (Miller and Saxton 2011, p. 127).

Conditional language

Conditional statements, offered in direct oral or written material, seem to induce a cognitively mindful state that evokes the active engagement of the student's own mind.

Daniel Siegel 2007, p. 232

Another essential component to encourage participants' creative imagining is the use of conditional language not only in instruction but also in prompting, responding and reflecting (Chanowitz and Langer 1981). Words such as 'might', 'may', 'could be' and so on elicit divergent thinking and engage 'a more complex set of neural associations' (Siegel 2007, p. 233) as the experience is included in memory. 'The cumulative effect,' write Ritchhhart and Perkins (2000), 'of such open and active instruction is to make students more aware of or sensitive to the ambiguous or conditional nature of the world—that knowledge and understanding are always in flux' (p. 34). And it is ambiguity that keeps us in the active role of mental processing as we try and make sense of content and its context. It seems, writes Daniel Siegel (2007), that, 'creative uncertainty appears to strengthen learning' (p. 234). Certainly, if we look at the kinds of prompts that are used by many practitioners in their recorded practice, they reflect a use of the conditional so clearly illustrated by Neville Hatton and David Smith in their 1995 report on reflective practice in teacher education. Looking to our own discipline, we find the following transcriptions:

Jonothan Neelands (1984, p. 22):

. . . now some of you have not been before. You may not know that we always speak the great oath of the Geats before we go. Perhaps some of the more experienced, of the oath . . . who can remind us? . . . perhaps you remember parts of it only? . . .

Carole Tarlington (1991, p. 94):

It's an interesting story which always makes me think. The thing that I wonder about most is what effect the children's leaving had on the town of Hamelin . . . it might be interesting if we made a list on the board of all the people who might have been affected by the children's disappearance . . . .

Cecily O'Neill (Scheurer 1998, p. 42):

It may be possible to voice that dissent through graffiti. We have lots of walls—you could spray paint your message and then say it. If anyone thinks they can do that, go ahead.

In this last example, the author noted that participants 'hesitated' to take up O'Neill's offer 'because they did not want to deface their town.' Without that conditional phrasing, students would not have been able to suggest a different choice.

In a series of research studies with a variety of subjects, ranging from the elderly to college and medical students (Langer 1997, pp. 67–75), it was found that the responses to learning offered conditionally resulted in better memory and more enjoyment. Conditional language presents learning in ways that encourage openness to novelty, sensitivity to different contexts and implicit, if not explicit, awareness of multiple perspectives (Langer, cited in Powers [nd.]). Conditional learning, posits Siegel (2007), involves concepts such as intelligent ignorance, flexible thinking, the avoidance of premature cognitive commitments and creative uncertainty. It directly contrasts with absolute learning (generated by absolute language): 'intelligent sureness, clearly defined routes of analysis, categorical clarity, and a sense of certainty and predictability' (p. 234). Of course, there are many who prefer learning this way, as Jonathan Haidt (2012) points out in *The Righteous Mind*, and are happy to let invariant representations do their thinking for them. While it is possible to have an almost immediate change of mind (See Ravich 2010), change is more likely to be incremental. It comes about, as we know and as Haidt suggests, when we take the time to listen and get to know the other side in order to arrive at what Neelands (1984) calls a 'conspectus' which leads to new understanding. What interests us is that there is so little research on offering instruction/discussion/ reflection and so on in a conditional way.

Metaphor

A metaphor serves to illuminate a concept by saying that one thing is another. Its structure is composed of two images having sufficient in common to highlight their differences.

Gavin Bolton 1990, personal conversation

Our last lens is metaphor. In theatre and drama we are always working in the 'as if' fictional world of the narrative; it is a foundational construct of our art form and interestingly, the third concept we address. The archaeologist Steven Mithen (2004), in his discussion of the evolution of mind, suggests that:

> . . . the emergence of metaphorical thought might be as significant for cognitive and cultural evolution as that of language itself. I expect that it relates to a major re-organization of human mentality away from one of a domain specific nature to one that is cognitively fluid (p. 34).

Keith Oatley (2009) goes further to suggest that it was this interpenetration of our cognitive structures that gave birth to metaphor: 'marks on the wall of a cave could become a rhinoceros' (np).

Metaphors offer new and different ways to experience life – at once clearly understood and, at the same time, ambiguous. 'Narratives are fundamentally social in nature in that almost all stories concern relationships between people; understanding stories thus entails an understanding of people and how their goals, beliefs and emotions interact with their behaviours' (Mar et al. 2006, p. 696). The research of Oatley (2009) into theory of mind shows that the effects of fiction, 'enhance our abilities to empathize with other people and connect with something larger than ourselves' (np). Although these theorists are using narrative fiction as the basis for their discussions, it seems to us that their findings have equal, if not greater, application to our field in that the responses within the dramatic context are embodied. 'Advocates,' writes Raymond Gibbs (2008), editor of the *Cambridge Handbook of Metaphor and Thought*, 'readily acknowledge metaphors' ability in both verbal and non-verbal forms to create new modes of understanding often accompanied by special aesthetic pleasures' (p. 5). It is through the embodied metaphoric acts of the imagination in drama and theatre that we create internal models that result in increased social and empathic awareness.

We have provided a theoretical framework through which we can now explore our practice with specific examples. We use Margaret Wild and Anna

Spudvilas' *Woolvs in the sitee* (2007), a picture book that comes to us from Australia. According to Bruner (1986), 'stories of literary merit . . . are about events in a "real world" but they render that world newly strange' (p. 24) and this text allows us to examine how we might interrupt that capacity for sameness, or, as Coleridge (1817) put it, the 'lethargy of custom.' We then consider the value of conditional language to generate a disposition to explore a range of ideas critically and creatively. Finally, we look at the motivational power of metaphor as that paradoxically boundless container for enactment.

Articulation of practice

We explore the three initial drama strategies of this story drama structure that enable participants to imagine, create and build together the metaphoric world of the protagonist. Without this preparation of the fictional world that is now evolving out of the collective imagination, there is no possibility of authentic engagement. What is interesting about these strategies is that they all operate as the means by which perspectives are deliberately shifted in order to enlarge and deepen understanding. The language challenges, the writing itself and the ambiguous meanings in Wild's text, coupled with the illustrations of Spudvilas, are rich in possibilities for imagining self and other.

***Strategy one*: an example of disturbing and pushing against what Louis Cozolino (2002) refers to as 'a hardening of the categories' and defined by Duffy (2012) as 'pre-conceived representations of reality that are not attuned to the particularities of a given situation' (p. 283).**

Task 1: I am going to give you a piece of writing. Your first task is to read it. [They do]

There are woolvs in the sitee. Oh, yes!
In the streets, in the parks, in the allees.
In shops, in rustee playgrownds,
in howses rite next dor

And soon they will kum.
They will kum for me and for yoo

and for yor bruthers and sisters,
yor mothers and fathers, yor arnts and
yor grandfathers and grandmothers.

No won is spared.

Lissen to me.
Lissen!

I yoosed to hav a familee, a home.
These streets wer my rivers,
these parks my vallees.

Now I am scrooched up in won room
in a mustee basement, heavy kertins across
the window.

Task 2: Perhaps it would help you to know that this was written by a boy named Ben. Now, I am going to ask you to read it again but, this time, as if you were a professional who has been called upon to provide expertise in order for us to understand a little about the person who wrote it. What professionals might be called upon in this way? [They respond]

The helping professions such as psychologists, social workers, teachers, therapists, medical personnel, school counselors and so on, would all be appropriate.

Choose one of those professions. When you have decided, just write down the profession you have chosen at the top of the page. Then, as you read, make any notes based on your professional expertise that could be helpful to our understanding. You might consider such things as cognitive development, emotional health, physical sense of security and so on. [They respond]

Task 3: Just talk to the person next to you about the assumptions you are making about the boy, Ben, based on what you have read and what your professional expertise suggests. Here, of course, I am talking about such things that you may have noticed, such as self-esteem, family background, educational development and so on. You may wish as you talk together to make some notes based on your professional reading of the material that *could be* useful to us in a minute. Just use the other side of the page of text. [They talk and make notes]

Analysis

In the initial task, while there is familiarity with the letters in the words, their arrangement requires that participants take on the task of translation in order to make meaning of the text. Immediately, we are put off balance by this need to decode. In the second task, the reading stance of professional expertise, known to us as Heathcote's early use of Mantle of the Expert (Wagner 1976/1999; Morgan and Saxton 1987, p. 31), demands a deliberate shift in perspective. Mantle of the Expert forces the brain to reconsider initial reactions that then become another layer that expands our information about the young person represented through this text. The taking of the role of expert is not about outward appearance (in theatre, characterization is a requirement) but, rather, is a response generated internally, a response driven by mirror neurons. It is the mirror neurons, neuroscientists Giacomo Rizzolatti and Laila Craighero (2005) tell us, that enable 'individuals to understand the meaning of actions *done by others, their intentions, and their emotions*' (p. 107, italics ours). In the third task where participants share their understanding by reflecting through imagined roles, it appears that their emotional understanding is deepened and broadened. The work of Seja and Russ (1999) and Taylor and Carlson (1997) on play and fantasy as they relate to emotional understanding support our experience.

The strategy that follows, Role on the Wall, is one in which participants fill in the outline of a paper 'person' with words and phrases that make evident our assumptions about the character.

Strategy two: **An example of the use of conditional language, modelling how to work in an open structure in which all suggestions become possibilities**

Task 1: I am now going to put down an outline that represents this young boy, Ben. Having discussed your assessment, please come and write on this outline the words or phrases that, as professionals, you would use to describe him. Many of your contributions *may be contradictory* and *ambiguous* but we know that that is the nature of our work. It is, of course, the exposure to these differences that heightens our awareness of the possibilities that lie within this boy – Is he a poet or is he illiterate? Can he be both? This is *perhaps* an unusual way of collating our data but it will serve as an *informal* reference for our continued work. Who will make the first contribution?

Thank you. The rest of you choose a pen – there are many colours to choose from and this *may be* important to you. You *may have* to wait a moment for a space. {They begin]

As they are working,

You *may see* a word or phrase that triggers another idea for you that you *may want* to add.

When everyone has contributed,

It is important that we all have a chance to read what has been written. We're going to walk around this outline so that we all have the opportunity to see our collective impressions of this young boy. Note any contradictions and ambiguities, anything that surprises you.

Option: It may be appropriate to ask participants to read aloud the words or phrases that 'pop out' for them.

Thank you. Just talk to the person next to you about anything you've read or heard. While you are conferring, I will hang up our outline so that should we need it, we can use it for our reference.

Analysis

Role on the Wall is dependent upon the sorts of scaffolding through communication and collaboration that the brain as a social organ so much enjoys (Eisenberger and Lieberman 2009). Daniel Goleman (2006), citing the work of Daniel Stern (2004), posits,

> . . . the neurons for mimicry are at play whenever we sense another person's state of mind and resonate with their feelings. This interbrain linkage makes bodies move in tandem, thoughts go down the same roads, and emotions run along the same lines. As mirror neurons bridge brains, they create a tacit duet that opens the way for subtle but powerful transactions. (p. 43)

In terms of our use of conditional language, it may be more evident in the italicized words in the first three tasks of *Strategy one* where the deliberate use of the conditional is an effective means of keeping the work open and flexible. In *Strategy two*, the focus is on the invitational environment that works against self-censorship in terms of contributions. Brainstorming words and phrases is designed to model subtly how drama works – to hold back and constrain our natural tendency to create 'the narrative'; we are not yet ready to draw conclusions (in this case, to define a character). The instructional language acknowledges contradiction and ambiguity as present and welcome while, at the same time, enabling and encouraging the social nature of the work by accepting all ideas.

In looking at the instructions for these strategies, it is very clear that when there is a specific requirement, the language used is what Ellen Langer and Alison Piper (1987) call 'absolute instruction'. For example, 'Your first task is to read it' is a clear teacher direction for getting started. Conditional language is used when participants are working creatively and imaginatively, where the need for wider, flexible considerations may lead to unexpected surprises. This language creates the 'conditions' for the 'tacit duet that opens the way for subtle but powerful transactions' to which Stern (2004) is referring.

Tableau, the final strategy we describe, focuses our attention on looking from the inside to the outside (visually and metaphorically) in order to interpret further information about the life of the boy whom we now know as Ben.

Strategy three: A projection of the outside world that Ben sees as he looks out from his window provides a visual metaphor for exploration leading to embodied interpretation through tableau

Task 1: Let's have a look at this picture. What do you see? What is the mood? In your mind's ear, what sounds do you hear? [They say]

As you continue to look at this picture, listen to the text that accompanies it.

Teacher reads from, **"I peers throo the kertins . . . to . . .But the seasons are topsy-turvee. Nothing is rite."**

Task 2: Working in your groups as artists and taking the essence of how you read the illustration, you are now to respond as visual artists and, using your bodies, you will interpret what, for your group, represents the meaning of the picture. Think of this as an abstract painting that might hang in a gallery dealing with contemporary issues. We are not expecting to see a recreation of this illustration but, rather, your artistic interpretation of the mood generated by this picture. Is everyone clear about this task?

Analysis

As we uncover what is going on in this illustration, the tension that the picture conveys allows us to imagine the soundscape Ben hears when he looks out at his world. After an initial deconstruction of the picture, the meanings and feelings inherent in it for participants become the material from which they will respond; the tableaux become artistic interpretations of the mood generated by Spudvilas' illustration. Participants in the tableaux are involved in complex layering as they are asked to interpret a two-dimensional visual image into a three-dimensional interpretation relating what they see in the picture book illustration to contemporary issues in the world today. Goleman (2006) reminds us that, '[t]he human brain harbors multiple mirror neuron systems, not just for mimicking actions but also for reading intentions, for extracting the social implications from what someone does, and for reading emotions' (p. 42).

In tableau, we are relying on the pre-frontal cortex's executive attention when we ask students to focus, interpret and re-create (Baars 1997). 'It is essential to see, not merely to look' (p. 419) and 'seeing necessitates looking and thinking,' writes Macaulay (1991, pp. 419/420). Paradoxically, the brain needs movement to maintain attention and to create memories but movement can refer both to physical and to mental movement (Zull 2002). While the tableau itself is still, the creating process demands trial, rehearsal and observation from different perspectives. As ideas are refined, shifts in placement and levels occur as memory becomes the resource for comparisons. The 'finished' tableau embodies a dynamic energy by which spectators read the 'picture' as a moment in a process. The reflection on each tableau layers further possibilities of meaning that now set the context in which the exploration of the story will evolve.

Latest research (Lacey et al. 2012) suggests that metaphor comprehension is grounded in our sensory and motor experiences. In these tableaux, participants are working through multiple modes of sensory experience – visual, auditory, olfactory and kinaesthetic. We 'draw upon sensory experiences to achieve understanding of metaphorical language,' notes Sathian, (in Emory 2012). The use of metaphor and language that, 'by presenting ambiguities, by using words in unfamiliar ways, by juxtaposing elements of perceptual reality in new combinations, by evoking imagery, [offer] fresh, novel possibilities for experiencing life' (Siegel 2007, pp. 54/55).

Discussion

The language challenges, the writing itself and the ambiguous meanings in Wild's text, coupled with the highly sophisticated illustrations of Spudvilas, are rich in possibilities for imagining self and other. It seems to us that a pedagogy that consciously includes the use of conditional language, metaphor and opportunities to subvert taken-for-granted responses has significance not only for arts educators. The implications of research into these areas and others now under study have, we believe, wider resonances for professional development; indeed for all those who hope to help learners reframe, reimagine, and continue to question the templates of how we live and may best live in a world of challenge and opportunity.

Dorothy Heathcote's advice to the Duke's players has led us to think differently about our spaces. Classrooms and theatres (indeed anywhere) as blazing fish and chip shops? Why not? We now have a richer understanding of how those fires can, must and should be lit!

References

Baars, B. (1997), *In the Theater of Consciousness: The Workspace of the Mind*. New York: Oxford University Press.

Bruner, J. (1986), *Actual Minds, Possible Worlds*. Cambridge, MA: Harvard University Press.

Chanowitz, B. and Langer, E. (1981), 'Premature cognitive commitment'. *Journal of Personality and Social Psychology*, 41, 1051–63.

Coleridge, S. (1917), Biographia Literaria. Retrieved 22 January 2013, from https://notes.utk.edu/Bio/greenberg.nsf/0/

Cozolino, L. (2002), *The Neuroscience of Psychotherapy: Building and Rebuilding the Human Brain*. New York: Norton.

Damasio, A. (2010), *Self Comes to Mind: Constructing the Conscious Brain*. New York: Pantheon.

Dobson, W. (2012), 'In memory of Dorothy Heathcote, MBE (29 August 1926 to 8 October 2011)'. *Research in Drama Education: The Journal of Applied Theatre and Performance*, 17, (1), 8–34.

Duffy, M. (2012), 'Narrative approaches to therapy with trauma victims', in A. Lock and T. Strong (eds), *Discursive Perspectives in Therapeutic Practice*. Oxford, UK: Oxford University Press, pp. 269–87.

Eagleman, D. (2011), *Incognito: The Secret Lives of the Brain*. Toronto, ON: Viking.

Eisenberger, N. and Lieberman, M. (2009), 'The pains and pleasures of social life'. *Science*, 323, 890–1.

Eriksson, S. (2009), *Distancing at Close Range: Investigating the Significance of Distancing in Drama Education*. Vasa, NO: Åbo.

Gibbs, R. (ed.) (2008), *The Cambridge Handbook of Metaphor and Thought*. New York: Cambridge University Press.

Goleman, D. (2006), *Social Intelligence: The New Science of Human Relationships*. New York: Bantam Books.

Haidt, J. (2012), *The Righteous Mind: Why Good People are Divided by Politics and Religion*. New York: Pantheon Books.

Hatton, N. and Smith, D. (1995), 'Reflection in teacher education: Towards definition and implementation', [accessed 13 May 2011] http://alex.edfac.usyd.edu.au/localresource/study1/hattonart.html

Hawkins, J. and Blakeslee, S. (2004), *On Intelligence*. New York: Times Books.

Heathcote, D. (1978), 'Of these seeds becoming', in R. Baird Shuman (ed.), *Educational Drama for Today's Schools*. Metuchen, NJ: The Scarecrow Press, pp. 1–40.

Kahneman, D. (2011), *Thinking, Fast and Slow*. Toronto, ON: Doubleday Canada.

Kang, M. J., Hsu, M., Krajbich, I. M., Loewenstein, G., McClure, S., Wang, J. T., and Camerer, C. (2009), 'The wick in the candle of learning: Epistemic curiosity activates reward circuitry and enhances memory'. *Psychological Science*, 20, (8), 963–73.

Lacey, S., Stilla, R., and Sathian, K. (2012), 'Metaphorically feeling: Comprehending textural metaphors activates somatosensory cortex'. *Brain and Language*, 123, (3), 416–21.

Langer, E. (1997), *The Power of Mindful Learning*. Reading, MA: Addison-Wesley.

Langer, E. and Piper, A. (1987), 'The prevention of mindlessness'. *Journal of Personality and Social Psychology*, 53, 280–7.

Macaulay, D. (1991), 'Caldecott acceptance speech'. *Hornbook Magazine*, 67, (4), 410–21.

Mar, R., Oatley, K., Hirsh, J., dela Paz, J., and Peterson, J. (2006), 'Book worms versus nerds: Exposure to fiction versus non-fiction, divergent associations with social ability, and the simulation of fictional social worlds'. *ScienceDirect, Journal of Research in Personality*, 40, 694–712.

Miller, C. and Saxton, J. (2011), ' "To see the world as if it were otherwise": Brain research challenges the curriculum of "organized chunks"'. *NJ*, 35, 118–32.

Mithen, S. (2004), 'Human evolution and the cognitive basis of science', in P. Carruthers, S. Stich and M. Siegel (eds), *The Cognitive Basis of Science*. Cambridge, UK: Cambridge University Press, pp. 23–40.

Morgan, N. and Saxton, J. (1987), *Teaching Drama: A Mind of Many Wonders*. London, UK: Routledge.

Neelands, J. (1984), *Making Sense of Drama: A Guide to Classroom Practice*. London: Heinemann Educational Books.

Oatley, K. (2009), 'Changing our minds'. *Greater Good: The Science of a Meaningful Life*, 5, (3). [accessed 12 May 2012] http://greatergood.berkeley.edu/archive

Powers, R. (nd), 'Conditional vs. absolute learning: The power of uncertainty', [accessed 6 June 2012] http://socialdance.stanford.edu/syllabi/conditional_learning.htm

Ravitch, D. (2010), *The Death and Life of the Great American School System: How Testing and Choice Are Undermining Education*. New York: Basic Books.

Ritchhart, R. and Perkins, D. (2000), 'Life in the mindful classroom: Nurturing the disposition of mindfulness'. *Journal of Social Issues*, 56, (1), 27–47.

Rizzolatti, G. and Craighero, L. (2005), 'Mirror neurons: A neurological approach to empathy', in J-P. Changeux, A. Damasio, W. Singer and Y. Christen (eds), *Neurobiology of Human Values*. Berlin Heidelberg: Springer-Verlag, pp. 107–23.

Sathian, K. (2012, Emory University, February 3), 'Hearing metaphors activates brain regions involved in sensory experience'. *Science Daily* [accessed 18 September 2012] http://www.sciencedaily.com/releases/2012/02/120203182623.htm

Scheurer, P. (1998), 'The poetic artistry of Cecily O'Neill', in J. Saxton and C. Miller (eds), *Drama and Theatre in Education: The Research of Practice/The Practice of Research*. Victoria, BC: Idea Publications, pp. 30–47.

Seja, A. L. and Russ, S. W. (1999), 'Children's fantasy play and emotional understanding'. *Journal of Clinical Child Psychology*, 28, 269–77.

Siegel, D. (2007), *The Mindful Brain: Reflection and Attunement in the Cultivation of Well-Being*. New York: W.W. Norton and Company.

Stern, D. (2004), *The Present Moment in Psychotherapy and Everyday Life*. New York: W.W. Norton.

Tarlington, C. and Verriour, P. (1991), *Role Drama*. Markham, ON: Pembroke.

Taylor, M. and Carlson, S. M. (1997), 'The relationship between individual differences in fantasy and theory-of-mind'. *Child Development*, 68, 436–55.

The President's Committee on the Arts and Humanities (2011), *Reinvesting in Arts Education: Winning America's Future through Creative Schools*. Washington, DC [accessed 14 September 2011] <www.pcah.gov> the website of the President's Committee on the Arts and the Humanities.

Wagner, B. J. (1976/1999), *Dorothy Heathcote: Drama as a Learning Medium*. Portsmouth, NH: Heinemann.

Wild, M. and Spudvilas, A. (2007), *Woolvs in the Sitee*. Asheville, NC: Front Street.

Zull, J. (2002), *The Art of Changing the Brain: Enriching the Practice of Teaching by Exploring the Biology of Learning*. Stirling, VA: Stylus.

9

Drama as Critical Pedagogy: Re-imagining Terrorism

Peter O'Connor

Introduction

On the morning of 12 September 2001, my family and I woke up to news on the radio of the attacks on the Twin Towers and watched the CNN reports on television before we went our separate ways for the day. I was working for the Ministry of Education as the National Drama Facilitator and spent the day planning a process drama on *The Three Billy Goats Gruff*. Before I had started my contract with them the Ministry had planned a unit of work which involved children trotting across a make-believe bridge. It was the sort of drama exercise that demonstrates how meaningless and trivial drama education can be. I was thinking of ways to work in a more meaningful way to engage with the story, and also with ideas that sat beneath the surface.

When my 14-year-old daughter returned home that afternoon, I asked what had happened at school in response to the terror attacks. She said they had spent most of the day, in each class, watching the live CNN feed. The next day when I asked what they did, she said that her teachers had said, 'It is time to get back to the curriculum.' In the remaining 4 years she spent at school, there was never an opportunity to think about, reflect, consider, question, to critically challenge or talk again about this event, possibly the greatest conflict of our times. School had nothing to say about her present world as it was busily preparing her for the future. True to form, school remained for my daughter a 'rehearsal room for a future that never arrives' (Heathcote 1984).

The responses of artists to the events of that day varied, with the ideas of Karlheinz Stockhausen being perhaps the most radical. He argued on 17 September 2001 that the attack on the World Trade Center was, the greatest work of art that is possible for the whole cosmos. Something in one act what we in music cannot dream of, that people practice madly for 10 years, completely, fanatically, for a concert, and then die. Just imagine, you have people who are so concentrated on one performance, and then 5,000 people are dispatched into eternity, in a single moment. I couldn't do that. In comparison with that, we're nothing as composers' (Tommasini 2001, p. 28).

The response to this deliberately outrageous and provocative statement was swift and almost uniformly condemnatory. The New York Times response was to challenge, and ultimately dismiss, the notion of art's transformative potential.

Mr. Stockhausen has long been fired by the idea that art should transform us "out of life" itself, as he said at the press conference; otherwise "it's nothing." Obviously, any artwork, from a short Schubert song to a long Dostoyevsky novel, can have a transforming effect. But Mr. Stockhausen has dangerously overblown ambitions for art. Even Wagner, another egomaniac who controlled every aspect of his opera productions, was mostly trying to provide audiences with an absorbing evening in the theater. He did not necessarily expect you to walk out a better person. Writing the operas certainly didn't make him a better person (Tommasini 2001, p. 28).

The lack of engagement in schools in addressing the complexity of terrorism, either by ignoring it completely or by reinforcing simplistic binary notions of good and evil, motivated me to create a process drama to build student resistance to these discourses. I too wanted to engage in social transformation. Unlike the New York Times, I believe that the arts are our greatest hope for creating social change.

Critical pedagogy

At the very least, critical pedagogy proposes that education is a form of political intervention in the world that is capable of creating the possibilities for social transformation (Giroux 2004, p. 34).

Critical pedagogy is founded in the hope of Marxist revolutionary praxis, with the goal of overthrowing oppression and creating a more democratic and just social order (Kellner, Mclaren). It originates from the work of Paulo Freire (1972). Centred on an impulse to challenge dominant ideologies, it seeks to empower those systematically excluded from civic participation. It is rooted in notions of social justice and equity (Kincheloe and McLaren 2000).

Mclaren (2000) argues that increasingly schools are reduced to preparing students as part of the capitalist machine that dehumanizes and disempowers young people across the world. Critical pedagogy is offered as an antidote to an education system that replicates social inequity and creates an unthinking consumer class. It is, therefore, also interested in replacing the rehearsal room with an active engaged curriculum that enables children to question, challenge and remake their reality. Paradoxically, this chapter talks of the attempt to remake this reality through creation in the imagined worlds of process drama.

Process drama

Process drama is a genre of theatre with improvised role-play at its core. It is episodic and engages in non-linear narrative. This distinguishes it from single or brief improvisation exercises or scenes. The non-linear narrative allows for other kinds of exploration into the narrative and its meaning. Process drama shifts the role-playing from an acting *out* of a story to an acting *as if* approach to the narrative. Its origins are in the work of Dorothy Heathcote's notions of drama as a learning medium (Wagner 1976) and Gavin Bolton's (1979) theorizing of drama for understanding. In this genre, meaning making is created through improvisation; where students and teachers co-create drama for themselves rather than for an outside audience. Process drama follows in the tradition of Brecht's lehrstuck theory where he 'postulated drama of this type, without an audience, as a way in which the actors themselves could learn about the world, about how the victim as well as the executioner felt, by playing these parts in turn. Here the players form their own audience' (Esslin 1987, p. 130).

Like Brecht's theatre, the participants in process drama 'observe and simultaneously participate in the narrative before them. The participation takes the form of ongoing criticism of causes and effects of selected human predicaments' (Errington 1992, p. 44). Central to process drama is the sequencing of dramatic conventions to generate new understanding. Jonothan Neeland's and Tony Goode's seminal text, Structuring Drama (1991) introduced to teachers a series of conventions 'which are Brechtian in the sense that they disrupt realism and make strange' (O'Connor 2010, p. 4).

There has been surprisingly little research into the relationship between critical pedagogy and process drama. Although, for example, Cecily O'Neill (1986) draws attention to Mclaren's notion of teachers as a liminal servant as a way to explain the role of the drama teacher and others have explored implicitly the relationship (Aitken 2009; Nelson 2011), Edward Errington's Towards a socially critical drama education (1992) and Clar Doyle's Raising curtains on education: Drama as a site for critical pedagogy (2003) are the most systematic explorations of the relationship.

Troll School

Preceding the liberation/invasion of Afghanistan, CNN images of Taliban terrorist training camps showed people systematically training in a range of skills to scare, intimidate and kill. The connection I saw between terrorists and the central character from the story of the *Three Billy Goats Gruff* led me to create a process drama that explores the ideas of how trolls learn to become trolls, what it means to be a troll, and what it means to be a terrorist. It was a process drama I hoped would be a form of critical pedagogy that would challenge and disrupt the dominant ideologies that framed the discourse on terrorism.

I envisaged a range of dramatic conventions that could be used to establish a picture of how trolls might learn and how they may become acculturated to the notion of terrifying goats. The process drama would be framed when asking students to create a school curriculum for trolls. This framing would be crystallized dramatically in a series of still images from within a troll classroom, designed as part of the Troll School prospective. The drama would move to improvised scenes of a parent troll packing their troll child's back pack as s/he heads to the bridge for his/her first assignment. Following this, participants construct a letter that the parent troll writes to put into the back pack. A conscience alley created by the reading aloud of the key lines from the letters would conclude the drama, with me in role as the troll arriving at the bridge and the start of the story. I planned to stop the action sporadically throughout the drama to ask what we were learning about trolls and what we thought trolls valued. These ideas would be recorded on large sheets of paper. It was my intention to draw the analogy across to the real-world training camps once the active part of the drama had been completed. Throughout my planning of the drama, I wondered if such an approach might simultaneously humanize, and provide a richer and more critical understanding of those whose job in life is to scare others. I was interested in creating empathy for, and a felt understanding of what it is to be a terrorist.

The first time I ran the workshop was with a group of New Zealand Drama Advisers in 2002. They leapt at the opportunity to experience what it was like to be trolls. Their improvisations and freeze frames, of classrooms within a Troll School, had them considering issues around education and schooling. As we worked on uncovering what it is to be a troll, the lists of attributes included: bravery, loyalty, pride, a sense of purpose and mission, a sense of ownership towards the bridge, and a need to protect what is rightfully theirs. The conscience alley had parents reminding trolls that they were being counted on for protection against the goats, and that they must be prepared to die in the cause of their duty – protecting the bridge. The bridge was symbolized by two chairs at the end of the alley and the sombre tones of my silent walk to the bridge, in role as a troll, signalled a shift in the manner in which the group engaged with the story. As we reviewed the list of troll attributes, I spoke softly about the troll camps in Afghanistan that I had seen on the television just weeks before. The room was silent in thought for some time. Then we started to talk, and we talked about the importance of the work we had done, about how confused we were by terrorism, and about how it was good to begin to challenge ideas about what a troll/ terrorist is. From the relative safety of New Zealand, it seemed a fairly powerful drama. In the coming years, as I took the drama to other cultural contexts, the responses to the drama shifted.

Troll School in different cultural contexts

During 2004, I work-shopped the drama on a marae with a group of mainly Maori youth and community workers, in the Far North of New Zealand. The drama provided an opportunity for a lengthy and fierce debate about who the trolls are within New Zealand history. The colonizer and how the colonizer is seen, or more importantly not seen, became the focus of the debate. How Maori are presented as trolls who terrorize and scare the settler population became the focus of more debate. An American participant in the workshop had played along happily as a troll, but was clearly disconcerted by the analogies I drew from the drama. I remember her discomfort as the group decided the trolls had every right to be angry with goats who wanted all of the grass to themselves. When I asked who the group thought would be most likely to succeed in the conflict, they answered that the trolls had a greater sense of identity and a clarity of purpose while the goats had nothing but their greed to sustain them. We considered what this might mean in the real world of trolls/terrorism.

I have run this workshop on three separate occasions in Singapore, most recently in 2011. Work-shopping this story in an island state, separated from its closest neighbour by heavily guarded bridges, the drama provokes discussion around the importance of defence and security. Participants talk of being strong enough to scare those who might invade. They discuss costs that might need to be paid when living under the threat of goats, which could come and take all of the grass. We talked about who are seen as trolls and goats, within the Singapore context. How the need for security might become a national obsession lurked underneath our conversations. What prices people are willing to pay for security has also been a common talking point as a result of the drama. During the Singapore workshops, Muslim participants have talked about the manner in which Muslims are seen as trolls throughout the United States. In this context, the CIA and their activities were thought of as troll like too. We have wondered what CIA training camps might look like. And we have wondered why it is that goats are so determined to assert their rights to cross bridges to feed on other's lush fields.

In 2007 and 2010, I worked with teachers and applied theatre artists who were enrolled in the University of Victoria Summer School, in British Columbia, Canada. Their list of troll-like attributes included a sense of needing to fight back against how they are seen by goats, and a sense that trolls needed to be trolls because goats gave them no other choice. Perhaps most telling in terms of Canada's position on the war on terror, they were reminded that there were only two sides to the story; goats or trolls and without any room for anyone to be in the middle. The discussions that followed on both occasions focused on the impact of their neighbouring country's foreign policy, and its impact on Canadian perceptions of their own position in the world.

In 2008, I presented the workshop with a group of graduate students in the United Kingdom. Following the 2005 London underground bombings, the packing of the backpack in the drama had a significantly different resonance in the United Kingdom. Within the British context, this moment led to a discussion around suicide bombing. I remember the huge weight of expectation as I put the bag on my back and walked down the conscience alley. As the participants spoke the lines from the mother's letter, I was reminded of my duty as a troll, of my need to honour those who had been before me, of my sense of belonging, and of my pride in who I was. As I climbed under the bridge to wait for the goats to come, the last line of the conscience alley was stage-whispered to me; 'Remember who you are, and where you are from. You must be prepared to die for us all'.

At that moment I understood how it was possible to train people to terrorize and to kill. From my role as a troll, trained in the manner in which the participants had shown throughout the few hours of drama, I understood how others in similar circumstances had loaded their packs with explosives.

I remain morally revolted by anyone's desire to kill innocent people. Despite this, as I removed my backpack under the bridge, I knew I would do my duty, as a troll. The participants in the drama spoke of how they were convinced I would do whatever it took to defend the bridge. I felt deeply challenged by the emotional intensity of the session, as did many others in the room. An Israeli student and a Palestinian student took the opportunity to discuss how each of them could be seen as either goats or trolls. One student asked, 'What is the point of feeling empathy to the trolls?' It provoked a storm of responses with one I clearly remember; 'Because if we don't empathise, or chose whom we empathise with, we become terrorists ourselves.' This new narrative, a form of critical pedagogy in action, counters the simplicity of nation states' responses to acts of terrorism perpetuated on them, although of course not to those they perpetuate.

Trolls and empathy

In the heated emotions of the aftermath of the 2001 terror attacks, the Mayor of New York City, Rudy Guiliani made the following statement to the UN General Assembly only weeks later:

> Let those who say that we must understand the reasons for terrorism, come with me to the thousands of funerals we're having in New York City – thousands – and explain those insane maniacal reasons to the children who will grow up without fathers and mothers and to the parents who have had their children ripped from them for no reason at all . . . There's no excuse for mass murder, just as there's no excuse for genocide. Those who practice terrorism, murdering or victimizing innocent civilians, lose any right to have their cause understood by decent people and lawful nations . . . The era of moral relativism between those who practice or condone terrorism and those nations who stand up against it must end. Moral relativism doesn't have a place in this discussion and debate. There's no moral way to sympathize with grossly immoral actions (Guilliani 2001).

The United States has barely softened in its refusal to see beyond the simple binaries posited by Guiliani , Bush, Cheney et al. During 2010, a hardening of attitudes towards mainstream Islam was evidenced in the debate over the close proximity of a Muslim prayer centre to the site of the former Twin Towers on Manhattan Island. Threats of Koran burning have been supported by right wing media outlets as a form of American free speech while empathy within general life is considered to be suspicious. President Obama's suggestion in 2009, that empathy was a key attribute for a Supreme Court Judge, was met with derision and scathing criticism from the Republican party and its mouth piece Fox News. Fox News commentator, Glenn Beck, in a bizarre and convoluted piece of logic, suggested that empathy had caused the holocaust and suggested Obama was a neo-fascist because of his attachment to empathy (Beck 2009).

Paulo Freire argues that the purpose of living is to become more fully human (1972). An empathetic response which humanizes the terrorist, rather than demonizes him, creates the possibility of making and remaking all of ourselves as human beings. In this sense alone, the work we engaged in was critical pedagogy in action.

Drama as critical pedagogy

Yet empathy alone is not enough to explain the possibilities of process drama acting as a form of critical pedagogy. Vygotsky's (1933) concept of 'dual affect' whereby the person is directly engaged with what is happening in the drama, and at the same time is distanced from it, as he or she watches his or her own engagement with the drama is central to an understanding of process drama as a form of critical pedagogy. The educative function of role taking in process drama relies on the ability of the drama participant to also be the percipient of their actions (Bolton 1986). Bolton saw this 'dual affect as the tension which exists between the concrete world and the "as if" world, sometimes leading to contradictory emotions' (1986, p. 87). The dual affect is possible in process drama because participants simultaneously experience and empathize with the role they are playing. As themselves, they are able to enjoy, and analyse, the different emotions they experience. Process drama provides the possibility of distancing and empathetic responsiveness, within the same action. The framing and Brechtian distancing devices borrowed by Neelands in the development of process drama are based on his assertion that 'process drama is mimetic, but it doesn't deny the possibility of there being a metaxis between the dramatic and the real. The idea that life and art are rigidly separate areas of experience, and cannot coincide, is challenged in educational drama' (1994, p. 10). Errington suggests process drama provides 'an opportunity to observe and simultaneously participate in the narrative before them. The participation takes the form of an ongoing criticism of causes and effects of selected human predicaments' (1992, p. 44).

When the participants took on the role of being a troll, they embodied an understanding of what it is to be a troll/terrorist. Brechtian distancing conventions mediated this process because they allowed for simultaneous critical reflection on both the actions and the beliefs of the troll. The distancing conventions are essential to the troll drama as they free participants to explore the issues of terrorism by looking obliquely and tangentially to the issue through the fictive process. In this manner, participants are able to both empathize and critically examine the nature of terrorism. Central to a critical understanding of terrorism, the word itself was troubled and complexified and the simplicities of dominant ideologies and discourses were overthrown.

Despite the desire of Guiliani to simply reduce terrorism to unspeakable evil, the need to understand why it is that some train to kill innocent people still remains. The simple and emotional language used in response to terrorism needs to be tempered with a discourse that allows for the complexities of terrorism, and its response, to be articulated.

The troll drama has created forums for people to discuss the war *on* and *of* terror – an opportunity that seems to be rarely afforded. The distancing of the fiction provides an opportunity for short-circuiting the political correctness and fear people can have about expressing ideas that may conflict with the state's position. Talk, which Dewey (1936) argues to be the centre of democratic action, flows freely as a result of the fictional engagement with the issues. Talk which challenges and critiques terrorism, from within a felt understanding of its force and horror, is the true democratic response to the great issues of the early twenty-first century.

Despite the derision that now routinely seems to greet ideas such as the willingness to understand others, to negotiate difference and to give space for alternative understanding, these ideas still remain as cornerstones of hope for a world that might be capable of transformation – a transformation that is not based on the horrors of terrorism which derives from the Taliban or the White House.

The alternative to an empathetic and compassionate approach to conflict is only too clear; a lack of empathy allows us to consciously plan to destroy the lives of others, to create pieces of terror theatre that are morally reprehensible for all their effectiveness. Rather than simplifying the issues, the complex responses of process drama are able to engender a felt understanding of the humanity of all involved and fulfill the need to move beyond moral outrage to moral responsibility.

The manner in which drama in education can act as a critically engaging pedagogy that challenges and interrupts the way in which dominant discourses are perpetuated in schooling needs further examination. Case studies that tease out further the relationship between critical pedagogy and drama education are necessary, but a more philosophical questioning of the relationship would also bear fruit.

References

Aitken, V. (2009), 'Coversations with Status and power: How Everyday Theatre offers spaces of agency to participants'. *RiDe; The Journal of Applied Theatre and Performance*, 14, (4), 503–29.

Beck, G. (2009), www.youtube.com/watch?v=h7lq4mS76MQ. Accessed 13 Januray 2011.

Bolton, G. (1979), *Towards a Theory of Drama in Education*. Harlow: Longman.

—(1986), *Towards a Theory of Drama in Education*. Harlow: Longman.

Dewey, J. (1916), *Democracy and Education*. New York: MacMillan.

Errington, E. (1992), *Towards a Socially Critical Drama Education*. Victoria Australia: Deakin University.

Esslin, M. (1987), *The Field of Drama*. London: Methuen Drama.

Freire, P. (1972), *Pedagogy of the Oppressed*. Harmondsworth: Penguin Books.

Giroux, H. (2004), 'Critical Pedagogy and the Postmodern/Modern Divide'. *Teacher Education Quarterly*, Winter, 31–47.

Guiliani, R. (2001), *New York Times*, 1 October 2001.

Heathcote, D. (1984), *The Collected Writings*. London: Heinemann.

McLaren, P. (2000), *Life in Schools: An Introduction to Critical Pedagogy in the Foundations of Education*, 4th edn. Boston: Pearson Education Inc.

—(1994), 'Theatre Without Walls'. *Drama One Forum: Many Voices*, 2, (2), 1–14.

Nelson, B. (2011), *Drama and Multiculturalism: Power, Community and Change*. PhD thesis, University of Warwick.

O'Connor, P. (2010), *Creating Democratic Citizenship Through Drama Education: The Selected Writings of Jonothan Neelands*. Stoke on Trent: Trentham Publishers.

Tommasini, A. (2001), *Music – The Devil Made Him Do It, The New York Times, 30 September, P. 28*. Retrieved from http://www.nytimes.com/2001/09/30/arts/music-the-devil-made-him-do-it.html on 25 July 2012.

Vygotsky, L. (1993 orig., trans. 1976), 'Play and its Role in the Mental Development of the Child', in J. Bruner (ed.), *Play: A Reader*. London: Penguin Books.

Wagner, B. J. (1976), *Dorothy Heathcote: Drama as Learning Medium*. Washington, DC: National Education Association.

10

Drama and Beauty: Promise, Pleasure and Pedagogy

Joe Winston

Although postmodernism has long sought to discredit goodness, truth and beauty – that traditional triad of western cultural values – beauty for one has been making something of a comeback in recent years. Elaine Scarry (2001) has re-emphasized its significance as both a cognitive and emotional force that helps us to understand ideas of social justice rather than simply distracting us from them; John Armstrong (2005) has re-examined what key western philosophers have had to say about beauty and has demonstrated how their preoccupations are still of significance to contemporary culture; and, closer to our own field, James Thompson (2009) has invited us to reconsider the significance of 'the call of beauty' as a valid expression of the hopes and desires of those who create art, including the young and the marginalized. I will propose in this chapter that, rather than being some elitist concept, old-fashioned and displaced by the more popular (if at times nebulous) duo 'culture and creativity', an idea of beauty can help focus on key concerns to sustain educators and practitioners as well as students in their quest for real value in the drama classroom. To do so is to move away from the technical demands and reductive vocabulary of current curricula and instead to attend to the language that good drama teachers often use anyway – vocabularies of pleasure, hope, passion, emotion, experience and togetherness. My argument is that beauty can bring a conceptual coherence to the values articulated in such a language; and that its virtues are already present in the work of both educators and students when the practice is good. For, if beauty can provide a language of value for drama educators, it can also help us to connect with key aspects of our practice.

We need to talk of beauty as well as the aesthetic to remind ourselves to concentrate on the affective power of experiencing the art form and not merely to intellectualize it into a set of technical qualities. In other words, if drama is to teach *about* beauty then it must also teach *through* beauty, which means that we must conscientiously find ways to help our students experience its sensual lure, its affective appeal, to identify and discuss its charms without denying that element of mystery that will always persist in anything we find beautiful.

This chapter begins by exploring what we might mean when we talk of beauty and how its diverse manifestations can be seen to impact on the drama classroom. I then proceed to look at a particular example of teaching about and through beauty through extracts from a scheme of work based upon Ted Hughes's poem *Midas* before briefly considering how beauty as a concept can be seen to have practical implications for researching drama in educational settings.

The language of beauty

There are different kinds of beauty

Beauty in the arts is often associated with gentle qualities such as delicacy, balance and harmony – qualities that were central to the concerns of western art, at least, until the late nineteenth century. But Crispin Sartwell (2004) has argued that there are all kinds of beauty that can appeal to us – the disturbing beauty of a Picasso painting, the terrifying beauty of the gothic, the messy natural beauty of the rainforest, the simple austere beauty of a Mark Rothko painting, the charming and domestic beauty of a Renoir. Certain cultures or epochs or social groups may well favour one form over another, but individuals are always more than the predetermined expression of a particular, dominant culture; they are idiosyncratically individual, or, to borrow a phrase from Louis NacNeice, 'incorrigibly plural'.[1] Drama, too, can be beautiful in a variety of ways – in its language, visuals, austerity, lavishness, spiritual vision, capacity for expressing compassion or its potential to be shocking. Its aesthetic pleasures can be many and varied and thus of broad appeal to the incorrigibly plural tastes of young people.

Beauty is a relational experience

We will all have seen on television the type of arts programme, where experts explain to us why a particular museum piece is exquisite or a certain painting is a masterpiece. They will often use formal language to help us – the intricate carving, the delicacy of line, the structural balance and so on – in their attempts to educate our eye so that we begin to see what they see. Sometimes this will leave us cold – perhaps we are put off by their supercilious air; perhaps we are unappreciative of the artistic virtues they are describing; or perhaps we are preoccupied with other concerns. Whatever the reasons, any beauty that can be found in a work of art will not be recognized or come to life for us unless we are able to feel it for ourselves. We will not *know* it to be beautiful unless we *feel* it to be so, which is another way of saying that we will not know it at all. Such knowledge can be informed by critical instruction but can never only consist of it. So if, for example, as teachers we want our students to appreciate Shakespeare's language, we will never manage this by simply telling them how or why it is so powerfully beautiful; we must find ways of making them feel it for themselves. Beauty in this sense is never solely in the eye or the ear of the beholder or in the object of study; it only exists when the two come together in a state of balance and harmony.[2]

Beauty is sensual and passionate

Part of the problem we have with beauty is that we have inherited a particular understanding of it from influential eighteenth- and nineteenth-century philosophers. Schopenhauer, for example, saw beauty as an escape from life, as a peaceful, contemplative experience to remove us from the troublesome world of desire. But that is only one type of beautiful experience. For the early Greek philosophers, by contrast, beauty was sensual and erotic, even in its most intellectual forms, as it was inextricably linked with desire and love, and the hopeful energies they generate that stir us to action. This idea of beauty is relevant to us as drama practitioners because it values the body and what the body can feel and do. It reminds us how we can learn through the body and thus validates the intensely physical and actively playful approaches we bring to experiencing and creating drama. It also reminds us that learning to love can stimulate a desire to know and a passion to learn. It reminds us, too, of the power of desire inherent to the experience of watching or being part of a performance and the positive effects this can have on young people, for whom it is quite natural to love and want to be loved.

Beauty is a social as well as an artistic value

The philosopher Schiller turned his attention to beauty after the profound disappointment he and many progressive thinkers of his era felt when their great hopes for the French Revolution evaporated as it descended into terror, violence and anarchy. Beauty mattered in education for him as it was, he felt, the best way for humans to apprehend what a good society would actually feel like should we be able to bring it about. Beauty he saw as an experience in which our contrasting drives for sensation and reason, action and order were brought into balance and harmony through a third drive, that of play. 'Beauty alone makes the whole world happy', he wrote, 'and each and every being forgets its limitations while under its spell' (Schiller 1967, p. 213). The fact that Schiller saw art as intrinsically playful should give any drama teacher pause for thought as such a definition is congruent with the playful approaches at the heart of our pedagogies. But what is particularly interesting here are the social implications of what he claimed and how these are reflected in the classrooms and studios of the best drama practitioners. Whatever the world is like outside the studio for themselves and for the young people they work with – the pressures, the quarrels, the conflicts, the unhappiness, the preoccupations, the loves, the enmities – they work incessantly at creating an ethos in which these external factors can be temporarily put aside as new worlds are imagined, experienced and reflected upon. These sites of practice become spaces in which young people are called upon to watch, listen, respect and praise one another – and it is the reciprocal nature of this contract, its ethical balance, that is crucial. The aesthetic pleasure young people can derive from creating and watching drama, then, is mirrored and enhanced in the ethics of the social space that makes such pleasure possible. These values, inherent to the ideals of the ensemble, are part of a social ideal of beauty at odds with the overly competitive demands we find in the cult of the virtuoso, where the skills of the brightest and the best are nurtured to the exclusion of the potential of the greater number.

Beauty is not synonymous with perfection

Why do some performances by young people move us while others, technically more skilful, leave us cold? It is largely because, as drama educators, we share some insight into the creation of such performances and what they might mean for those involved. Some years ago, I witnessed a group of young male offenders perform a piece of drama in which they presented a very simple story of crime and its effects, one they had devised themselves. Technically the acting was poor but emotionally it was extremely powerful. I was almost moved to tears as I watched these boys, who had been written off by practically everyone, pretend to fight yet exercise great physical restraint, show off what they could do on a skate board, and generally work together in a disciplined way for 20 minutes. Apparently their head teacher had felt the same. She had wept openly as she had praised what they had achieved, they told me after the performance, something they were evidently quite proud of. When beauty moves us to tears in this way, it is making a profound connection with some fundamental values. It is reminding us of our deepest ideals, of the teacher we always wanted to be, and re-affirming that this goal can at times be realized, despite the frustrations and disappointments that are inevitably part of the job. Moments such as these are moments of beauty that can help keep the professional spark within us alive.

The 'tense' of beauty is the future[3]

If the experience of beauty, the joys and pleasures it affords, are intensely felt in the present, Denis Donoghue insists that 'its apprehension is propelled by a politics of hope and anticipation, a surge of feeling beyond the merely given present moment' (2003, p. 86). The language of aspiration has been embraced by government policy makers worldwide, of course, but the politics of hope bring to mind Paulo Freire (1996) and his insistence that it is as necessary to human flourishing as water is to fish. We can urge young people to work hard for some future career-oriented reward, of course, but the urgings of beauty are different. Take the rewards on offer to a group of drama students intent on creating something beautiful for others to watch and appreciate; the future here is more immediate, more realizable and promises the sensual rewards of the aesthetic rather than the distant and increasingly doubtful rewards of eventually finding a good job. And yet the demands of the work remain high and consist of virtues that could find a place in any business or vocational training manual – commitment to task, working on a joint project, developing a shared vision, having high production values, and so on. In this way, the pleasures of beauty can keep alight the spark of hope in young people rather more than the sterner admonitions of duty while, at the same time, developing social and work-related virtues of use to their future lives.

Beauty in the drama classroom: An example

Many of the qualities that I am associating with beauty need to be developed over time in the classroom, but some can be made demonstrable within a scheme of work. The poem *Midas* by Ted Hughes (1997) provides an eloquent pre-text for how this might be done. It tells of how the God, Bacchus, grants King Midas a wish for restoring his old friend, Silenus, to him. Midas reacts on impulse and requests for everything he touches to become gold 'the purest, the finest, the brightest' (p. 201). The folly of this soon becomes apparent as, not only do leaves and grass become gold as he brushes his fingers against them, but also anything he tries to eat and drink: a roasted chicken drops with a heavy clunk on to his table and those of his subjects watching are aghast as he spits out gold mush that had seconds before been wine. In desperation the king prays to Bacchus to take away this gift that he had preferred above all other possible wishes. The God relents and tells Midas to bathe at the source of a river so that the last trace of the gift might be washed away. Midas does as he is bid and is suitably chastened by the shocking experience but, we are informed, sadly no wiser.

The beauty of this poem lies largely in the language, of course, yet the vocabulary is simple and readily accessible to young people of secondary school age. It is the elegance of its rhythms and its phrasing and the detail it effortlessly evokes that make this telling of the well-known legend so striking. But the poem also allows for the exploration of a theme resonant with the call of beauty – what in our lives and in our desires is truly beautiful and what is deceptively so? Below I present a selection of activities (not the complete scheme of work) that are designed to 'dance' with this theme through encouraging students to become physically and sensually immersed in the language and imagery of the poem.

1. In groups of four, students are asked to create images, each within 10 seconds, in response to lines or phrases called out from the poem. There should be five or six in all, none too explicit; the phrase describing Silenus in the opening verse: 'They chained him in flowers and dragged him' (p. 201) is a good example, as are the words of Bacchus near the poem's conclusion: 'Let that river carry your folly away.' (p. 205) This ensemble exercise calls for students to physicalize the image spontaneously and to listen to the language intently as you repeat the phrase. Such a sensual response can precede a more reflective consideration if, after the exercise, you ask students to consider what kind of story they feel is evoked by these images.

2. I now give an oral presentation of the poem, having chosen to learn it by heart. This is a more powerful experience for the students than if they, or I, merely read it. It has also led me to internalize the subtle choices of phrasing

and the exact order of the words that the poet has chosen. In other words, it has sensitized me to the beauty of its rhythms and imagery through a process Iris Murdoch describes as 'unselfing', the 'self-forgetful pleasure' (1991, p. 85) that is part of the aesthetic and also, for Murdoch, the moral force at the heart of the experience of beauty. Such experiences, she suggests, help us temporarily to forget the petty distractions that characterize day-to-day living, putting us in touch with more vital forces that provide us with spiritual sustenance. Dare I suggest that a drama teacher might gain more sustenance from such an exercise than from the endless meetings, planning, documentation and policy initiatives that currently plague their non-teaching time? However, if the exhausted teacher truly cannot find the time to learn the poem by heart, she might listen with her class to Ted Hughes' own reading, freely available on you tube.

3. Students are grouped in a circle and each handed a copy of the lines which show Midas's request to be the expression of a mad fantasy that had long obsessed him. (From 'A certain fantasy . . .' to '. . . the fate I shall describe,' pp. 201–2). Standing shoulder to shoulder, the class reads round the circle from punctuation mark to punctuation mark. Then, in twos or threes, still in a circle, each group is given one of these lines and asked to choose a word from it to speak and to physicalize in a form they feel to be particularly apt. This physicalization can be abstract or mimetic. Going round the circle again, the whole class copies the way each word is presented. When the exercise is finished, students can be asked the simple question: 'Any discoveries?' to invite them to discuss first of all in their small groups and then with the whole class what they have learned about the nature of Midas's obsession and of his folly. This instinctive, sensual immersion in the language of the poet as precedent to reflection and response is, of course, informed by the pedagogies promoted by the Royal Shakespeare Company in the UK[4]; but it is also very much in line with Iris Murdoch's proposition that we should reverse the particularly modern tendency 'to talk of reasons rather than experiences.' (Ibid, p. 84) This exercise foregrounds experience to ensure that beauty is not by-passed by dull and worthy rationalism.

4. Students in new groups of four are presented with the task of tracing Midas's emotional journey through the poem. Each is presented with one of the following 'moments' – elation, doubt, fear, regret, panic,

supplication, and redemption. They are asked to choose two or three lines of narration from the poem that match this emotion and present a short snippet of action, vocalized and physicalized as they see fit, thus mapping out the subtle aesthetics of the plot and making this accessible for consideration.

5. Midas, upon realizing the full implications of his folly, utters what is, in effect, a six-line prayer to Bacchus, begging for forgiveness and redemption (from 'I have been a fool. Forgive me, Bacchus' to 'Nothing can live, I see, in a world of gold', p.204). Students can play with different possibilities of sculpting Midas and Bacchus for the performance of this prayer. Bacchus, in particular, can demonstrate different emotions – pity, contempt, mercy, disappointment, disdain, amusement – for them to play with and consider. This can be followed by a striking 'switch'. Have the students sit in a circle and remind them of the later, popular variation to this tale in which Midas has a daughter who runs in to greet him; but, as she hugs him, she too turns to gold.[5] Have students sculpt a volunteer into a statue of the daughter at the moment of this innocent expression of love for her father. Then utter the words of the prayer yourself from outside the circle, replacing the phrase 'Forgive me, Bacchus' with 'Forgive me, daughter', asking the class to concentrate on the image of the statue as you speak the lines. You can then discuss the difference between the two images; which they found more striking, or moving, and why; and what it tells us about the things that are truly precious, truly beautiful, to Midas. Further discussion and creative work can emanate from this, exploring issues of beauty, desire and self-deception closer to the students' own lives. Then, remembering that Midas is no wiser, they might imagine and enact what similar follies such a foolish leader might be capable of and how they could impact to the detriment of those he rules.

The poetics of the drama lesson: An example of how beauty might impact on research

'A practice comes to be seen as the mechanical application of technological rules, so its expressive, aesthetic aspects are consigned to a separate domain of "art" – a concept once synonymous with technical skill but whose meaning is now constituted by its opposition to technology on precisely the same grounds that music, in the modern conception, is constituted by its opposition to language.' (Ingold 2000, p. 413)

It is an argument well-rehearsed that the dominant metaphors for teaching today are drawn from the technical rationalism of managerialism, in which a series of terms such as targets, objectives, outcomes and performance indicators have effectively subsumed the idea of teaching as a *practice* into that of teaching as a *technology*. The quote from Ingold above suggests that we are mistaken if we divorce art from technique or the aesthetic from the rational, thus regarding their pleasures as unnecessary extras. His parallel with the musical qualities of language is particularly helpful. Just as the students' experience of the musical qualities of the language of *Midas* – its rhythms, stresses, alliterations and assonances – cannot be disassociated from the poem's transactional meaning, neither should the aesthetic be separated from the technical when considering the practice of teaching.[6]

As an example of this let us consider the drama lesson – that delimited period of minutes sandwiched between other activities somewhere within the school day – as a potential area for research. Of course there will be technical demands, but current models of planning concentrate exclusively on such demands – on objectives, learning outcomes, behaviour management, assessment criteria and the like. What if we were to reconceive of the lesson as the kind of performed narrative we have in a play? Those of us who work in the form of process drama are well used to this. We plot our lessons as much as we plan them, thinking of them as unfolding stories as well as learning activities, and planning for the pleasures of surprise, plot reversal and shifts in energy as well as for more usual activities such as discussion and writing. Aesthetic considerations such as these also impact on the structure of any good drama lesson, however – on its rhythms (shifting from high energy, physical games to quieter, reflective activities, for example); on its tone (from boisterous laughter to quiet moments of wonder, perhaps); or on its sensuality (isolating or combining in different ways verbal, aural, visual and tactile experiences). In this way, the artistry of the drama educator can be compared to that of the playwright or to that of any other artist who works through live action performed in narrative time. This is surely an area ripe for research and one which would explore what Philip Fisher has called 'that lively border between an aesthetics of wonder and what we might call a poetics of thought.' (1998, p. 6). It would be one significant way in which the concept of beauty could be brought into the practice of research.

Notes

1 From the poem *Snow* in MacNeice (1964), p. 26.
2 See Winston (2010), pp. 52–3 for a lengthier explanation of this proposition.
3 This phrase is taken from Donoghue (2003), p. 86.
4 See RSC (2010). See also Berry (2008) and Winston and Tandy (2012).
5 This originates from Nathaniel Hawthorne's tale 'The Golden Touch', first published in 1852 in *A Wonder Book for Girls and Boys*.
6 See Winston (2011) for a further consideration of the points raised here about the potential for beauty to influence ideas of teacher research.

References

Armstrong, J. (2005), *The Secret Power of Beauty*. London: Penguin.

Berry, C. (2008), *From Word to Play: A Handbook for Directors*. London: Oberon Books.

Donoghue, D. (2003), *Speaking of Beauty*. New Haven, CT/London: Yale University Press.

Fisher, P. (1998), *Wonder, the Rainbow and the Aesthetics of Rare Experiences*. Cambridge, MA: Harvard University Press.

Freire, P. (1996), *Pedagogy of the Oppressed*. London: Penguin.

Hughes, T. (1997), *Tales from Ovid*. London: Faber and Faber.

Ingold, T. (2000), *The Perception of the Environment: Essays in Livelihood, Dwelling, Skill*. London: Routledge.

Murdoch, I. (1991), *The Sovereignty of Good*. London: Routledge.

MacNeice, L. (1964), *Selected Poems of Louis MacNeice*. London: Faber and Faber.

RSC (2010), *The RSC Shakespeare Toolkit for Teachers*. London: Methuen.

Sartwell, C. (2004), *Six Names of Beauty*. New York: Routledge.

Scarry, E. (2001), *On Beauty and Being Just*. London: Duckworth.

Schiller, F. (1967), *On the Aesthetic Education of Man in a Series of Letters*, ed. and trans. E. M. Wilkinson and L. A. Willoughby. Oxford: Clarendon Press.

Thompson, J. (2009), *Performance Affects: Applied Theatre and the End of Effect*. Basingstoke: Palgrave MacMillan.

Winston, J. (2010), *Beauty and Education*. New York: Routledge.

—(2011), 'Beauty: A concept with practical implications for teacher researchers'. *Educational Action Research*, 19, (4), 579–86.

Winston, J. and Tandy, M. (2012), *Beginning Shakespeare 4–11*. London: David Fulton.

11

Drama and the Audience: Transformative Encounters in TheatreSpace

Penny Bundy, Robyn Ewing and Josephine Fleming

While there is a great deal written about how powerful engaging in process drama can be, there is less research about the transformative potential of engaging in live theatre performance as an audience member. This chapter focuses on the experiences of spectators at live theatre events. It begins by drawing on the literature to discuss the nature of aesthetic engagement as a response to live theatre highlighting the link between engagement and the possibility of changed understanding. It then offers a brief overview of the TheatreSpace project, an Australian Research Council funded project that investigated the engagement of young people (teenagers and young adults) as audience of live theatre. It then turns to discuss the way young people in that study described their transformative experiences of live theatre. It concludes by drawing a direct link between possible experiences of young people attending live theatre and the goals of transformative learning.

The nature of engagement

There is no doubt that engagement as an audience member can have intellectual, sensory and emotional dimensions (Hurley 2010). Hurley argues that the emotional component is central to the experience and to the emergence of new awareness or understanding for spectators at live theatre events. Such a claim resonates with the ideas of a number of earlier scholars who focused on the role of emotion in facilitating changed awareness or understanding.

Lawrence, for example, (1981, pp. 24–5) claimed that there are three ways a change of understanding might occur in response to drama. The first he suggests is contextual and at a surface level where we might learn new facts. Like Bolton (1984, pp. 144–5), he suggests that the second involves a change of understanding at a universal level and involves generalizing beyond the specific event portrayed on stage to make broader links with our own experiences. He argues that a more profound change of understanding requires the spectator to be engaged at a feeling level and that 'without endeavour to engage this "feeling" level of experience, any change in understanding will be largely cognitive in nature, or may not be possible to achieve at all' (Lawrence 1981, p. 25).

In a similar vein, Koestler (1975) suggested that a spectator must be engaged at a feeling level if new awareness or understanding is to emerge. If new understanding or awareness is to develop, the mental and emotional energies of the participants or spectators must be engaged. The purpose is to not to encourage emotional experience for its own sake, but for the potential to bring to living consciousness the experience in a new way in the mind of the spectator. As Bentley (1965, pp. 53/54) claimed, art is not a matter of cognition but of re-cognition. '. . . it does not tell you anything you didn't know . . . it tells you something you know and makes you realize'. In a sense, live theatre can make the familiar strange, and the strange familiar, so that the audience member can examine and reflect on the taken for granted.

A strong sense of intellectual and emotional engagement can thus encourage us as audience members to link ourselves to the work. We wonder about why people behave in the way they do. We consider how we might respond in such circumstances, or we wonder about the implications of various ideas or actions. We contemplate if things could have occurred differently and if so, how and why. And we consider these ideas about humanity in relation to ourselves.

Spectators at live theatre events see the performed work and are simultaneously aware of themselves and other audience members experiencing the work. They can see themselves as part of the action and therefore make links between the work and themselves. In the process, they are encouraged to learn about their relationship to others. Such strong response opens audience members to new ideas about the world and humanity. In a sense, metaxis can happen through vicarious engagement as an audience member.

In this way, our most profound theatre encounters shed light on experiences, illuminating them in ways previously not contemplated. We become more alert, more open to ideas and possibilities. We may be challenged to think more broadly and more deeply. We make new links, connections and associations. We become more critically aware. We grow to understand human interaction in new ways and in the process gain greater insight into the human world of which we are a part. Some (see Gallagher 2005, p. 83 drawing on Bruner) describe this as a shock of recognition, we see how things are and we can imagine them differently. Radford (2000 in Gallagher 2005, p. 83) describes it as 'something speaking to something "within us"'. Even as spectators, such insight comes to us as an embodied experience. We perceive the work and the ideas of the work through the whole body. We feel a sense of exhilaration that occurs in those moments when we make a new kind of sense of something, and we experience a wholeness.

Just as Egan (2007) reminds us how important the imagination is in the cognitive as well as the affective dimensions of our thoughts, Beardsley (1970/1982, p. 292) states that he hadn't realized the importance of the cognitive act in aesthetic experience until he reconsidered the ideas of Gombrich, Goodman and Arnheim. He claims that 'the experience of discovery, of insight into connections and organizations – the elation that comes from the apparent opening up of intelligibility' is central to aesthetic engagement. He calls this 'active discovery'. We actively work to make sense of something and experience a thrill, a sense of achievement in the discovery. Once again, these understandings permeate Bruner's (1966) early work on discovery and process learning.

There is a direct link between the experience that is possible for an engaged spectator at live theatre and the goals of transformative learning. While there are many definitions of transformative learning, Mezirow's (2003, pp. 58–9) definition is helpful:

> Learning that transforms problematic frames of reference, sets of fixed assumptions
> and expectations (habits of mind, meanings, perspectives, mind sets) to make them
> more inclusive, discriminating, open, reflective and emotionally able to change.

Ewing (2010, p. 32) describes transformative learning as 'learning that moves beyond traditional notions to provide the stimulus for individuals to make significant shifts in their understandings of themselves and the worlds in which they live.' She draws on Mezirow's work to suggest that learning is transformative when individuals experience some kind of profound and structural shift to their core thoughts, feelings, actions. Such a shift of consciousness alters our way of being in the world and changes our fundamental beliefs alongside our understanding of ourselves, our relationships with others and with the natural world. It can also alter our understanding of power relationships and how they work in relation to class, race and gender. It can impact on our body awareness, our visions of alternative approaches to being and our sense of identity and belonging.

The TheatreSpace project

We now examine young people's experiences of live theatre by drawing on the findings of the recent TheatreSpace research project undertaken in Australia. One of the largest Australian Research Council linkage projects, TheatreSpace drew together researchers[1] from Griffith, Melbourne and Sydney Universities and 13 industry partners representing a significant sample of Australia's flagship theatre companies, cultural venues and major funding organizations. Over a 4-year period (2008–11) the research pursued two primary lines of enquiry: the effect of various factors on young people's attendance or non-attendance at live theatre and young people's experiences of live theatre, the latter being the focus of this chapter. The research used a mixed methods approach and was designed around 21 in-depth case studies of selected industry partner productions and a small 3-year longitudinal study which included data from three Australian states: New South Wales, Queensland and Victoria.

The case studies, which were conducted over a 2-year period, provided the project's major quantitative and qualitative data. The research team, in consultation with the nine partner theatre companies and performance venues, selected a case study research night or school matinee performance of at least two of their productions over a 12- to 18-month period. The productions chosen for the case study performances were diverse in terms of genre. They included traditional period productions (e.g. *The Importance of Being Earnest*), contemporary interpretations of classics (e.g. *Anatomy Titus Fall of Rome: A Shakespeare Commentary* and *The Threepenny Opera*), Australian classics (e.g. *God of Carnage* and *The Removalists*), contemporary plays from Australia and other western countries (e.g. *The True Story of Butterfish, Dead Man's Cellphone* and *Up Jumped the Devil*) plays targeted at young audiences (e.g. *The Shape of a Girl* and *Moth*) and a musical (*Wicked*). With perhaps one exception, *Yibbiyung*, all plays were sourced from Western cultures, which did not reflect the diversity of cultures represented in the school audiences. The fieldwork required detailed logistical planning, as the research team had to quickly distribute participant information to the target audience of young people to gain their consent to participate in the survey and, if possible, the post-show interviews. Table 11.1 gives an overview of the data collected.

The case study research consisted of two phases. The first phase applied a mixed methods approach, and the methods included using a survey, focus groups and document analysis of relevant organizational materials and policies. The survey

Table 11.1 Data collected from 21 case study performances during 2008–11, TheatreSpace project

Case Studies	21
Pre-show surveys	N = 1881
Post-show interviews	N = 795
Two-week post-show interviews	N = 225
Six-month follow-up interviews	N = 144
Key informant interviews	N = 85
Schools involved	N = 51

was administered prior to the performance to collect baseline demographic and cultural participation data, which would enable later comparison across the case studies and assist in the recruitment of a representative sample for the second qualitative phase of the research. For example, the results of the survey revealed that school matinee audiences across the three states had a greater spread of geocode, cultural background and arts attendance patterns than was the case for evening audiences. Observation field notes were taken during the performance and focus group interviews were held, when possible, immediately following the performance.

The second qualitative phase aimed at exploring the research questions in greater depth. Participating young people were interviewed at 2-weeks and 6-months following the performance. Obtaining a representative sample of the attendant, school audiences was particularly critical to understanding the factors that both encouraged and inhibited engagement as school audiences included a great range of young people, from those who attended theatre regularly with their families and schools through to those who were attending theatre for the first time. The semi-structured interview questions initially focused on the participants' responses to the case study performance and then probed more broadly for their attitudes towards theatre and how it fitted within the cultural life of their peer group. The 6-month interview was designed to explore participant reactions to the production from a distance (such as what they remembered and whether their views had changed) and to find out what cultural activities, including theatre they had taken part in with their families and friends since the case study performance. Interviewers were sensitive to probing references to the qualities respondents associated with their engagement and disengagement with theatre and to factors that impeded the engagement of themselves, their families and their peers. Key informants from the participant partner organizations were also identified and interviews were conducted with directors, education managers, performers, designers and senior management, as well as the teachers who had facilitated and/or attended the schools' performances with their students.

As noted by Robson, case study design focuses on a 'particular contemporary phenomenon within its real life context using multiple sources of evidence' (Robson 1993, p. 146). In this research each case study was built around the analysis of survey data, observation field notes, organizational documents and interviews with respondents who came from a range of perspectives such as the audience (young people interviewed), the theatre-makers (industry partner key informants) and the facilitators (teacher key informants in the case of school excursions). This resulted in 21 highly contextualized and detailed accounts. The overall research framework that guided the data collection and analysis provided the basis for comparison across the case studies (Stake 2006).

Data from each case study was separately analysed and detailed individual reports were completed for the industry partners. Because the commencement and completion of the case studies was staggered over a 2-year period, the accumulation of findings from multiple completed case studies allowed emergent patterns and themes to be explored in later case studies. This iterative approach was built into the research design. For example, it was intended that the industry partners would be provided with their first case study reports in time to feed into their programme decision-making for their following season, from which the second case study performance would be chosen. In reality, the programme decisions required a much longer time frame and these expectations were unrealistic. The follow-up of emergent themes, however, became a critical part of the process and even led to the decision to include a specific case study, *Wicked* after the popularity of musicals across a very broad range of our participants became apparent.

The collected case study reports were then re-analysed through the lens of 11 research questions. The questions that addressed the notion of engagement and in particular what encouraged and what inhibited the engagement of a large and diverse sample of young attendees (14–30 years) were:

1. How do the performance choices of teachers and caregivers influence the theatre-going experience of young people?
2. To what extent does membership of particular sociocultural groups impact on young people's engagement with the performance event?

3. What is the impact of a young person's education on his/her experience of the performance event?
4. Is theatre literacy a significant factor in influencing a young person's response to the performance event?
5. What elements of a theatrical experience engage young people?
6. What do young people respond to and value in the theatre experience?

In the following section we offer insights gained from the project on the relationship between engagement and learning with a particular focus on the centrality of emotion in this process. To do this we unpack the concepts of theatre literacy, theatre confidence and theatre etiquette to assist in differentiating between passive and active reception, the latter being necessary to activating deep understanding and learning. We then turn to describe the way young people articulated their experiences of engagement at live theatre events.

Theatre confidence, literacy and etiquette

In our research the young people, as well as the key informant teachers and industry partners, often spoke of theatre attendance as requiring a set of behaviours that were usually learnt through prior exposure to theatre with family and/or school excursions. In fact this emerged as a significant theme, which we defined as *theatre etiquette* – knowing and observing the protocols of theatre attendance. Whereas an understanding of theatre etiquette indicated familiarity with theatre attendance, it did not necessarily indicate engagement nor lead to a more focused appreciation of the production. Theatre etiquette did, however, appear to be linked to *theatre confidence*. We used this term to describe feeling comfortable attending and responding to a performance event as an audience member and having a sense of agency in constructing meaning from the experience. Our analysis demonstrated that having an understanding of the etiquette of attendance contributed to a young person's theatre confidence.

Theatre confidence links to trust. In an earlier study, Bundy (2003) noted that while the notion of trust is commonly associated with participation in drama workshops, its experience is also necessary if spectators are to experience meaningful engagement as a response to live theatre events. Spectator experience of trust is linked to perceptions of integrity. The necessary perception of integrity occurs at several levels. They must perceive integrity in the dramatic action, in their ability to read the work and in their emotional response to that action. Theatre confident young people are more likely to be open to the experience than their less confident peers.

There was evidence that lack of familiarity with theatre attendance had a distancing effect on young theatregoers and created a barrier between watching the performance and receiving meaning from the performance. Not understanding the codes and protocols was a cause for concern in some of the young people. For example, when asked about her response to the venue one respondent focused on her self-consciousness at being dressed more casually than the other theatregoers, leaving her to stand outside until her classmates arrived. She said: 'I was really confused and I was so scared, because I did not expect (pause) I don't know what I expected'. It was clear over the course of two interviews (taking place over a six-month period) that her negative feelings towards the other audience members, who she viewed by and large as being elitist, had a negative influence on her experience of watching and synthesizing meaning from the production. Other examples given by young people included being unsure of how to respond when actors addressed them directly during a performance or when the staging meant that other audience members were in their sightlines. Common to many of these responses was the feeling of self-consciousness and this arguably impeded their ability to respond and engage with the meaning of the production.

Transgression of the codes of attendance led to censure by other young people. For example, one respondent who was asked why she was annoyed when people spoke in the theatre responded that it was 'breaking the etiquette' and was 'disrespectful to the live performers'. While being entirely understandable, such a comment does lead one to question whether understanding the codes can also impede deep involvement, as focus moves from reception of the production to the behaviour of offending audience members and concern about the impact their behaviour has on the live experience. This was the case for some young audience members as well as teachers and industry key informants who were distracted by others sending SMS text messages while watching a performance. This was a somewhat complex issue because in some instances it appeared that the SMS messaging between audience goers was related to what was happening on stage and therefore could be argued was a part of the process of engagement.

For the theatre confident young people who attended theatre regularly, theatre was a natural part of their cultural landscape. In this context, they were constantly evolving skills and vocabulary to engage with theatre in nuanced and meaningful ways. They were conscious of a shared experience inside the theatre and discussions that took place after the performance formed part of their engagement with the work. Post-show interviews with school groups of theatre confident students were peppered with excited interjections, comparisons, confident opinions, careful listening and camaraderie. Finding new ways to see the experience and new words to describe it was part of their development as theatregoers. They valued both the emotional and intellectual components of their response as audience. As one young person observed, 'you can reflect on it and it draws your emotion'. Young people were aware of the significance of their emotional response in their engagement as spectators often describing it as compelling.

Conversely, the groups of young people with little familiarity with theatre-going were sometimes lost for words when they were asked to respond to a performance. When the focus shifted to a more familiar territory such as their experiences of stadium concerts or musicals, the discussion became more animated. However, this did not necessarily mean that they were not engaged by the theatre performance, as teachers sometimes noted after the event. What it did mean was that these young people did not have the confidence and/or the language to articulate their experiences of the event and in many instances they had not had the opportunity to discuss their reactions in class. For learning to be activated for these students, further scaffolding of the theatre event might be required.

Articulating engagement in the live theatre experience

In the following section, we draw on the statements made by young people in the TheatreSpace project about the nature of their engagement at live theatre events. We focus in particular on how they describe the emotional, sensory and intellectual components of their response as audience.

Frequent comparisons were made between attendance at live theatre and watching film, which was described as more passive. Young theatregoers saw theatre as more unpredictable than film and valued this. We were told that part of the thrill of theatre is that 'you don't know what the experience will be before you get there and have it' and that each theatre performance was unique. They also described theatre as more intellectual. Speculating about why they believed there was this difference, they commented that 'theatre reaches you on a level that other mediums can't because it's real emotions being portrayed by real people'.

The atmosphere of sitting in the theatre with other spectators was also noted as contributing to their engagement. We were told:

> There's more buzz, you can feel the energy and excitement;
> The buzz of being there with all those elements coming together;
> It's more thrilling when it is there in front of you; and
> It feels more real.

They described such experience as personal and intimate. The feeling was heightened when young people attended a live theatre event in a smaller venue. One person discussed enjoying being so close to the stage action that she felt like she was in the story. They also told us that the atmosphere contributed to their focus encouraging further attention to the work. One young person described an 'eerie feeling sitting in a crowd but the crowd is so quiet that you feel like you're the only one there'.

The enjoyment of being confronted; of experiencing an emotional roller coaster, a rush, a wholesome feeling was highlighted by many young people. They indicated that they reacted differently to confronting events on the stage than they might do if the same event was to be witnessed on screen. They indicated that their response to the stage action was more intense and more thrilling, hence more real, more emotional and more engaged.

> On stage you're part of the moment, you can't really ignore it.
> You feel like a part of it, you feel like you're actually experiencing it.

Recognition of the realness 'out there' made them feel more like they were part of that realness. One young person referred to this quality as being 'more 4D'. Actor presence also strengthened focus. Other comments that directly reflect the transformative nature of the experience included statements such as 'you learn new and different things because it's different to normal life'.

We were also told that the spectator's gaze at a live event is more intense and more focused. This intensity of focus draws the spectator's attention to the ideas and questions raised by the work.

> Because it's there in front of you (it) forces you to confront something you might
>> normally just take for granted or ignore.
> A live event is a richer experience. It is more interesting and more intellectual;
>> (it) makes you want to talk about it.

Being present in the same space and at the same time as the actors was important to young people. It intensified the perception of realness, a quality that many young people admired. Several people told us that 'you pay more attention because they're real people'. Their use of the term 'realness' should not be equated with realism or naturalism. Rather, they used the term to refer to the presence of real people. Their attention was drawn to any occurrence on stage that heightened awareness of the humanity of the actors. They noticed (often with delight) actor sweat and spit. Their attention was drawn to the broken arm of an actor. Terms used by young people to describe their experience of the quality of 'realness' across a number of the case studies included rawness, immediacy and grittiness.

A further quality of engagement at the live theatre event that influences the nature of the experience is the perception that there is a relationship between the spectator and the work, usually expressed as being a sense of connection between the actor (not character) and themselves. Comments of this kind were noted following most of the case study performances.

> You feel a sense of the connection to the actors on stage and there are emotions and feelings in that sense of connection.
> It feels like you're involved a bit more; almost in the play with the actors, they can make eye contact with you.
> You feel like you could interact even if you can't; and
> It feels like it's reaching out to include you to see what you think.

We were told that other mediums lack a sense of relationship between the performer and spectator.

> There is a relationship, a real relationship, like a now relationship between what's happening up there and what's happening in the auditorium.

Across the case studies, proximity to the action was noted by a number of young people as impacting on their engagement. Physical proximity was usually (though not always) described as a desirable element. It seemed that the closer to the action a person was, the more involved they felt. Quite often the word 'immediacy' was used to describe this. Young people referred to the power of immediacy, the way it increased their emotional response and their attention to the work.

While people recognized that their proximity to the action impacted upon them, the specific response related to the particular work and the degree of comfort individual spectators felt witnessing such content in the public space of the theatre. When a work is experienced at close hand, spectator attention is drawn to the humanity (and probably vulnerability) of the performers.

I think it's the experience, because, I love the idea that you are right there in the experience, and you can see like the sweat lying there on the actors forehead and like the spit flying from their mouth.

In our study, young people often referred to the notion that something might go wrong and recognized this uncertainty as a positive quality of their engagement. Not only do spectators seem to take pleasure from the perception that a mistake is possible, they also take satisfaction in attempting to spot the error and observe how the performer recovers from it. They respected and admired the stage actors' vulnerability and skill and indicated that the risks taken by the actors made them seem more human. Some young people described placing themselves imaginatively in the shoes of the performers to consider how they might have responded, indicating that when they do this their engagement is further increased.

Several young people spoke about being aware of the responses of other audience members. Some indicated that they experienced pleasure when their own responses were affirmed by other people's apparently similar reactions. Some indicated a sense of intrigue in the way people around them were responding. Experiencing a work among the company of others offered a sense of connection and a sense of community to some of the young people we spoke to.

There's more of a human element not only people on stage but people all around you; (it) feels like a group experience, it is not an individual experience;

There is a feeling of connection and communication when you sit in a theatre audience; you watch the audience and you have a sense of the audience's emotional response.

Engaged spectators sometimes spoke about feeling respect. They respected other spectators and felt that this was returned. They respected the performers and felt that was returned, that those performers were creating this show especially for them. Some indicated that they were consciously aware that being in the same space as the actors meant the possibility that the actors could directly interact with them. This in turn heightened their engagement.

Conclusion

Engagement in live theatre as an audience member can be life changing. It can transform our understanding of the world or of who we are in the world. Our work in the TheatreSpace project strongly supports Hurley's (2010) assertion that intellectual, sensory and emotional dimensions are embedded in the responses of young people as audiences of live theatre. Furthermore young people who participated in the TheatreSpace research were able to articulate the way they experienced these transformative moments and how they interacted with them. In the foreword to Hurley's (2010) book, Bogart (p. xiii) claimed that 'Experience and sensation become memory via emotion. The more emotion that is generated in the heat of the experience, the more likely the memory is to "stick"'. To feel free to experience this emotion, theatregoers need to experience trust. Our research suggests that trust is more likely to be experienced by more confident theatregoers. Further work needs to focus on the relationship between theatre confidence, theatre literacy and how trust can enhance the transformative potential of being a spectator at live theatre.

Note

1 TheatreSpace chief investigators included Professor John O'Toole, Associate Professor Michael Anderson, Associate Professor Penny Bundy, Professor Bruce Burton, Associate Professor Kate Donelan, Professor Robyn Ewing, Dr John Hughes, Associate Professor Angela O'Brien, Dr Christine Sinclair, Dr Madonna Stinson, with partner investigator Noel Jordan.

References

Beardsley, M. (1970/82), 'The aesthetic point of view', in M. Wreen and D. Callen (eds), *Monroe C. Beardsley: The Aesthetic Point of View: Selected Essays.* Ithaca, London: Cornell University Press, pp. 15–34.

Bentley, E. (1965), *The Life of Drama.* London: Methuen & Co.

Bolton, G. (1984), *Drama as Education: An Argument for Placing Drama at the Centre of the Curriculum.* Essex, England: Longman.

Bruner, J. (1966), *Toward a Theory of Instruction.* Cambridge, MA; New York: Belknap Press of Harvard University.

Bundy, P. (2003), 'Aesthetic engagement on the drama process'. *Research in Drama Education*, 8, (2), 171–81.

Egan, K. (2007), 'A brief guide to imaginative education'. *Imagination in Education Research Group (IERG)*. Accessed on 22 June 2009 from http://www.lerg.net

Ewing, R. (2010), *The Arts and Australian Education: Realising Potential.* AER 58, Melbourne: Australian Council of Educational Research.

Gallagher, K. (2005), 'The aesthetics of representation: Dramatic texts and dramatic engagement'. *Journal of Aesthetic Education*, 39, (4), 82–94.

Hurley, E. (2010), *Theatre & Feeling*. Houndsmills, Basingstoke, Hampshire: Palgrave Macmillan.

Koestler, A. (1975), *The Act of Creation*. London: Pan Books Limited.

Lawrence, C. (1981), 'Layers of meaning: A case study of Tynewear theatre company's junior programme, "Geordie's lamp"'. *SCYPT Journal*, 8, 21–31.

Mezirow, M. (2003), 'Transformative learning as discourse'. *Journal of Transformative Education*, 1, (1), 58–63.

Robson, C. (1993), *Real World Research: A Resource for Social Scientists and Practitioner-Researchers*. Oxford, UK: Blackwell.

Stake, R. E. (2006), *Multiple Case Study Analysis*. New York: The Guilford Press.

12

Drama, Speaking and Listening:
The Treasure of Oracy

John O'Toole and Madonna Stinson

Section 1: A quiet classroom is a good classroom (?)

We live in an age where two giant modes of communication vie for supremacy and also combine to rule much of our lives – printed books and papers, and computers. However, the vast majority of human communication is still done face-to-face, by mouth, eyes and ears, through the spoken word and accompanying gestures and body language.

Oracy, the forgotten basic (O'Toole 1991)

The 20-year-old paper from which this quotation is taken contended that Oracy, or the ability to communicate effectively by speaking and listening, is more basic than the '3Rs', and went on to assert that it is largely untaught and often inhibited or discouraged in schools. At the time, there was an international groundswell of interest and concern in English-speaking countries about the state of speaking and listening in schools, with major research and development projects happening worldwide (e.g. in Canada: Booth and Thornley-Hall 1991; in the United Kingdom: McLure et al. 1988; in United States: Harste et al. 1984). The Australian state education system which commissioned the paper received it with enthusiasm. However, for most of the next two decades, oracy received no increased attention in the schools and in some of the above countries the imposition of compulsory regular written testing narrowed both notions of literacy and the opportunities for independent use of language (Alexander 2010). In the political rhetoric and the dominant curricula, 'literacy' still almost invariably means the ability to master written text and also occasionally computer technology.

Oracy has remained prominent in academic publication, such as Robin Alexander's (2005, 2008) extensive work on dialogic teaching. In a comparative international study, he notes that in English and American classrooms, talk is initiated and dominated by the teacher in contrast to a tradition of 'oral pedagogy' (2005, p. 99) evident in French, Indian and Russian classrooms. Alexander promotes such an oral pedagogy in a 'dialogic classroom' involving talk in the classroom that is collective (involving teachers and children in partnership), reciprocal (talking and listening and sharing ideas and viewpoints), supportive (without fear of 'wrong' answers), cumulative (building on each other's ideas) and purposeful (with educational goals in view). In the United Kingdom, Alexander's work has influenced some policy and curriculum relating to literacy, for example, the UK Government's *Talk for Writing* (DCSF 2008); however, that material has been further criticized by Carole Bignell (2011), for reinforcing Bourdieu and Passeron's 'cultural arbitrary' which perpetuates social reproduction rather than the dialogic classroom proposed by Alexander. Another indication of current interest in oracy is the 2007 publication of a special edition of the international journal, *Early Childhood Development and Care*, the editors of which recognize that "the oral competencies children need to become fully participative citizens in a highly mobile global context cannot be left to chance" (Evans and Jones, 2007, p. 559). This extensive collection ranges throughout the fields of language development (including environmental factors, and language delay), second and additional language learning and speaking and listening for the development of literacy.

Drama research has a place here too. Betty-Jane Wagner (1998) reported a range of studies that concluded that drama experiences impacted positively on language learning. The results of the research studies that she analysed strongly indicate that learning in drama improved spontaneity, fluency, articulation, vocabulary and use of diverse language registers. In addition, more abstract thinking and expressive language was produced as well as indications of increased use of rarely accessed vocabulary, improved grammar and understanding of narrative structures. Ann Podlozny (2000) undertook a meta-analysis of 80 studies into drama and language learning, concluding that drama had a positive impact on a range of outcomes, particularly those relating to oral language. Of special interest to us is that, in this article, she went on to say that those studies employing 'unstructured enactment' (p. 259) rather than reproduction of script had greater effect. In the decade since those extensive collections the research into language and drama has intensified in the academies.

Something else has happened in the last 20 years, however, that makes addressing our forgotten basic even more important and much more urgent. That is the incorporation of the computer and the internet into our family lives, and the difference it has made to the way children learn to express and communicate in the world. Copious research (e.g. Christakis et al. 2009, 2004; Ward 2004) confirms what is only too plain: children nowadays spend much less time conversing with friends and family, and a great deal more in front of a screen. It is true that with their computer they are learning all sorts of communication, reading, recognition and writing skills, but they are having significantly less opportunity to practise the live skills and constraints of listening, turn-taking, practising registers of spoken language, expanding their verbal and expressive vocabularies, and the dialogical skills of argument, negotiation and questioning. This is taking its toll on children's natural acquisition of oracy.

Drama and oracy

The studies referred to by Wagner and Podlozny show drama's contribution to oracy, and it is not hard to see how it works. As the late Dorothy Heathcote, one of those most responsible for drama's re-invention as pedagogy, memorably put it: 'Drama is a real man in a mess . . . And the students have to talk and argue their way out of it' (1971). Numerous drama theorists have considered the contribution of spoken language to the production of dramatic meaning and applied that to schools contexts (e.g. Haseman and O'Toole 1988; Kempe and Holroyd 2004; Winston 2004; Dickenson and Neelands 2006; Anderson et al. 2008; Baldwin 2009; Stinson and Freebody 2009). Drama is, after all, the art form of the spoken word and of gesture and the body. More than that, the very basis of drama is putting ourselves in other people's shoes to imagine human situations and contexts that are or might be. Dramatic play, which is a richly embodied and oral medium, is among the primary ways in which children together explore their world, invent new worlds, try out models of behaviour and communication. Pretty well all drama and theatre (which, simply defined, is the public expression of drama for an audience of others) start with a fictional model of a human situation that is then complicated in order to explore the causes and consequences of action and relationships and these are expressed nearly always in combinations of spoken words and/or gestures. Because they are fictional and leave no negative consequences when the players step back into their real world, the behaviour of the characters and their settings can be altered, played with, re-examined, new logics and imaginative connections found. In the next section of the chapter, we will illustrate drama's connections with oracy through the analysis of a sequence of drama lessons requiring the student participants to create oral texts and discuss, challenge, construct persuasive speeches and arguments, and explanations, all in order to 'talk and argue their way out'.

Section 2: A case full of treasure

This study took place in an urban government school close to the centre of Brisbane, Australia. The school, which we will call Miller State School, was established in 1920 and is situated in what might be considered a reasonably well-off middle class area, though students come from a range of home circumstances. Miller is proud of its supportive school community and employs a range of specialist teachers and programs to assist students with learning difficulties. There is also an established program for gifted and talented students. We were invited into the School to help promote oracy, which the school leaders considered an important but under-resourced area of the curriculum. Our aim was to deepen our own understanding of *how* drama supports oracy, by demonstrating just how many aspects of oracy can be practised in a single coherent unit of drama whose primary purpose is the teaching of something else – and then analysing how effective the practice was in terms of four dimensions of oracy skills and capabilities. The culture of contemporary and traditional India provided both the pre-text for the drama and its content.

We co-taught with the classroom teacher and 22 students from a Year 4 (9–10 years) mixed gender cohort. The students had little or no prior experience of drama despite the teacher's interest in the area. We planned and implemented eight lessons (each lasting 1–1½ hours). Each session was video- and audio-recorded; students, the classroom teacher and parents were interviewed; and we audio-recorded an in-depth reflective discussion after each lesson. The discussion in this chapter draws on the analysis of all the data.

Oracy skills

We devised a comprehensive checklist of oracy skills to drive both our planning and analysis. We identified four dimensions of oracy: *functional, dialogical, linguistic* and *paralinguistic*.

Dimension	Category
Functional	informing (and responding to information)
	controlling (and responding to control)
	negotiating
	imagining
	feeling

Our *functional skills* model was one previously derived for a textbook on drama and oracy (Haseman and O'Toole 1988 adapted from Gordon Wells 1986), identifying as the five distinct functions of any live communication: *informing, controlling, negotiating, feeling* and *imagining*. One of the most important aspects of this is the notion of sub-text, when one function is explicit and primary, but conveys one or more other functions by implication and inference. Most spoken conversation entails speakers conveying messages about relationships, power and feelings, at the same time as they are primarily engaged in informing or speculating. A conventional school lesson is overwhelmingly biased towards the language of informing and controlling, initiated and sustained by the teacher, with limited negotiating, and imagining and feeling mostly inhibited (though often present in the sub-texts of student response!). However, we designed the drama to contain opportunities for the students to practise both initiating and responding in all five primary functions.

Dimension	Category
Dialogical	listening
	responding
	turn-taking
	leading
	narrative

The next dimension of oracy is the *dialogical skills* – those which enable two or more people to sustain an encounter that fulfils the speakers' purposes. Prime among these of course is the ability to *listen* clearly, accurately and perceptively (including for sub-texts). Next is the ability to *respond:* offering, questioning and proposing in order to sustain a conversation. *Turn-taking* is another key skill: contributing appropriately without blocking, interrupting, pre-empting or cutting others off. So too is *leading* – initiating ideas, sustaining and advancing conversation and encouraging response. Finally comes creating coherent *narrative*: telling a story interestingly and with appropriate elaborations.

Dimension	Category
Linguistic	diction
	vocabulary
	grammar and syntax
	register
	colour
	public address

Our third dimension comprises the *linguistic skills*: *diction* – clarity, articulacy, speed and projection; *vocabulary* – the breadth, richness and detailed understanding of words and their meanings; *grammar* and *syntax* – structure, complexity (the elaboration and flow of sentences) and articulacy; *register* – the control and variety of language suited to particular situations and social contexts; *colour*: the ability to choose a suitable level of vivid or expressive language, and use live metaphors and other figures of speech. As important as all of these is the skill of *public address* – the ability to express ideas confidently and hold an audience.

Dimension	Category
Paralinguistic	vocal expression
	non-verbal and gestural
	proxemics
	energy
	silence

The final dimension is the bits beyond the words, or *paralanguage* as they are called, where, it is variously estimated, between sixty and ninety per cent of meaning is conveyed, including all those sub-texts. In this dimension, we identified five categories: *vocal expressions* – volume, pace and tone and pitch and emphasis, and how and when we pause; *non-verbal* and *gestural* – what we do with our body, arms and hands, how we stand or sit, our faces and most significantly our eyes; *proxemics* – physically how we place ourselves or are placed in relation to others; *energy* – often expressed through the tempo or the volume of the conversation; and (not to be overlooked, just as artists and designers must consider the meanings of negative space) *silence* – how to use and to interpret it.

A lot to incorporate in a single unit? We didn't think so, as all these components are present in almost any complex live human interaction and managing them, rather than being managed by them, is the key to agency which all young people need. The students understood that our overarching aim was investigating this theme, and we reinforced that at the end of each lesson with a reflective discussion, led for consistency by Madonna, that always started with gathering their immediate thoughts about the lesson content and activities, and moved on to discussing the extent to which they had felt enabled to practise the specific speaking and listening skills.

Planning the drama

We organized our planning to ensure maximum opportunities for students to practise initiating, responding in and sustaining all the *functional* categories, all the skills of *dialogue*, and apply a range of specialized *registers* and *public address*. These created challenges for them in all the other categories of *language* and *paralanguage* (How do you respectfully contradict a Maharajah, or start and sustain a vox pop interview?).

We found a topical pre-text and a hook for the drama in a brief, graphic news item.

> Waiting in the musty darkness beneath one of India's most secretive Hindu temples this month, a team of experts prepared to prise open the granite door of Chamber A, a vault that had been sealed for a century . . . they emerged shocked and speechless . . . The value of the treasures hidden beneath the temple in Trivandrum, the capital of Kerala, has been estimated at $18 billion (The Australian, 11 July 2011)

The article went on to note that soldiers had been placed round the Sree Padmanabhaswamy temple, as debate about what to do with the treasure hotted up, and the traditional guardian of the treasure, the 91-year-old Maharajah, was 'worried about the consequences now the world knew about the treasure'.

In the following account of the drama, the box on the right indicates the *functional* categories being foregrounded in each activity (including *specialized register* and *public address*):

The treasure of Trivandrum drama

The plan	Oral language focus
We started as usual with some preliminary games, a treasure hunt and some freeze-frames to uncover, decode and piece together the basic story of the find.	informing, negotiating
Next we enrolled all the class as 'top investigative journalists from Radio India' – the main role they would hold and frequently come back to throughout the eight lessons. One of us (Madonna) took role as the radio program producer Marni, gently authoritative but as ignorant as the journalists about the emerging story, and all the students chose from a range of gender-appropriate Hindu names, whose meaning they were encouraged to find out; they did, and wore their badges with pride and growing belief.	imagining, feeling, negotiating
They next held vox-pop interviews with the local populace (working in pairs, with one of them at a time swapping roles to provide opinions from a wide range of citizens and stakeholders). We encouraged the interviewees to make it more difficult in the second round, in a multitude of ways, so that the interviewers had to deal with difficult, unwilling (and a few unhinged) respondents. This they then all 'reported back to the studio'.	Reporters: negotiating, controlling Interviewees: informing, imagining, feeling, *specialized register* Report back: informing *public address*
That was a prelude to a special press conference, interviewing Sri Tirunal the Maharajah (John in role, grave and rather daunting) with strict protocols. He revealed that he had been there as a 9-year-old boy the last time the chamber was opened (true, he had, in 1931) and was concerned both about the insult to the priests, and the lack of respect shown this time, as the doors had just been battered down. He announced that he would only consider allowing chamber B to be opened if it were done with respect, and challenged the journalists to help or demonstrate to the people how it should be done.	informing, feeling, negotiating *specialized register* *public address*

(Continued)

The plan	Oral language focus
The drama convention shifted as the journalists, without explicitly dropping their roles, effectively morphed into the designers and performers, in four groups, of a suitable ceremonial to the temple god, Vishnu, complete with dance, chant, oath and procession. They learned some simple kathakali dance steps (coincidentally one girl was just learning it at her dance school and was able to offer some advice and modelling – a little 'mantle of the expert' for real). Then negotiating in groups, they designed and practised their procession.	imagining, negotiating, feeling *specialized register*
With solemnity and great tension, they performed it to the Maharajah. Mollified, Sri Tirunal promised to consider their request to open the other Chamber, providing all the treasure would be used to the greatest benefit of the community. For a second time he challenged the journalists to help him decide between four worthy causes: • Kerala State government – for infrastructure: roads, schools, hospitals; • Kerala Opposition Party – for all Keralans to benefit directly with an equal shareout; • Indian Tourist Board – to build a 'Treasure' centre, to attract people from round the world; • Sri Padmanabhaswamy Temple priests – some to repair the temple, most kept sacred to Vishnu	imagining, informing, negotiating *specialised register* *public address*
The journalists, in four groups, now had quite a different task, each to create a brief but persuasive news item or feature, promoting one of these options. This task proved very challenging for the students, but they managed it, and presented their features once again to the Maharajah (as live performance – video was beyond the class's resources, and not necessary to sustain the fiction anyway). He promised to go away and think about it.	negotiating, informing *specialized register* *public address*
Before he was fully out of earshot, Marni (Madonna in full flight of outrage) burst out that 'that stupid old man' had completely missed what the treasure should be properly used for, which was to address India's greatest shame: child labour, and the exploitation, torture and murder of millions of children in fields, factories and sweatshops. This outburst stunned the journalists, as intended; Marni promised to bring in a child worker for them to talk to, and they prepared their questions.	feeling, informing

(Continued)

The plan	Oral language focus
The stakes were now much higher . . . especially as the next session started with John in the new role of a very junior producer delivering the news that the furious Maharajah had insisted that Marni be sacked for her disrespect to him. The interviews went ahead, with Madonna in a new role as a child working in a sweet factory (owned, they discovered, by a company allied to the Maharajah's family) and the classroom teacher bravely and quite successfully taking role as the child's mother. The dramatic tension was almost palpable throughout.	negotiating, informing, feeling *specialized register* *public address*
Following the interviews, the excited but sobered journalists reported back to the studio what they had heard, and together with their new producer decided what they should do about it. This decision was to confront Sri Tirunal – respectfully but firmly. They also insisted that the mother and child should be brought in to see him too – entirely their idea, which they stoutly defended.	informing, negotiating *public address*
The confrontation was theatrical, powerful and totally committed. The Maharajah made it very hard, but the journalists stuck to their guns and the protocols, and he slowly relented, especially when they told him of his own family's involvement. As their piece de resistance they dramatically produced the family – and became its spokesperson. Sri Tirunal revealed that he was as shocked as they were to discover this source of his wealth and agreed to develop a 5-year plan to use the treasure to alleviate this scandal. The journalists even persuaded him (reluctantly) to agree to reinstate the insolent Marni, as it was she who had revealed the scandal.	informing, negotiating *specialized register* *public address*
Following this entirely satisfactory climax, going into the last two sessions our neat plan came unstuck for the first time. We had intended to loosen the structure to permit the children to take over the direction of the narrative of the drama. We switched the focus of the drama right back to their original major interest and mystery at the start of the drama: What was in Chamber B? The students had lost interest and focus on that plot, and invented and enacted frozen effigies with little real imagination or commitment, and many humorous and superficial ideas.	imagining, negotiating *public address*

(Continued)

The plan	Oral language focus
We therefore switched back to the Maharajah's 5-year plan, much more successfully, with a series of small-group role-plays: • as labouring mother and child deciding what to do with their share • as labouring children egging each other on to more ambitious dreams • as wise family friends who foresee possible trouble • as reporter and angry factory owner, faced, without child labour, with closing the factory and making hundreds unemployed	imagining, negotiating, controlling *specialized register*
We next led a discussion out of role, about what might have happened 5 years on to those families, in the light of the previous role-plays.	imagining, negotiating
In fours, two returned to their reporter roles, and two became the labouring mother parent and child, interviewed (after preparation by both groups) about their lives 5 years on, to report back to the Maharajah.	informing
Finally, with all re-enrolled as Radio India journalists, each was required to report carefully to him, in one or two sentences, the most important thing that they had learned from their interviews. This was done with great seriousness – and to our ears very mature and unromantic realism: most outcomes were very positive, but some reporters had really taken the pitfalls to heart. At the end the Maharajah reminded them of the other four official requests five years earlier, and left them with a question: did we do the right thing with the treasure?	Informing, imagining *public address*

Section 3: Data, analysis and implications

The data from our journals and video observations and from the student, class teacher and parent interviews showed clearly that our oracy aims were achieved. All the functions indicated in the right-hand column operated as we expected, and our observations and the video clearly identified, in almost every lesson, examples of opportunities for practice, challenge and extension in all the other dimensions. Because of limitations of space in this chapter we have selected only a few extracts that we believe are illustrative of the dimensions. We hope the extracts give you a sense of the powerful dialogue from which they have been taken.

Functional

As part of the ceremony to convince the Maharajah that they would treat the opening of the chamber with respect, the students set to work in groups on the task of creating a chant to be performed at the opening. The following two samples of student work (done without teacher input) clearly show their attempt to work with the poetic, imaginative, affective language suggested by the task:

Lord Vishnu	*Lord Vishnu Lord Vishnu*
Lord Vishnu	*shine down on us*
The sun sparkles	*Please open chamber B*
The moon shimmers	*to let the dark see the light*
Please open chamber B	*Namaste*
and let the statue glimmer	*Namaste*

The young participants (each group of two girls and two boys), worked together with seriousness and focus as they negotiated the exact language they thought would be the most convincing. We can see that they were imagining themselves 'into' the situation: 'the sun sparkles; the moon shimmers' and 'to let the dark see the light'. The repetition of the respectful address to Lord Vishnu and 'namaste', together with their personal focus, facial expression and concentration

Figure 12.1 The children perform their ritual.

on gesture that we can see on the recording (Figure 12.1) as they presented these short rituals give more evidence of imagination and feeling at work.

Dialogical

In the following extract, we trace the work of one group of boys through three stages of the drama. In this first extract they are reporting back to Marni. In groups, the reporters have been sent to interview various interested parties and this report relates to the government position:

> M. *Did anyone hear from the state Government? Badri?*
> R1. *Yeah, build better hospitals.*
> R2. *Build better hospitals in the city, better roads in the country and clean up the sewage industry, new arts and sports centres and put computers in schools._*

In the next extract the same group of boys is working, out of role, to discuss how the reporters might present the information they have gathered from interviews – negotiating and planning together:

> S1 *Ok, who's reading what guys?*
> S2 *How bout we just have one person reading it?*
> S1 *All people*
> S3 *We need someone to introduce us, like someone who goes, 'we are the state government and we will help India by blah-blah-blah-blah-blah'.*
> S1 *[using eyes, and gesture to control the group] Jeez, we gotta make up our minds. We're not gonna worry about ME! We're gunna share it around.*
> S4 *We'll go Addy, James, Rhys, me and then you.*

Linguistic

They go on to plan the presentation in detail. In this next extract, you can see the change in register, as they move *into* role and rehearse the material. They have made careful selection of language to persuade the audience. We have indicated by R when the students are speaking in role:

> S2/R *. . . we'll use this money for good.*
> S4/R *Such as?*
> S2/R *Such as new and better hospitals to help sick people; new roads in the country will cause less accidents. A clean up of our cities, the rubbish and the sewage in the streets, will cause less infections.*

S4/R	*New arts centres and sports centres will bring more people to India. Um . . .*
	more computers in the schools, more children can learn on computers. Will . . .
S3	*[prompt] equal*
S4/R	*equal happy Indians.*
S1/R	*which brings . . .*
S4	*And someone will have to add . . .*

When they returned to the studio they continued to negotiate and discuss their presentation of the report with great commitment, as was evident from their intent facial expression, concentrated gestures, and purposeful discussion.

Paralinguistic

In the following extract, the student in role as a member of the community supporting the temple priests (R3) is being interviewed by one of the reporters (R4). The recording of the interview is striking because of the range of vocal modulatory devices which R3 uses to indicate the depth of her character's feeling. She uses pitch, pause and volume to particular effect:

R3.	*Because the chamber is <u>falling down!</u> It needs to go to the priests because*
	they can build it back up again ... and because the priests [should] *have the*
	money because THEY <u>built</u> it.
R4	[very respectfully and with 'microphone' in hand] *May I ask why do you*
	need to repair the temple?
R3	[clearly frustrated] *Because it is CRACKING! Well <u>obviously</u> it is cracking!*
	Haven't you <u>seen</u> it?

Reflection in and on language

In addition, we found that students became much more conscious of language, how it impacted on meaning and their own processes of working with language. Here are two extracts from the reflective discussions at the end of each session. The first extract illustrates the students becoming conscious of a number of language processes (negotiation and informing – for the purpose of persuasion):

| S5 | *I thought it was kind of hard to do an argument.* |
| M. | *Why?* |

> S5 *Because well like I thought it was hard because you wanted to put it together and you only had a short amount of time.*
>
> J. *Would you have liked more time?*
>
> [General agreement].
>
> M. *How did you go with one of the big Cs: Cooperation?*
>
> S6 *Pretty well.*
>
> [General agreement] *Yes, uhuh etc.*

And in the following extract, we can see students' developing awareness of the emotional impact of language (following their interviews of the child worker and her mother), and evidence of a developing consciousness of different points of view:

> M. *What was interesting?*
>
> S7 *I thought the mother because she sounded so sad and serious about it. She had to so do much hard work.*
>
> S8 *I thought it was interesting that the child said working in the sweet factory was very dangerous and the mother thought the child was lucky to have such a good job.*

How drama activates oracy

Our research suggests that the activities planned by us, and enacted in partnership with the teacher and students, had significant impact on the students' skills in oracy, with three contributing factors: the targeted linguistic practice identified above; our more general choice of a dialogical pedagogy encouraging student talk; and some specific characteristics of drama which support challenge and risk-taking in language. In drama, the activators of learning are *role* and *dramatic context*. Many of the students commented on the power of role to diminish the personal risk involved in interaction:

> *Because you did not have to be yourself; because you could act like another person . . . you can make them look like whatever you wanted.*

One student, an *extremely* shy girl, surprised the regular classroom teacher (and her parents) with her willingness to participate in the drama work. She was one who identified that when in role she was able to do things she could not do in 'real' life and in the final reflection session, told us:

I liked . . . um . . . the role . . . when we were interviewing people. Like . . . when I am myself I am not very confident . . . but when I was in role it was easier.

Added to this is the importance of teacher in role (TIR). Working in role with the students allows the teacher to model language and paralanguage and, importantly, puts the teacher on the same level as the students thus diminishing the 'teacher as authority' relationship evident in so many classrooms. The students in this drama really enjoyed us 'playing alongside' them and took that playing very seriously:

I was worried about really stuffing it up and Sri Tirunal [TIR] might be angry . . . I was very nervous – everyone was nervous. Because if you are basing it on real life he might not be very happy.

I remember . . . when Marni [TIR] got angry – it was a bit funny and scary at the same time.

Dramatic context provides both purpose and opportunities for specialized genres in language use. In this drama, the purpose is driven by the need to deal with the particular dramatic tension/s involved (e.g. in this drama the participants needed to persuade the maharajah to open the second chamber, they wanted to find out the circumstances of the workers in the interview with the mother and daughter, and they had to meet the time and task demands of the roles they were undertaking as reporters). And in this dramatic context, the students had many opportunities to play and experiment with a large range of language registers (talking with the maharajah, with the other roles they encountered, and with each other, both in and out of role).

Other contributing factors, not necessarily related to drama but of importance in this study, were the careful *changing of groups* and partners for various activities; and the *fun* of participating in the work. We deliberately chose to change the grouping and grouping patterns in this drama because we wanted the students to need to negotiate with a range of other students in the class, and not fall into familiar patterns of friendship group interactions. Consequently, we sometimes allocated partners, and sometimes allowed free choice, drawing on our day-to-day observations of student–student interactions to guide our decision. This meant that, even when out of role, the functional and dialogical dimensions were prominent:

S: *There were lots of ideas and we argued a bit . . .*
M: *How did you get around that?*
S: *We just had to make a decision and get on with it*

These comments were made as part of one of the regular *reflection* sessions held at the end of each lesson. We believe that these were vital to the development of the oracy skills of the students as they allowed the students themselves to identify their learnings, and pinpoint when and why they happened. And, last but by no means least, is the capacity for learning to be fun and enjoyable. We know that we cannot claim that drama alone, of all the disciplines, offers this opportunity, but the purposeful play we undertook with the children in this class was highly enjoyable for all. Even the parents noticed that their child was enjoying school more and that this was contributing to their oracy more broadly:

P1 *[He] felt happy at school and that the others in the class were listening to him and respecting his ideas.*

P2 *For the first time in her life, she led the dinner table conversation.*

P3 *She talked about these classes every night – normally school is forgotten [when she gets home].*

One student expanded on this, giving a vivid insight into his expectations of education, and unwittingly putting his finger on why this experience was different:

Learning and having fun are different things and you can't have them together but this is out of this world [our emphasis] and you can have them together in drama.

This single study does not provide definitive answers to the question of *how* drama activates learning in oracy but it does suggest that there are a number of contributing factors. We should acknowledge that the drama work undertaken here was planned and implemented by two very skilled and experienced drama educators; that we had effective support from the school and the classroom teacher (who enthusiastically participated in every lesson); and that the drama work took place in large blocks of time (over 3 hours per week for three weeks). However, there are some strong indications from our data that give clues to what is actually activating the learning. The first of these is *role*, both for the students and the teacher, and the capacity for role to allow for modelling and experimentation with language, and the safety of role whereby the act of taking on role gives permission to be someone different to oneself. The second is *dramatic context* that provides purpose and opportunities for specialized language. The students were motivated by the purpose and tension of the drama and were conscious of the need to switch language registers when needed within the context. The constant changing of groups and working partners within the drama meant that oral discussion and negotiation were foregrounded, and the students had many practical opportunities for purposeful talk within the drama sessions. Regular reflection at the end of each session was vital for the students to identify their own learning and, therefore, be more conscious of how and when they might learn better in future. Finally, the drama sessions were enjoyable: the students wanted to participate; and they had much to talk about following the lessons, both at school and at home.

We would like to suggest that more drama educators take up the challenge to research the practice of drama teaching, not just to determine learning outcomes, but also to take us all further on the journey towards identifying why and how those outcomes may be achieved.

How else, we wonder, might it be possible to achieve the necessary changes in systemic policy, school curriculum and classroom structures, teacher education and re-education, the culture of schools and the practices of teachers, in order to encourage the use of dramatic pedagogy for oracy, and kill the lingering notion that a quiet classroom is a good classroom?

References

Alexander, R. (2005), *Towards Dialogic Teaching: Rethinking Classroom Talk*, 2nd edn. United Kingdom: Dialogos.

—(2008), *Essays on Pedagogy*. London and New York: Routledge.

—(2010), *Children, their World, their Education: The Final Report and Recommendations of the Cambridge Primary Review*. London: Routledge.

Anderson, M., Hughes, J., and Manuel, J. (2008), *Drama and English Teaching*. Melbourne: Oxford University Press.

Baldwin, P. (2009), *School Improvement through Drama: A Creative Whole Class, Whole School Approach*. London: Continuum.

Bignell, C. (2011), 'Talk in the primary curriculum: Seeking pupil empowerment in current curriculum approaches'. *Literacy*, 46, (1), 48–55.

Booth, D. and Thornley-Hall, C. (1991), *Classroom Talk*. Portsmouth NH: Heinemann.

Christakis, D. A., Gilkerson, J., Richards, J. A., Zimmerman, F. J., Garrison, M. M., Xu, D., Gray, S., and Yapanel, U. (2009), 'Audible television and decreased adult words, infant vocalizations, and conversational turns'. *Archives of Pediatrics & Adolescent Medicine*, 163, (6), 554–8. Available at: http://archpedi.ama-assn.org/cgi/content/full/163/6/554#AUTHINFO

Christakis, D. A., Zimmerman, F. J., DiGiuseppe, D. L., and McCarty, C. A. (2004), 'Early television exposure and subsequent attentional problems in children'. *Pediatrics*, 113, (4), 708–13.

DCSF (2008), Talk for writing [Electronic Version], from http://www.education.gov.uk/publications/eOrderingDownload/Talk-for-writing

Dickinson, R. and Neelands, J. (2006), *Improve your Primary School through Drama.* London: Fulton.

Evans, R. and Jones, D. (2007), 'Perspectives on oracy – towards a theory of practice'. *Early Childhood Development and Care,* 177, (6–7), 557–67.

Harste, J. C., Woodward, V., and Burke, C. (1984), *Language Stories & Literacy Lessons.* Portsmouth, NH: Heinemann.

Haseman, B. and O'Toole, J. (1988), *Communicate Live!* Melbourne: Heinemann.

Heathcote, D. (1971), (Verbatim, in) *Three Looms Waiting.* Film: Directed Richard Eyre. London: BBC Films.

Kempe, A. and Holroyd, J. (2004), *Speaking, Listening and Drama.* London: David Fulton.

McLure, M., Phillips,T., and Wilkinson, A. (eds) (1988), *Oracy Matters.* Milton Keynes: Open University Press.

O'Toole, J. (1991), *Oracy: the Forgotten Basic.* Brisbane: Minister's Council on Curriculum.

Podlozny, A. (2000), 'Strengthening verbal skills through the use of classroom drama: A clear link'. *Journal of Aesthetic Education,* 34, (3/4), 239–75.

Stinson, M. and Freebody, K. (2009), 'The contribution of process drama to improved results in English oral communication', in R. Silver, C. Goh and L. Alsagoff (eds), *Acquisition and Development in New English Contexts: Evidence from Singapore.* London: Continuum, pp. 147–65.

Wagner, B.-J. (1998), *Drama and Language Arts: What Research Shows.* Portsmouth, NH: Heinemann.

Ward, S. (2004), *Baby Talk.* London: Arrow Books.

Wells, G. (1986), *The Meaning Makers: Children Learning Language and Using Language to Learn.* London: Hodder and Stoughton.

Winston, J. (2004), 'Integrating drama and English: Literacy and oracy in action'. *English Drama Media,* 1, (1), 26–7.

13

Drama for Health and Human Relationships Education: Aligning Purpose and Design

Helen Cahill

Introduction

Health and Human Relationships (HHR) educators aim to educate their students about social, physical and mental health issues, and to promote the adoption of healthy practices. They are in the business of influencing behaviour. They use drama-based strategies to help bridge the gap between health knowledge and its application within the social and relational contexts of everyday life.

In their efforts to influence health-related behaviour, HHR educators face significant competition from the global marketing machines which provoke dissatisfaction with the self in order to create desire for those commercial products which promise results in the area of personal beauty and social status. Giroux (2000) argues that 'as culture becomes increasingly commercialised, the only type of citizenship that adult society offers to children is that of consumersim' (19). Given this social context, educators need pedagogical methods that will assist students to engage critically with the discourses that make them vulnerable to market culture and to the adoption of associated risky health practices.

People are sometimes sceptical about whether an education programme can have an effect on health-related behaviour, particularly in the face of the onslaughts young people face from the media. However, there is now a considerable evidence base that shows that well-designed and well-implemented prevention programmes can improve students' social skills (Durlak et al. 2011), diminish body image distress (O'Dea and Maloney 2000), reduce sexual risk-taking (Kirby et al. 2007), reduce risky approaches to drug use (Tobler et al. 2000, Wood et al. 2006) and reduce rates of school bullying (Smith et al. 2004). This evidence base also demonstrates that participatory pedagogies are integral to the effectiveness of these programmes. Didactic approaches, which pivot on the transmission of knowledge, tend to have a weak or null influence on health-related behaviours. The programmes that do produce positive behavioural outcomes are those which provide a combination of relevant information, exercises to enhance positive coping, opportunities to engage in collaborative problem-solving, critical thinking tasks and rehearsal of the assertiveness and help-seeking skills needed to negotiate health-promoting choices (Hopfer et al. 2010). Simulations, skills rehearsal and problem-solving exercises are key among the components of such programmes (Soole et al. 2008). This substantial evidence-base demonstrates that drama-based tasks are integral to the efficacy of these programmes.

Purpose and pedagogy

There are many different drama conventions available to the educator, and they can be used to fulfil different pedagogical purposes. It is useful for health educators to categorize these different functions, so as to be clear about why a particular technique is chosen and what educative purpose it is expected to fulfil. Ideally there should be a close relationship between the objective of the learning activity and the selection of the particular drama-based convention.

Drama techniques can be employed to serve five important functions in the Health program. These include: (a) *describing*: students use the drama to report on their experiences; (b) *rehearsing*: students practice skills such as assertion, help-seeking or problem-solving; (c) *critical thinking*: students explore the way in which broader social and political forces influence health behaviour; (d) *deconstructing*: students analyze the way in which societal expectations are internalized and shape desires, fears and behaviour; and (e) *envisioning*: students imagine new possibilities for action.

Drama for description

One of the key benefits of using drama for descriptive purposes is to provide fictional scenarios for class discussion. Students can be called upon to construct scenarios which show situations in which health-related choices are played out, or which pinpoint the moment in which a decision is made, or its effect is felt. A set of freeze frames may be used to catalogue different manifestations of school yard bullying. A more extended role-play can be used to show how a particular interaction plays out. When students fashion their scenarios, they take an active role in constructing meaning and representing their experience. Those who watch the dramatic play also develop a sense of ownership because they have witnessed something happening. The embodied and immediate nature of drama-based tasks helps to build engagement and the sense of being involved in a shared experience.

Health education programmes call upon students to deal with sensitive material. Students engage with issues relating to bullying, body image, racism, sexuality, drugs and mental health. Given the personal nature of many of these issues, there is particular need for well-being educators to use fictional scenarios as the focus for enquiry so as to protect the privacy of their students and to provide some level of distancing from the material under discussion. The process of constructing a fictional scenario provides a useful form of distancing. When students co-create a fictional scenario, it is both 'theirs' in that they made it, but 'not theirs' in that it is a fiction. They draw from their experience of the world, but without having to re-tell their own story.

The potency of descriptive drama work depends largely on whether it is used in a summative or investigative manner. Ideally the descriptive drama tasks form the platform for subsequent enquiry. It can be tempting for an educator to accept the construction of the dramatic artefact as the culmination of the learning activity. There can be a sense of completion once students have constructed and shown their work, and the teacher may be unsure about what to do with the offering. The teacher may even be reluctant to invite children to critique the ideas represented in their work lest they be seen to be diminishing the value of the students' response. However, the response to the initial dramatization should involve enquiry about the health and relationship issues represented in the presentation. Where a drama class might be called upon to appraise the aesthetic quality of the work, and the performance decisions made, the HHR class will be asked to enquire into the issues raised through the drama.

When the teacher uses the descriptive scenario as the basis for discussion, they lead the class from an experiential mode of learning to a reflective mode of learning. This positions students within an enquiry. Once a line of questioning is in place, students are re-positioned from creators of the scene to investigators of the material. This shift in positioning from representing to analyzing is integral to the effective use of drama as a tool for HHR education.

In leading the follow-up work, it is particularly important for the educator to be aware of the tendency people have when working in a naturalistic mode to call upon simplistic storylines or to create stereotypical characters. This may show up as a relegation of characters to positions based on traditional gender roles, or assignation of negative characteristics to persons in positions of authority. There may be a tendency to play out simplistic binaries such as good–bad, cool–uncool and guilty–innocent. Driven by their urge to create a tell-able tale, the players may fashion an exaggerated narrative, with the worst-case scenario presented as if it was a typical occurrence (Elliott 2005).

It is important to counteract this trend towards simplification or exaggeration as it may work against the health-promotion goals of the curriculum. Techniques available to the teacher include use of reality-testing questions to ask students about the accuracy, frequency, prevalence, reach or impact of the phenomena represented in the scene (see Table 13.1). The process of review and an associated re-shaping of the scenario may help students to recognize the effect that dominant stories have on the way in which we make sense of what happens in our world.

Drama as rehearsal for life

HHR educators have a strong interest in developing the capacity of their students to negotiate for their own health and safety. Rehearsal techniques are integral to the effectiveness of HHR education programmes. It is not sufficient just to talk about what should be done. Students need also to practice how to convert advice to action. Drama strategies provide the opportunity for students to try out

Table 13.1 Analyzing images

Following construction of a representational freeze-frame or scenario, ask about	
Accuracy	Is this how it usually happens?
Location	Where do these things tend to happen?
Frequency	How often do these things happen in everyday life?
Reach	Is everyone involved? Who is affected?
Impact	What are the consequences? Who is affected and in what ways?
Focus	Whose point of view is privileged? What can be seen from other perspectives?
Intention	What did the makers of this scene intend to communicate?
Audience	How is the audience affected?

solutions-in-action, test the viability of their strategies and in doing so develop their communication, assertiveness and problem-solving skills.

Rehearsal exercises are commonly conducted within a naturalistic performance genre. Players perform 'as if' in real life. They are provided with a typical form of resistance and must practice ways to address obstacles as they pursue their health-related choices. Within the narrative, emphasis tends to be placed on the moments in which the individual must make a decision, exert a choice or manage their behaviour. Commonly this is presented as a conflicted or obstructed choice, leading to struggle on the part of the individual. Students may additionally be faced with the challenge of transacting their choice in a situation of unequal power relations.

Rehearsal techniques may be used for a number of different purposes. They may be used to pursue a rights or liberation agenda; they may be used as exercises within a more psychologized approach to developing social and emotional literacy; or they may be used as a mode through which to practice technical skills.

The educator working from a *rights-based* interest in health promotion will focus on equipping students to resist or redress the types of oppression that are routinely experienced by members of a particular group. The role-play exercises will be used to reveal the practices and effects of oppression and to rehearse resistance skills. The educator will emphasize the connection between the personal and the political, and seek to heighten awareness of the way in which a particular narrative is routinely replicated within a broader pattern of oppression. For example, a rights-based approach within a sexuality education programme may lead to rehearsal of a scene in which a young woman refuses to have sex unless a condom is used or seeks help to address the gender-based harassment she has experienced in the workplace.

An empowerment approach can be heightened through the selection of forum theatre techniques. In this approach, the students play and re-play the scenario, experimenting with different ways to deal with resistance. The focus within this mode of approach tends to centre around agency and liberation (see Table 13.2). The process of naming the abuse of rights and working overtly to address this oppression can help students to realize the effect of both subtle and overt forms of discrimination. The drama helps to reveal the mechanisms of oppression.

Social and emotional literacy programmes tend to take a *personal* rather than a political approach to understanding human development. Within such

Table 13.2 Drama as rehearsal for life

When using drama to rehearse for change, consider the following strategies	
Role-swap	Swap roles so as to develop empathetic engagement with both positions in the dyad
Re-play	Play the scene over to examine the effect of different interventions
Coaching from observers	Ask the observers to advise the character about different ways to pursue their wants
Role-replace	Ask an observer to enter the scene to demonstrate their advice in action
Rewind	Move forward or backward in time to investigate causes and influences and potential opportunities to change direction
Fast forward	Move forward in time to investigate the longer term effects and consequences of people's actions
Re-frame	Move the focal point away from the initial framing of the action and view the situation from a different perspective
Cartoon frames	Present the change actions in a series of cartoon style freeze frames to show key steps in change efforts
Advice from player to character	After the player has worked in role, ask them to provide their character with some advice

programmes the educator may call upon rehearsal techniques to develop the skills of self-awareness, self-management, social awareness and self-expression (Payton et al. 2008). Rehearsal tasks may be used to have students practice their communication skills. The teacher may set out to invoke compassion through the experience of playing a certain role, and ask students to talk about how being in a certain situation makes them feel. There may be an emphasis on role-rotation or role-swapping so as to help students imagine what it is like to be in a particular situation. Students may be asked to practice expressing their emotions, needs or wants in a respectful, assertive or considerate manner, or to learn conflict resolution techniques.

Rehearsal exercises may also be highly *pragmatic* in nature and include exercise of utility skills such as obtaining medical help in an emergency or cleaning up a blood-spill. These exercises are used to practice prescribed procedures. However there is also a potential to build a narrative around the exercise to add a more realistic sense of the social pressure that might be experienced while carrying out the activity. This can be done by introducing competing needs and priorities, or to engage with a moral dilemma such as whether to maintain loyalty to a friend who has attended a party without parental permission, or to call for medical help to deal with the injury they sustained while intoxicated. In this case the dramatic narrative can strengthen the simulation exercise.

While rehearsal is a useful strategy for well-being educators, there is also the possibility that use of drama for rehearsal can work *against* the health promotion goals of the curriculum. Just as with the use of drama for description, this can occur when characterization inadvertently normalizes or reinforces limiting stereotypes, when it glamorizes the behaviour it aims to reduce, and when it demonizes or pathologizes certain subject positions. Constant replaying of 'problem' scenarios can also make a negative contribution when this contributes to pessimistic thinking about the possibility of change, or when success stories are excluded, thus unnecessarily problematizing a situation. A worst-case situation commonly requires a different response to the everyday scenario and it is not helpful to confuse the two when rehearsing response strategies.

There are many strategies the teacher can use to counteract a possible drift towards the demonizing of certain persons, the glamorizing of risk behavior or an excessive problematizing of everyday challenges. Chief among these is the use of critical thinking strategies. The following section introduces the way in which drama strategies can be used to engage students in critical thought.

Drama for critical thinking

Critical thinking is a key skill for health literacy. In an era of media saturation, this has become a particularly important skill. Students need critical literacy skills to detect the underlying messages beneath the texts that they encounter. Critical enquiry is political in nature (Kincheloe and McLaren 2003). It requires people to consider the way in which power relations, social conditions, institutional practices and media messages function to influence health-related behavior. Critical enquiry calls for students to focus on the way in which ideology, class, race, ethnicity, location and systems work to shape expectations, desires and behaviour.

Critical theorists argue that to make change we need to detect and dislodge the patterns that hold things in place. Kincheloe and McLaren (2003) argue that we live now within a 'hyper-reality' in which we are bombarded by images and representations through the media. They argue that one of the effects of living within this hyper-reality is that 'the distinction between the real and the simulated is blurred' (p. 442). Young people come to presume that if their own lives are to be 'normal', they should resemble those they encounter via the electronic mediums. This can place a particular pressure on young people as they negatively assess their appearance, relationships, portfolio of life experiences and possessions, unfairly comparing them with the benchmarks established in the worlds they encounter within the shared hyper-reality. When their sense of what is normal is colonized by airbrushed images and inflated storylines, their own lives appear trite, meaningless and ugly in contrast. It is important then that young people are invited to use their critical faculties to detect and combat this assault on their sense of self and on the standards they use to assess their own position in the world.

In Western modernity, young people are increasingly expected to manage their own biography, chart their own pathway and create and live into their own personal future. Sociologist Ulrich Beck uses the term 'individualization' to define the way in which people have become forced to construct their own lives, given the erosion of the social traditions which once prescribed roles and pathways (Beck 1992). In the Western world, class, gender and family no longer dictate choices; rather, these are encountered at an individual level. The escalation and dominance of the market economy has led to a breakdown in older markers of social identity such as class and gender. The individual believes they must choose and shape their future, even when the availability of choice is more an illusion than a reality. The individual as choosing agent feels increasingly responsible for managing their image. They become increasingly vulnerable to a sense of meaninglessness and failure. A concern about their failure to construct a 'successful' life-path may pervade their sense of self and leave them vulnerable to commercially driven quick fixes.

To re-dress this impact of hegemonic storylines about what it means to 'have a life', it is important to activate a critical and politicized sensibility. Drama-based approaches can be used to help with activation of the political imagination. Drama strategies can help to make visible the powerful marketing forces that shape consumer desire. Surrealist techniques can help with this (see Table 13.3). Imagine, for example, that your students 'become' multinational companies. One plays Alco-Whole, a multinational alcohol manufacturing company, and another Glamour-Whirled, the leading company selling cosmetics to the young. In the conversation in which they attempt to out-boast each other about their success, they will articulate the strategies they have honed to manipulate the thinking of their potential consumers so as to create a desire for their products.

Drama-based methods such as these can help to make visible the circulation of power that tends to remain invisible when the individual experiences

Table 13.3 Drama for critical thinking

When using drama to promote critical engagement, consider the following strategies	
Anthropomorphosis	Adopt the role of significant objects who can report on the human behaviour observed in a particular situation
Parody	Distort the characters to heighten what is distinctive about their position and function within the decision-making process
Interview the character	Interview the character about how they have experienced their situation, what they are hoping for and what influences their choices
Relative positions	Adopt the physical position which illustrates the character's relative power and status and play the scene from that position
Advisory panel	Establish a panel of 'experts' to give conflicting and positional advice on the matter
Nightmare	Play the situation in the style of a nightmare in which the underlying fears are realized
Documentary	Create a series of documentary-style interviews and images to report on an occurrence
Animal kingdom	Play the scene as if the animal that best represents your character. Adopt the animal's characteristics. Discuss the patterns of behaviour exhibited.

themselves as the sole site of will and agency. It can be hard to engage students in an abstract discussion about consumer culture. However, a dramatized scenario is entertaining and immediate. It can use metaphor, archetypes or analogy to make the complex issues more accessible. Surrealist techniques are particularly useful for this purpose. They invite students to engage with ideas and issues rather than with the personalities or narrative lines that are privileged within the naturalistic performance tradition.

Deconstruction is vital to the work of critical enquiry. It is important to identify how is it that the external operations of the world around us manage to affect our thinking, expectations, preferences and sense of priority. How does this happen? What can we do about it? The following section deals more specifically with the way in which drama strategies can be used to help people understand how they come to internalize dominant storylines and discourses and how these thought patterns work to influence health-related behaviour.

Drama for deconstruction

The poststructuralist tradition of thought invites us to focus on the way in which our sense of identity influences our health-related choices (Davies 1993). Our sense of identity is personal, social, cultural and historical. Who we think we are, and who we desire to be, has a lot to do with the world we are born into. In poststructuralist theory the term 'subjectification' is used to refer to the way in which people ongoingly gain a sense of who they are and what it is appropriate for them to do or desire (St Pierre 2000). For example, people learn gender scripts which teach them about what it is 'appropriate' for a man or a woman to do or to think (Davies et al. 2001). They learn storylines which position the Prince as the active and the brave, and the Princess as the beautiful and the passive. They learn that if they are not beautiful (or brave) they will be neither desirable nor chosen. From the poststructuralist feminist tradition we learn that social norms are absorbed and internalized, working to shape the very desire to play ourselves in certain ways (Butler 1999). Thus we become complicit in playing into the standards that surround us, seeking to fit and to belong.

Research into the effectiveness of body image programs has highlighted that it is important to apply critical thought to the way in which beauty standards are internalized, and conflated with ideas of goodness and worth (O'Dea and Maloney 2000). Once students become alert to the way in which they are influenced by the standards of beauty that are crafted in the media, they are more able to challenge the way in which the beauty myth governs their thoughts and actions.

When educators use the concept of subjectification as a way to understand the shaping of identity, they see the need for enquiry techniques that will help students to identify the raft of standards against which they measure and moderate themselves. They seek methods to reveal the way in which these standards are internalized and work to shape the expectations that people place upon themselves (Cahill 2012). The theory is that once these discourses are detected, it becomes possible to contest and resist them (Davies 1994).

Deconstruction does not mean dismissal or destruction. We cannot swipe away the mechanism of definition whereby distinctions such as beautiful–ugly, truth–lie, teacher–student, fat–thin or right–wrong are held in place by our very language structures. Rather, Derrida proposes that deconstruction involves pulling the assemblage apart to see how it is constructed (Derrida 1978). He uses the metaphor of the palimpsest to conjure a picture of how this might happen. The palimpsest is a manuscript made of parchment that has been scraped back and written over, with new text replacing old. However traces of the old scripts can be seen beneath the new script. The new and the old simultaneously occupy the same space and can be read in relation to each other.

When drama is used as a tool for deconstruction, the original scenarios provide the backdrop against which subsequent scenarios are read (Cahill 2011). They remain as the backdrop against which the subsequent scenarios are played out. The new scenarios are compared with the initial portrayal and the contrast provokes a re-thinking as the initial certainties are questioned and dislodged. The process of comparative analysis assists participants to critique and to see things differently. Alter-ego techniques are particularly useful in engineering the work of deconstruction as they can more readily allow for a complex and even contradictory interpretation of character. For example, the educator might initially invite a descriptive role-play showing a teacher–student conflict about late submission of an assignment. In a subsequent scene the teacher calls for additional players to enact the 'hidden thoughts' of the characters (see Table 13.4). The first scene portrays a conflict between surly student and scathing teacher. In the 'hidden thoughts' iteration, however, it becomes evident that both the teacher and the student are experiencing a sense of shame, a fear of failure, a sense of helplessness and a desire for support. A new knowledge is created about

Table 13.4 Drama for deconstruction

Use these drama conventions to assist with deconstruction of the shaping discourses	
Hidden thoughts	Interview players in role as the 'hidden thoughts' of the characters. Ask what the characters may have been thinking or feeling but not saying out aloud. Ask what the character is afraid of and what they are hoping for. Seek multiple answers.
Truth game	Have the actor re-play a scene without withholding their thoughts. Or have them give only truthful answers to the questions they are asked.
Decider game	Choose a dilemma. Cast one player as the affirmative side of the brain and the other as the negative, and ask them to argue their case, seeking to influence the ultimate decision made by the character
Types	Play the stereotype. Re-play the scene as the inverse of the type. Discuss the differences and the norms that inform these differences
Heritage of influence	Play a scene from a far distant time to show the mythic origins of the norms or expectations that govern the original scene

who these characters 'are'. This new knowledge abrades the initial certainty about the characters and has the observers re-think the student–teacher relationship.

Drama for envisioning

Deconstruction opens a space for reconstruction. Re-construction entails imagining the possibility that things can be done differently or that different meanings can be ascribed to a particular action or situation. Judith Butler discusses the role that the imagined plays in enabling change in the self, describing fantasy as a key tool in change work.

> Fantasy is what allows us to imagine ourselves and others otherwise; it establishes the possible in excess of the real; it points elsewhere, and when it is embodied, it brings the elsewhere home. (Butler 2004, pp. 28–9)

This notion of fantasy as allowing us to imagine ourselves otherwise may be at the heart of the transformative power of drama.

Commonly people presume that the future is created out of those actions taken in the present to rectify what has happened in the past. However, using Butler's theory that the imagined possibility is critical in change work, we might conceptualize that it is the image of the possible preferred future that calls forth the changes made in the present. The image of what is possible and desirable calls people to action.

In recent times, psychologists have become increasingly interested in the function of hope in promoting resilience and coping (Seligman et al. 2009). Given this, the educator may wish to specifically call upon envisioning work to invite participants to construct the possibility that there will be a future in which rights are realized, and in which people will effectively look after themselves and each other.

A range of drama conventions can be used to engage students in the construction of compelling images for a future in which transformation has taken place (see Table 13.5). The educator may use a performance sequence whereby the 'preferred future' is played first, with a subsequent playing backwards in time to demonstrate the phases of change in reverse order (Cahill 2010). Playing backwards from the future to the present reinforces the idea that it is the image of the future that calls forth the change efforts. The preferred future image is important because it shows how we believe things ought to be. To co-create a new possibility is also to produce hope – or the idea that something *can* be.

Table 13.5 Drama for envisioning

When using drama to create new possibilities for transformative change, consider the following strategies	
Super-heroes	Re-play the scene in role as a super-hero or fantasy figure. Discuss what makes this possible in the line of action. Compare with the original set of options created in the realistic scenario.
Surrealisms	Play the roles of non-human characters reporting on the recent transformation in human interactions.
Dreams	Play the interaction as a dream scene in which wishes and needs are fulfilled. Compare with the realistic scenario.
Preferred futures	Create the scenario that demonstrates that the preferred future is in place. Discuss what has shifted to make this possible.
Alternative endings	Re-play the scene a number of times to produce a worst-case ending and a best-case ending.

Conclusion

It is important for HHR educators to be informed by the growing evidence base which distinguishes the pedagogical elements found to be essential within effective prevention education curricula. This evidence base highlights the importance of including authentic and pragmatic learning tasks via simulation and rehearsal. It also highlights the importance of including critical thinking exercises to address the influence of social norms upon health-related behaviour. When deployed effectively, drama-based techniques can assist students to detect and critique the influence of harmful social norms and to envision and rehearse alternative modes of action. It is equally important for educators to embrace the theoretical turn and to be guided by the insights provided by those who engage philosophically with the way in which the internalization of social norms works to influence the sense of what is permissible and what is possible. Drama techniques can assist with the challenge of revealing the influence that these invisible thought lines have on health-related choices. When educators are well-informed about the range of methods available in the drama canon and the pedagogical functions they are suited to, they are better equipped to harness the potential of drama as a tool for deep learning and as a medium through which to achieve personal and social change.

References

Beck, U. (1992), *Risk Society. Towards a New Modernity*. London: Sage.

Butler, J. (1999), *Gender Trouble: Feminism and the Subversion of Identity*. New York: Routledge.

Butler, J. (2004), *Undoing Gender*. New York: Routledge.

Cahill, H. (2010), 'Drama for intergenerational dialogue: Researching youth views about the future'. *NJ Drama Australia Journal*, 33, 7–20.

—(2011), 'Drama for deconstruction'. *Youth Theatre Journal*, 25, 16–21.

—(2012), 'Form and governance: Considering the drama as a "technology of the self"'. *Research in Drama Education: The Journal of Applied Theatre and Performance*, 17, 405–24.

Davies, B. (1993), *Shards of Glass: Children Reading and Writing beyond Gendered Identities*. St Leonards, NSW: Allen and Unwin.

—(1994), *Post-structuralist Theory and Classroom Practice*. Geelong: Deakin University Press.

Davies, B., Dormer, S., Gannon, S., Laws, C., Rocco, S., Taguchi, H., and Helen, M. (2001), 'Becoming schoolgirls: The ambivalent project of subjectification'. *Gender and Education*, 13, 167–82.

Derrida, J. (1978), *Writing and Difference*. London: Routledge.

Durlak, J. A., Weissberg, R. P., Dymnicki, A. B., Taylor, R. D., and Schellinger, K. B. (2011), 'The impact of enhancing students' social and emotional learning: A meta-analysis of school-based universal interventions'. *Child Development*, 82, 405–32.

Elliott, J. (2005), *Using Narrative in Social Research: Qualitative and Quantitative Approaches*. London: Sage.

Giroux, H. A. (2000), *Stealing Innocence: Youth, Corporate Power, and the Politics of Culture*. New York: St Martin's Press.

Hopfer, S., Davis, D., Kam, J. A., Shin, Y., Elek, E., and Hecht, M. L. (2010), 'A review of elementary school-based substance use prevention programs: Identifying program attributes'. *Journal Of Drug Education*, 40, 11–36.

Kincheloe, J. L. and Mclaren, P. (2003), 'Rethinking critical theory and qualitative research', in N. K. Denzin and Y. S. Lincoln (eds), *The Landscape of Qualitative Research: Theories and Issues*, 2nd edn. Thousand Oaks: Sage.

Kirby, D., Laris, B. A., and Rolleri, L. (2007), 'Sex and HIV education programs: Their impact on sexual behaviors of young people throughout the world'. *Journal of Adolescent Health*, 40, 206–17.

O'dea, J. and Maloney, D. (2000), 'Preventing body image and eating problems in children and adolescents using the health promoting schools framework'. *Journal of School Health*, 70, 18–21.

Payton, J., Weissberg, R. P., Durlak, J. A., Dymnicki, A. B., Taylor, R. D., Schellinger, K. B., and Pachan, M. (2008), 'The positive impact of social and emotional learning for kindergarten to eighth-grade students: Findings from three scientific re-views', in *CASEL*. Chicago: Collaborative for Academic, Social, and Emotional Learning.

Seligman, M., Ernst, R., Gillham, J., Reivich, K., and Linkins, M. (2009), 'Positive education: Positive Psychology and classroom interventions'. *Oxford Review of Education*, 35, 293–311.

Smith, P., Pepler, D., and Rigby, K. (2004), *Bullying in Schools: How Successful Can Interventions Be?*. Cambridge: Cambridge University Press.

Soole, D. W., Mazerolle, L., and Rombouts, S. (2008), 'School-based adolescent drug prevention programs: A review of what works'. *Australia and New Zealand Journal of Criminology*, 41, 259–86.

St. Pierre, E. A. (2000), 'Poststructural feminism in education: An overview'. *Qualitative Studies in Education*, 13, 477–515.

Tobler, N. S., Roona, M. R., Ochshorn, P., Marshall, D. G., Streke, A. V., and Stackpole, K. M. (2000), 'School-based adolescent drug prevention programs: 1998 meta-analysis'. *Journal of Primary Prevention*, 20, 275.

Wood, E., Shakeshaft, A., Gilmour, S., and Sanson-Fisher, R. (2006), 'A systematic review of school-based studies involving alcohol and the community'. *Australia and New Zealand Journal of Public Health*, 30, 541–9.

Part Four

Activating Curriculum

14

Drama and History: A Kind of Integrity

Andy Kempe

Introduction

In Tom Stoppard's 'Rosencrantz and Guildenstern Are Dead' (1967) two of Hamlet's university chums meet a band of travelling players, the leader of which describes their job thus:

> We do on stage the things that are supposed to happen off. Which is a kind of integrity, if you look on every exit being an entrance somewhere else.

In turn, even the players get caught up in the unfolding tragedy of 'Hamlet, Prince of Denmark.' The difference between the players and the hapless students though is that at least they have control over the world they create and inhabit through their art. When the Player proclaims, 'We're actors – we're the opposite of people!', he is identifying both the limitations and potential of drama as a means of gaining insights into human experience through a process that Boal (1979) described as 'metaxis', that is, the ability to exist simultaneously in the real and fictitious world.

The value of drama as a method for exploring history has long been recognized. A concern with such work though is how the integrity of history may be retained in the process of dramatization given 'the thorny problem of *facts and authenticity*' (Woolland 1993, p. 112). One may similarly ask what the implications are for the integrity of drama when historical *facts* and *authentic* characters provide its content. The relationship between drama and history may be seen as a dance between the real and the fictitious. But this would be too simplistic and fail to acknowledge that just as dramatists are likely to proclaim that truth is found in fiction, many contemporary historians question the notion that history is concerned with indisputable facts. Rather, in what Raymond

Williams (1975) described as a dramatized world, it may be argued that all of our knowledge of the past is mediated through literary and non-literary texts. Even the experiences of first-hand witnesses are subject to semiotic influences. In commenting on the aesthetic relationship between content and form Zatzman (2003, p. 36) notes that 'the recognition that what we choose to tell, to whom we choose to tell it, and indeed how we choose to tell it, all matter'. Thus, behind the performative aspects of any testimony will lie the witness's attitudinal point of view and the accuracy of their recall, both of which will influence the degree of understanding and empathy experienced by the audience.

Drawing on a heritage

Arising from the movement towards a more child-centred approach to education and the influence of Dorothy Heathcote on the use of drama in education in particular, Fines and Verrier's *The Drama of History* (1974) may be recognized as a seminal work in the exploration of the relationship between these two disciplines. The book recommended 'an attitude to education that teachers of different disciplines may share usefully' (p. 11). Fines, a drama specialist, was primarily 'concerned with helping pupils understand themselves and the world they live in through setting up learning situations that could be explored through role-play method' (p. 9). For Verrier, a historian, 'true learning' consisted of, 'trying to feel what life-situations are like' (p. 13). While the first of these aims might be fulfilled without any reference to history at all, the second though can surely only ever be achieved given the proviso that the 'life-situations' are approximated and mediated, or, as Zatzman (2005, p. 95) puts it, in dramatic retellings of personal and public histories we play out 'that which cannot be represented'.

In terms of introducing children to such historical knowledge, Fines and Verrier contend that, 'information must come when they (the children) want it and when they are in a position to use it for themselves, and when they know why they are doing what they are doing' (p. 18). However, as a drama teacher fascinated with history and general knowledge I question this. I hoard snippets of information that I sense may have dramatic potential and believe that there is a value in introducing children to knowledge they may not consciously want or be in a position to use immediately. I reject the term 'trivial knowledge' believing instead that there is an intrinsic pleasure in having knowledge and finding uses for it. One of those uses may of course be to create drama. In response to a drama about the floods that hit the east coast of England in 1953, one Year 6 pupil wrote this to me:

> I loved learning through the drama. We usually do numeracy and literacy but the drama was an extraordinary change. We all learnt lots from the morning. You taught us about the flood in 1953. Firstly, that the flood even happened. I and the teachers had never heard of it!

The sentiment expressed here was apparent in many of the letters the class wrote in response to a one-off session devised as a 'hook' for a large group of 9- and 10-year olds embarking on a unit of work exploring natural disasters. In the first instance, the children were put into role as volunteer medics, fire and rescue specialists, police specials and social care workers, and discussed what skills they might need if they were called upon in an emergency. Using narration and a PowerPoint of images of England in the early 1950s, the children were taken through a 'time warp' and asked to imagine they were watching a television (a rare commodity) on the evening of 1 January 1953. In role as a weatherman, a teacher used the actual weather charts from that night to tell the children about a storm surge building in the North Sea. A further piece of narration took the children to a primary school hall near the estuary of the River Thames where they were told to prepare to receive people rescued from the flood caused by the storm surge. One of the victims was played by my colleague, drama educator Daphne Payne. Daphne is profoundly deaf. She brought her hearing dog along with her and told one group of children how she had been stranded on the roof of her chalet for hours in the freezing cold night because although a number of boats came offering to take her they refused to take the dog. The powerful effect of this encounter is captured in these children's comments:

> I enjoyed Daphne telling us about the flood. I know she was only acting as if she was in it but I thought she was actually in it. The way she showed her emotions was really good. She was crying but she hadn't really been in the flood. Even her dog looked like she was acting as well! It was immense!
>
> Having Daphne and Goldie in taught us about the friendship between humans and dogs. Everyone could see the friendship between you and Goldie and how you are responsible for each other. That's what everyone should be like.

From such tales, many developed from first-hand testimonies, the children dramatized their own stories of terror, tragedy and survival of that fateful night. The fact that neither the children nor their teachers had heard of the floods gave the drama an element of surprise and added to their fascination.

Commenting on a theatre project about a young victim of the holocaust, director Allan McInnes states that, 'When children make an emotional connection to a story, and especially a person, they can begin to truly care about outcomes and responsibilities and justice' (Hollis 2010, p. 26). Similarly, in her discussion of the centrality of narrative as a means of enhancing historical understanding, Little (1983) provides a number of examples of how they can be helped to realize that people read about in history books were real and had feelings. The fact is that deaf people didn't have hearing dogs in 1953 England, but I certainly wasn't going to tell the children who met Daphne that! The point is that the floods did happen and as a result of the drama the children's substantive knowledge developed alongside their empathetic response to a fellow human being.

Authenticity and integrity

Fines and Verrier sought to focus on history skills such as searching out all available evidence and producing a 'convincing and satisfying account which is as fair as possible to all sources' (p. 84). In their work, 'drama presented to children a remarkably faithful model of historical time: it happened at life-rate, was unplanned and often surprising, was sometime slow and sometimes fast' (p. 91). In this way the distinction drawn by Polyani (1959) between *explicit* and *tacit* knowledge were drawn together in order to develop children's historical understanding and knowledge. It should be noted though that the coherence of this 'knowledge-through-drama project' has not been without its detractors (e.g. Hornbrook (1998)). In bringing drama and history together in my work, I draw on a knowledge of how drama can be planned, structured and edited in order to elicit the tacit knowledge that arises from the proposition that, 'nothing that is said, written or printed, can ever mean anything in itself: for it is only a person who utters something – or who listens to it or reads it – who can mean something by it' (Polyanyi 1959, p. 22). In a similar vein, Zatzman discusses how narrative inquiry can support the surfacing of subtext so that, 'in the performance of memory, the "past is reinvented and textualised through the discourses and practices of the present"' (Zatzman 2006, p. 116). What appeals to me about this is the idea of subtext emerging from the reinvention of the past. An overt recognition that invention may replace recall suggests an integrity that is particular to the context in which stories from the past are explored in the present. As historical characters become the dramatis personae of re-enacted accounts, their stories are edited to both serve the agendas of the storytellers and meet the perceived needs of the audience. The process of popularizing history in this way thus becomes as much about the effects of events on people as the events themselves. In turn, these effects may be scrutinized and re-evaluated through drama. If empathy is an outcome then opportunities arise to examine how such a response was elicited. As the child in the drama cited above noted, 'The way she showed her emotions was really good.' Another example of this occurred at the end of a drama about the RMS Titanic. I had chanced upon a quotation from Fred Fleet, the ship's lookout on the night of the tragedy. Fleet was reported to have said that if only he'd had a pair of binoculars he could have saved the ship. Intrigued by this statement I researched further and devised a drama which focused on how the unfortunate seaman was initially held responsible for the tragedy until it came to light that others had played a part in there being no binoculars available in the crow's nest that night. In 1965, at the age of 77, Fleet committed suicide. By way of closing the drama, I presented the class with a mock-up of Fleet's gravestone and invited them to say something to it in response to what they had learned about him and the way he had been treated. The first few children stepped up and offered words of sympathy and comfort then one boy came forward and said:

> I'm sorry people blamed you for what happened, Fred, but I don't think that's why you killed yourself. It was a long time ago. I think other things must have happened to you.

The class were asked what they thought about this. They quickly came to a consensus that while me telling them about his suicide brought about a suitably dramatic ending to the session, they weren't convinced that something that had happened 53 years ago had been its sole cause, a conclusion that was quickly verified by Google!

Identifiable outcomes

Historian Christine Carpenter (DfEE 1999, p. 15) has attested that:

> History is an unusual discipline. Its core is hard fact that you cannot get away from and have to learn to master. At the same time you have to be deductive, perceptive and imaginative in the use of that fact.

Contemporary history educationalists have challenged the idea that 'hard fact' is the 'core' of their subject. McCrum (2012), for example, promotes a postmodernist perspective which 'rejects the possibility of a knowable past reality, instead conceiving of knowledge as the construction of the historian, gaining meaning only through narrative discourse'. In this, the work of the modern history teacher may be seen to parallel that of the drama teacher in many ways with both seeking to galvanize perception and imagination in order to inform, enlighten and enrich by mastering critical awareness rather than hard fact. Because drama, as an art form, seeks to entertain in order to achieve such aims, it gives a form to 'facts' that can invest them with greater meaning. Somers argues that, in this way, drama serves history well:

> Much of the content of theatre unravels and speculates on the personalities, motives and effects of individuals and groups from the past, whilst history benefits from drama's ability to reconstruct the human detail that fleshes out the facts of past events. (1994, p. 124)

An identifiable outcome of a drama lesson could be the extent to which this ability is realized. Goalen (2001) claims that children's historical understanding can be improved by using drama techniques rather than traditional teaching methods. The primary measure for this in his research was the content of the children's writing, the quality of which was also said to have improved as a result of the extensive use of drama strategies. In a drama about life in Victorian London, I asked the class to develop a character from brief pen portraits taken from Henry Mayhew's 'London Labour and London Poor' (Canning 1986) and devise a street cry to advertise their wares. The results confirmed that the children enjoyed committing their ideas to paper and had made connections between information gathered within the drama and knowledge acquired elsewhere:

> I have jaundice. A disease which I got because I don't eat the right diet. My body and eyes turn yellow. That's why my name is 'Lemonface'. I live on the edge of the River Thames. I collect what I find and call out 'Come and get your useful bits and bobs'.
>
> I catch rats in the sewers and sort them out for dog contests. I go down with my candle and a glove to pick them up then when I sell them I shout, 'get your rats for your dogs – let the pooches have a treat!'
>
> I know London is the richest place in the world but I live in the streets. People say it's lucky to touch me but they wouldn't want to squeeze up inside the chimneys like we do. 'Chimneys swept, chimney's swept. One a penny, two a penny, chimney sweeps for sale'.
>
> We look like normal people but by night we are the soil men roaming the streets collecting poo from chamber pots. It might be the worst job around but it's the

only job around for us. It makes money which is better than having nothing. What we call is, 'Come on, come on, don't be shy. Bring out your chambers, don't be shy.'

History educator Ian Luff suggests that a key issue for history teachers wanting to use drama as a method is to consider whether pupils are reflecting on the past or being asked to act as if they are 'in the past'. For him, the use of language is central to meaningful study of history:

> 'We can come closer to true empathy, for example, by attempting to articulate the ideas of a time in the language of that time. The condition is that the teaching of history must always be paramount in the history classroom' (Luff 2011, p. 11).

While being uncertain as to what constitutes 'true empathy', I accept that selecting language which sounds appropriate helps in the suspension of disbelief and contributes to the possibility of participants existing both within and outside the fiction, gaining insight from both positions, and being able to critically reflect accordingly. The teaching of drama should always be paramount in the drama classroom. The creation of something that looks, sounds and feels right, even if it may not be completely historically authentic, can be evaluated in terms of what it meant and how it felt to participants, audience or, in the case of the drama lesson, the spect-actors (Boal 1979).

Giving form to fact

Bolton (1984) argues that, in the first instance, the drama teacher's role is to help the students make drama happen so that it can happen to them. In order to achieve its full learning potential the drama lesson must move beyond the purely experiential and induce reflection and analysis. Exploring historical events through drama requires the participants to project their existing knowledge and experience into a fictionalized world and so develop new knowledge and experience as that world is reflected back at them. Both Aristotle and Brecht acknowledged in their different ways that drama requires engaging with emotions: dramas that fail to do this in some way are quite simply not very good dramas! Zatzman's work in drama and narrative inquiry recognizes how the gap between history and memory is 'the territory of many playwrights' (2003, p. 49). Indeed, historical dramas from Shakespeare's 'Richard III' to Joan Littlewood's 'Oh What a Lovely War' and Diane Samuel's 'Kindertransport' may be fictionalized accounts, but are no more fictional than any documentary in which some events are selected for representation while others are not with the aim of helping an audience 'know' the subject a little better.

The number of novels and plays about the World War II written for young audiences supports the contention that a great deal of children's knowledge comes either from fiction or dramatizations of first-hand testimonies (Kempe 2011). That such stories are told and reinforced in different media over time indicates a slide from 'fact' to 'legend' which in itself suggests a fundamental need to tell such stories. While the process may obfuscate one sort of historical fact it generates another, that is, the need for people to understand the past by organizing it into a narrative that simplifies events while elaborates on details which, for whatever reason, give the storyteller and the audience a purchase on their meaning. This same argument is used by Portelli (1998) in his defence of the importance of oral history and is implicit in these lines from David Greig's play 'Dr Korczak's Example' (2001, p. 12):

> Some stories – if you try and tell them exactly,
> Then somehow,
> You end up telling a lie.
> So it didn't happen exactly the way we tell it.
> But it happened.

Without selectivity, history is messy and discomforting. While selective histories may meet some needs in terms of stabilizing and reinforcing cultural icons and values, it is through acknowledging the messy jumble of different perspectives and interpretations that we come to know where we stand in relation to contexts past and present. In drama, what matters is not necessarily the authenticity of the historical fact but how the humanity in the history is forefronted by the integrity of the dramatic form.

Two case studies

1. 'BERT'S COUSIN BERT'

The evacuation of children in the World War II has served as the basis for many dramatizations (e.g. Kempe 2008, 2011). 'Bert's Cousin Bert' drew on a number of first-hand testimonies in order to extend the children's appreciation of both how close they were physically and temporally to a major historical event while explicitly 'setting up' a dramatic climax. The work was designed to fulfil requirements of the National Curriculum in both English and History in order to satisfy the school's needs and also to demonstrate to a group of trainee teachers how drama could be employed as a method while retaining its integrity as a subject in its own right. The project consisted of two 1-hour lessons. Lesson One was taught by me alone. In Lesson Two I was joined by 16 students training to be specialist drama teachers.

In the first lesson, I adopted the role of a man named Bert Hedges who told the children that he was visiting the school as he has discovered that his mother, Daisy, had attended it as an evacuee. He told them that Daisy had been close to her little brother after whom he was named. The brother had been evacuated to Canada and the two never saw each other again. A series of drama exercises helped the class explore what their school may have been like in 1940 (school records showed that it actually had received evacuees from London) and what it might have felt like to be told, as a 10-year old, that you were to have another child move in to your house.

In the second lesson, the class met a number of characters and worked in groups to discover who they were and why, at some time between 1939 and 1945, they found themselves travelling. Further exercises explored how these characters may have said their goodbyes and what their arrival at their new destination would have been like. The challenge of the exercises was to assimilate information gathered through hot seating and construct scenes that would have a predetermined effect on an audience, that is, to deliberately 'position' the audience emotionally.

Back in role as Daisy's son Bert, I explained that I had written a number of letters to people in Canada and the United States trying to discover what had happened to Daisy's little brother. The story was interrupted by the entrance of a character (a trainee chosen for the role because he was actually an American and only a little younger than me!) asking to speak to a Mr Bert Hedges. The character explained that he was from the United States and held a letter addressed to his father, a certain Mr Bert Hedges (senior), after whom he was named! Thus, the two cousins, both named Bert Hedges, were implausibly united to the cheers of the children. Cheesey it may have been, but the blend of tried and tested 'process drama' techniques with a pre-determined dramatic structure allowed for the learning objectives to be met, the time allowed for the workshop to be managed, and the whole thing to be informative and enjoyable. While no external audience was present, the conscious use of dramatic form in the planning and execution of the session gave the work an entertainment value for the young spect-actors.

2. MR MAYHEW AND MR TODD

I once had a heated argument with a chap (yes, we were in a pub!) who insisted that Sweeney Todd was a real person and that the remains of Mrs Lovett's pie shop still existed in a street preserved beneath Bell Yard near Fleet Street, London. Peter Ackroyd's study 'London Under' (2012) attests that there are indeed numerous relics of historical events entombed beneath the great city's streets. What is certain though is that the events depicted in George Dibden Pitt's 1847 melodrama 'The String of Pearls' and Christopher Bond's 1974 'Sweeney Todd: the Demon Barber of Fleet Street' (later turned into a musical by Stephen Sondheim) were entirely fictitious. Nonetheless, Sweeney Todd, like Robin Hood and King Arthur, has become such an integral part of English folklore that many people share the conviction that they were real people. What helps embed such characters into folk memory is that the events with which they are associated are plausible when set in the context of how the past has been depicted. Thus, exploring how the Victorian chronicler Henry Mayhew might have encountered Sweeney Todd served as a vehicle for the children to learn:

• who Henry Mayhew was and what he discovered about life in Victorian London;
• how the lives of young people 150 years ago were different from today;
• how Victorian melodrama worked as a theatrical genre and why it was so popular;
• how investigations into both real and fictitious events require interpretation not least because witnesses may have good reason to withhold information or be selective in the way they impart it.

Once again this was a two-lesson project which involved a number of trainee drama teachers. In the first lesson, the children created characters based on Mayhew's interviews with people he met on the streets of London and met both Mr Mayhew (me in role) and Mrs Lovatt (a trainee in role) who confessed, when interviewed, that she made the most appalling pies imaginable. In the second lesson, the class learned how easy it was to get into trouble with the law and what the conditions of Newgate gaol were like. The children thought of reasons why their character may have found themselves in Newgate and, in groups, created tableaux showing what it might have been like in there. Each group was given some information on a slip of paper and told to guard it carefully. Knowledge, even though we may not realize its value at the time, might at some point be power.

The class observed a scene in which Mayhew told six of his researchers (trainee teachers in role) how a man by the name of Sweeney Todd had been to see him. He was looking for his wife and daughter. He had, he said, been in Australia for some years 'fulfilling a contract' issued by Judge Turpin, a man known to be hard but not wholly honest and certainly not someone to cross! Mr Todd had given Mr Mayhew a picture of his wife as she looked before he went away. Mayhew asked his researchers to visit Newgate and probe the prisoners on what they know about Sweeney Todd, his wife and Judge Turpin. In the sequence that followed, the trainees worked hard to extract different snippets of evidence from the pupils: such knowledge could at once be valuable and dangerous depending on whose ears it reached! The researchers pieced together what they had learned and, with the pupils' help (out of role), reconstructed Sweeney's story. They told Mr Mayhew that Todd was really Benjamin Barker, a man transported to Australia so that Judge Turpin could seduce his wife. A pupil was chosen to play Sweeney. Mr Mayhew told him what he had discovered about the woman in the picture but did not reveal he knew Todd's true identity. The class considered what Sweeney might do next.

Mayhew told the class how, after Todd had left his office, he found a razor and a business card advertising his barber's shop in Fleet Street. He narrated how he went to the address and met none other than Mrs Lovatt. With a trainee in role as Mrs Lovatt, I acted out the scene. Her pie shop was being mobbed by people craving for her delicious pies. She revealed that she had gone into business with Mr Todd who was now working in the room upstairs. The drama stopped and the class were asked to fill in the gaps of the Sweeney Todd story before we discussed why such a story might have been so popular in Victorian England. The gory story of Sweeney Todd captured the attention of the class just as it has been capturing the attention of the public for well over a century, not least because there are elements of the grotesquely comic in the horror. Popular historian Tony Robinson, an actor famed for his portrayal of Baldric in the television series 'Blackadder', notes that, 'the opposite of trivial is serious, not comic. Comedy at its best has much to say about the human condition and often says it darkly and ironically.' (Vass 2008, p. 5). The Mr Mayhew and Mr Todd drama session sought to harness this very dynamic. Once again, the artful employment and examination of dramatic form took primacy over historical authenticity yet nonetheless historical knowledge and understanding was accrued by the participants.

From past to present to future

Santayana (1905) proclaimed that those who cannot remember the past are condemned to repeat it while a character in Alan Bennett's play 'The History Boys' defines history as 'just one fucking thing after another' (Bennett 2004, p. 85). In this chapter, I have sought to demonstrate that remembrance of things past is in itself as unreliable a means of learning as seeing history as no more than a succession of facts. Rather, by using their understanding of drama as an art form, teachers may invite children to exercise their imagination and critical awareness in order to achieve greater insights into the relevance of the past in shaping their future. Fines, alluding to Henry Ford's famous dictum, has noted that, 'Unless historical information is seen as something desirable, collectable, useful and unless it is used in an educational way, then it is merely bunk.' (1989, p. 17)

My research into what children may learn at the interface of drama and history is ongoing. The integrity of the art form of drama is that it is contained in time and place and like Stoppard's players its participants have control over the world they create and inhabit within it. I don't envisage my research will come to any grand conclusion any more than history itself will come to an end. Such is the integrity of history and indeed reflective practice in the classroom. Every exit is, after all, an entrance somewhere else.

References

Ackroyd, P. (2012), *London Under*. London: Vintage Books.

Bennett, A. (2004), *The History Boys*. London: Faber and Faber.

Boal, A. (1979), *The Theatre of the Oppressed*. London: Pluto Press.

Bolton, G. (1984), *Drama as Education*. Harlow: Longman.

Bond, C. (1974), *Sweeney Todd: The Demon Barber of Fleet Street*. London: Samuel French.

Canning, J. (1986), *The Illustrated Mayhew's London*. London: Weidenfeld and Nicholson.

DfEE (1999), *The National Curriculum for England: History*. London: Department for Education and Employment.

Fines, J. (1989), 'History in the National Curriculum – a reaction to the working party's Interim Report in Four Fits'. *2D*, 9, (1), 17–19.

Fines, J. and Verrier, R. (1974), *The Drama of History*. London: New University Education.

Goalen, P. (2001), 'The drama of history'. *International Journal of Historical Learning Teaching and Research*, 1, (2).

Greig, D. (2001), *Dr Korczak's Example*. Edinburgh: Capercaille Books.

Hollis, C. (2010), 'Hana's suitcase: Lessons from the past'. *Drama: One Forum, Many Voices*, 17, (1), 19–26.

Hornbrook, D. (1998), *Education and Dramatic Art*, 2nd edn. London: Routledge.

Kempe, A. (2011), 'Daisy's diary: Issues surrounding playing with the past in drama'. *Drama Research*, 2, (1).

—(2008), 'Playing with the past: Drama, history and critical literacy', in M. Parsons (ed.), *War and the Battle for Childhood: The innocent victims*. London: DSM.

Little, V. (1983), 'History through drama with top juniors'. *Education 3 - 13*, 11, (2), 12–18.

Luff, I. (2011), 'Beyond 'I speak, you listen, boy!' Exploring diversity of attitudes and experiences through speaking and listening', in *Teaching History*, 105, The Historical Association.

McCrum, E. (2012), *History as Methodology for Educational Research*, paper presented to the British Educational Research Association, Manchester, 5 September 2012.

Polanyi, M. (1959), *The Study of Man*. London: Routledge & Kegan Paul.

Portelli, A. (1998), 'What makes oral history different', in R. Perks and A. Thomson (eds), *The Oral History Reader*. London: Routledge.

Robinson, T. (2008), *Primary History*, vol. 48. The Historical Association, Spring 2008.

Santayana, G. (1905), *The Life of Reason*. London: Constable.

—(1998), *The Life of Reason*. NewYork: Prometheus Books.

Somers, J. (1994), *Drama in the Curriculum*. London: Cassell.

Stoppard, T. (1967), *Rosencrantz and Guildenstern Are Dead*. London: Faber and Faber.

Vass, P. (2008), *The Serious Business of Comedy: In Conversation with Tony Robinson*, *Primary History*, vol. 48. The Historical Association, Spring 2008.

Williams, R. (1975), *Drama in a Dramatised Society*. Cambridge: Cambridge University Press.

Woolland, B. (1993), *The Teaching of Drama in the Primary School*. London: Longman.

Zatzman, B. (2003), 'The monologue project: Drama as a form of witnessing', in K. Gallagher and D. Booth (eds), *How Theatre Educates*. Toronto: University of Toronto Press.

—(2005), 'Staging history: Aesthetics and the performance of memory'. *The Journal of Aesthetic Education*, 39, (4), 35–55.

—(2006), 'Narrative inquiry: Postcards from Northampton', in J. Ackroyd (ed.), *Research Methods for Drama Education*. Stoke on Trent: Trentham.

15

Drama for Additional Language Learning: Dramatic Contexts and Pedagogical Possibilities

Madonna Stinson and Erika Piazzoli

Introduction

Drama and additional language learning is a growing field of interest and inquiry, as can be attested by a recent wave of publications in the field.[1] In this chapter, we introduce this area of research, drawing on existing literature, and our own projects. First, we sketch out a succinct overview of Second Language Acquisition (SLA), next we provide a brief history of attempts at interconnecting the two fields, and finally we draw on our own research, to suggest some of the ways in which drama supports learning Additional Languages (AL). We acknowledge that this is a large and complex field of endeavour, and that justice cannot be done in only one short chapter so, for the purpose of this text, we will focus on four contributing aspects: the dual expertise of the teacher in both drama and language teaching; dramatic form and learner agency; scaffolding in both language and drama for dialogic learning; and the vital part played by the dramatic context.

Situating additional language learning

During the twentieth century, SLA theories have framed, and re-framed, the understanding of what it means to acquire a second language. Until the 1990s, language acquisition was conceived largely in terms of input and output, following Krashen's (1985) 'comprehensible input' hypothesis which suggests that learners acquire language by 'in-taking' (1981, p. 103). According to this hypothesis, if new language (input) is made comprehensible to the learner, acquisition will follow. Krashen's theory was based on the 'transmission' metaphor, positioning learners as receivers of information and gave rise to an influential branch of SLA research, mainly empirical and focusing on the 'input' of language (Pica 1994).

In contrast to this paradigm, Sociocultural Theory (Lantolf 1994, 2000) offers an alternative perspective, one that includes the social context of learning. Sociocultural theorists reject the transmission metaphor, arguing that it reduces SLA research to statistical 'input crunching' (Donato 1994). Instead, a sociocultural approach to SLA is based on social constructivism (Vygotsky 1978) and frames language learning as *a dialogic*[2] activity, reliant on communication, questions and dialogue as means of inquiry and action. As Morita (2000, p. 79) suggests 'language learning is not just an individual psychological process, but also a social process.' In this perspective, learning is envisaged as an active process of meaning-making, as opposed to an accumulation of linguistic items. Learning a language thus occurs through social interaction, involving scaffolding, and collaborative dialogue (Swain 2000). In a sociocultural stance, language learning is through the *agency* of the speaker, defined as the willingness to take initiative in the target language. Agency is framed as something learners 'do', coupled with an awareness of one's own actions on other speakers, in a social context (Van Lier 2008, p. 172). When language learning is considered as an *embodied* activity (McCafferty and Stam 2008), the focus shifts to include the use of gesture and body language as key mechanisms for language development.

Drama and Additional Language (AL) learning

Many approaches to the use of drama pedagogy in AL learning coexist, from scripted role-play, scenarios, to staged performance. For example, Haught and McCafferty's (2008) study involved six adult learners of English (AL), who participated in one semester of drama/language workshops. This research was based on improvisation, games, and the enactment of short scripts. The researchers focused on AL learning and embodied behaviour (gesture), filming the interaction and analysing each gesticulation and found that the drama work helped participants become active in their own learning. Miccoli (2003) taught acting skills to university students, culminating in a public production, and found that the students' own reflective journal was a vital contributor to their confidence in producing the target language and to understanding their own learning. In an action research study, Araki-Metcalfe (2008) investigated the application of drama as pedagogy for teaching English in Japan. Her study spanned a period of 12 weeks, using a range of games, exercises and role plays in a Japanese primary school. Data from video-recording, questionnaires, class discussion, informal interviews, students' work and the researcher's journal revealed that the students acknowledged the benefits of drama. Through the intervention, learners came to the realization they needed to become active, and, as a result, their level of emotional and cognitive engagement in learning increased.

In another relevant study, Yaman Ntelioglou's (2011) researched in the multimodal nature of drama and AL learning, with a focus on writing in role. Her ethnographic study involved 50 adult learners of English, in a Canadian adult school. Data from student/teacher interviews, focus groups, field notes, video recordings, photographs and artefacts suggest that drama had a positive impact on improving their writing (p. 609). Her research also highlights the importance of embodiment in role for representation and self-expression.

In this chapter, we refer to a kind of drama that is unscripted, operates without an external audience, stems from a pre-text and builds up from a series of episodes, but does not lead to a final performance. This form of drama has become known as 'process drama' (O'Neill 1995).

The first study to explore *process drama* and *AL learning* was Kao's (1995) research. This was a mixed-methods study, conducted at a Taiwanese university, with 33 undergraduate learners of English. Kao investigated the impact of process drama on AL discourse in terms of turn-taking, topic initiation, sequencing and effective activation of previous acquired knowledge. Her findings indicated a significantly higher percentage of spontaneous communication, when using process drama. Specifically, Kao noted that it was 'dramatic tension' that influenced motivation to communicate. In this context, dramatic tension can be defined as the energy that drives a drama forward, 'the gap between the characters and the fulfilment of their purposes' (O'Toole 1992, p. 27)

In 1998, Kao and O'Neill expanded Kao's study to create a rationale for AL/ process drama and AL teaching. In essence, Kao and O'Neill (1998) describe process drama as an 'activator' of learning, noting the importance of *dramatic tension*, *dramatic role*, and *reflection*. Since Kao and O'Neill's pioneering work, a number of studies have expanded their research, in a variety of contexts. For example, Bournot-Trites, Belliveau, Spiliotopolous and Séror (2007) conducted a mixed-methods study in a Canadian French Immersion context. They observed the difference between two elementary classes: one using a teacher-centred approach, the other using process drama. Data from pre-and post-testing, field observations and teacher journals revealed that motivation to learn the target language was significantly higher in the process drama group (p. 19). They also found that in the drama group, students were creating their own knowledge *through* the drama, while the other group was relying on the teacher as a source of knowledge. In other words, their research indicates that the kind of AL learning activated by process drama is constructivist in nature.

Rothwell's (2011) research highlights the function of process drama as an embodied pedagogy; in her own words, participants used the body as a 'tangible springboard for language' (p. 582). Her action research project involved 12-year-old students of German (beginner level), in an Australian school. Her data sets included two questionnaires, four focus groups, and video-recording of two terms of classes. Her analysis points to *dramatic role*, as an activator to create kinaesthetic interactions. The next study we review also investigated role, but from the teacher's perspective. Kao, Carkin, and Hsu (2011) researched the kind of *questions* AL/drama teachers ask, in and out of role during process dramas. The study spanned over a 3-week intensive course, in a Taiwanese university, with 30 (intermediate) students of English. Following a detailed analysis of the nature of questions, these researchers found that the teachers used a broader range of social registers, contexts and relationships (p. 511) when in role in the dramas.

The last study we discuss is To, Chan, Lam and Tsang (2011), who offer a comprehensive account of the benefits of AL/drama pedagogy. Their study stems from a year-long AL/process drama teacher development programme, with 160 teachers of English in Hong Kong. They investigated the perceptions of participants (principles, teachers, students and parents), through focus groups and private interviews. To et al. (2011) summarize the benefits of AL/ process drama as: motivation to learn, confidence in speaking, improvement in writing, using language in context with purpose, richer means of expression, engagement of students of different abilities, more active participation, better teacher-student relationship and more supportive and appreciative attitudes among students (p. 524).

To sum up, the studies above cover a broad spectrum of cultural contexts, research designs and language levels. In different ways, they all suggest that process drama can be a potent agent to activate learning in the AL classroom.

Four research projects

The heart of this chapter draws on four of our own research projects undertaken since 2004. Table 15.1 and the description below provide a brief overview of the research. In the discussion that follows, we draw on examples from each project to highlight key points in our arguments.

Research project A: Drama and Oral language (DOL) – promoting oral language learning through process drama (Stinson and Freebody 2006, 2009; Stinson 2008)

The DOL project took place in regular English language classes with Secondary 4 (16 year old) students in four schools in Singapore. Four process dramas made up the 10 lessons planned by the researchers and facilitated by trained and experienced drama teachers. The research measured oral language learning outcomes by applying the regular language tests used by the Singapore Ministry of Education; however, an important driving factor for the drama work was that the students experience high-quality drama pedagogy. For this reason, the lessons were planned by experts in process drama and implemented by experienced drama teachers. Findings gave unequivocal support to the process drama work, with the students in the drama classes gaining higher scores overall in their oral examinations, as well as higher scores in each of the separate criteria: clarity, vocabulary, relevance, interaction and the need for prompting; while the comparison classes, those without the drama intervention, showed no change. In addition, the students self-reported improved self-confidence, improved use of language, enhanced vocabulary and a greater capacity for cooperative work in the classroom. The teachers of the English classes unanimously supported the continuation of drama pedagogy.

Research project B: Speaking out – enhancing teacher pedagogy in English language classrooms (Stinson 2009; Dunn and Stinson 2011)

Following the DOL project, above, one of the principals of a participating school recognized the value of drama as pedagogy. She asked for research in a collaborative partnership to work alongside her English language teachers for a year, providing professional development and planning support. In this way it was hoped the teachers would develop skills in applying drama pedagogy within the language classroom. One of the measures used to chart progress in the project

Table 15.1 Summary of the four research projects discussed in this chapter

Research project	Length of the project	No. of participants (P)	Age of P	Language proficiency of P	P first language (L1)	P Target language (L2/AL)	Nature of the project	Location
Project A	1 hr × 10 weeks	~160	16 years	Intermediate-advanced	Malay Tamil Teochew/ Hokkien	English	regular classes government school lower stream students	Singapore
Project B	one school year	>600	13–14 yrs	Intermediate-advanced	Malay Tamil Teochew/ Hokkien	English	regular classes government school	Singapore
Project C	5 × 3 hours dramas	9	20–55	Intermediate-advanced	English, Japanese, Mandarin, Russian	Italian	Regular classes	Milan, Italy
Project D	5 × 3 hours drama	9	20–55	Intermediate-advanced	Arabic, Mandarin, Portuguese, Russian	Italian	Voluntary classes	Milan, Italy

was the same oral language test process used in the DOL project. The test was undertaken several times in the year to chart the students' progress alongside their teachers' development of facility in the drama process. Each teacher was supported by a trained drama teacher, to plan and implement drama pedagogy within their regular English classes across the first 2 year-levels of secondary school. Data included lesson plans, recordings of planning sessions with teachers, regular interviews with teachers and students, parent interviews and the sequence of oral examinations. In this study, the findings relating to language learning were uneven and results seemed to connect strongly to the quality of the drama lesson experienced, however, analysis of the data indicated that drama pedagogy enabled high levels of engagement, identification, motivation, collaboration and enjoyment.

Research project C: Buongiorno *process drama (Case study 2)*

This case study took place in an adult language school of Italian (AL) in Milan, Italy. It was part of a reflective practitioner, multiple case study research. The process drama intervention consisted of five workshops, for a total of 15 hours. The pre-text for the process drama was the short film *Buongiorno* (Prino 2005). As part of the research design, a group of AL teachers observed the teacher-researcher co-create a drama, with 9 adult learners of Italian (intermediate level). Data included video recordings, student/teacher interviews, teacher observations and a set of questionnaires where participants were asked to self-evaluate their engagement. Findings from this case study suggest that process drama was beneficial to activate dialogic learning. Significantly, the engine driving the learning process was *dramatic tension,* within a kind of social interaction that was *in role,* in a dramatic context.

Research project D: Buongiorno *process drama (Case study 3)*

This case study shares the same research design as project C, above, but was held at a different adult school, with different participants. As Table 15.1 shows, the main difference between the two case studies is the native language of the learners. Findings from this case study align with the previous one; in particular, through the manipulation of dramatic form, and reflection-in-action (O'Mara 2006), participants were empowered to exercise agency, leading to stronger engagement and motivation to communicate in the target language.

Drama activating language learning

Language and drama involve the skills of expressing meaning through words and action. However, combining the two is not a simple, mechanical action; it is not guaranteed that by implementing drama, a language is acquired. Below, we draw on examples from the four research projects described above to illustrate how drama can activate learning in AL. In particular, we focus on four aspects of drama pedagogy that we believe contribute to language learning outcomes. In brief we suggest that drama activates learning when:

- the teacher/facilitator is proficient in both drama and language pedagogy;
- learning is contextualized within a dramatic fiction;
- participants are able to work in embodied and enactive ways, contributing within the drama to develop agency in the target language; and
- learners are empowered to create their own dual scaffolding by applying their developing metacognition of language learning.

Teacher proficiency in both fields

Drama 'by itself does nothing. It is only what teachers do with drama that makes the difference' (Neelands 2009, p. 11). With these words Neelands reminds us of the centrality of the teacher and that the teacher's task is to enhance the learning for their students. When we talk about what teachers do, we acknowledge that they are skilful and knowledgeable practitioners of the craft of teaching. However, language teachers tend to specialize in language and drama teachers in drama. We want to consider the circumstances of drama being *applied* within a language-learning context. Art forms such as visual arts and drama are often used to enliven pedagogy in other discipline areas. Elliott Eisner (1994) has criticized an overly 'instrumental' approach to using arts in education, when the art form is subservient to the educational objectives of another area, and this is a challenge for the drama/language teacher to manage. We believe that teachers who use drama in the second or AL classroom need to have equal ease, confidence and facility in both areas because 'it is only when teachers/facilitators are able to hold both the artistry of the form and the intended learning in one hand, as it were, that the full promise of working with drama and additional language learning can be realized' (Dunn and Stinson 2011, p. 618) and this can only occur if the teacher has mastered the artistry of dramatic form. O'Toole (1992) defines 'dramatic form' as the negotiation and renegotiation of the elements of drama: role, context, focus, tension, mood, symbol, place, time, space, language and movement, which culminate in dramatic meaning.

Our concern with teacher proficiency in both fields is borne out by the results of the first two Singapore research projects above. In the Project A, the drama work was planned and implemented by expert drama educators, and the language focus was framed within well-constructed process drama plans. Student results in oral communication were overwhelmingly improved in every research school context, and in each of the criteria on the oral language tests, and the students learnt about drama and their own capacity as creators of dramatic work. On the other hand, Project B did not produce such strong language results, despite taking place over a longer period of time. A range of factors impacted on results of the project but the most dominant factor was the lack of skill in managing the dramatic form, demonstrated by the teachers. Bowell and Heap (2005, p. 64) talk of teachers adopting a process of 'quadripartite thinking' where they simultaneously wear the 'head of' the playwright, director, actor and teacher in order to manage the complexity, creativity and educative purpose of process drama. An educator who uses drama to teach language must manage the elements of drama suggested by O'Toole, above, as well as the functions of playwright, director and actor functions both in the preparation and implementation of the planned lesson. In addition they must draw on their deep knowledge of language teaching, so that the objectives of the language component of the lesson are met in, and through, the combined drama/language pedagogy. An alternative approach is to work in partnership, with each teaching partner sharing expertise in either drama or language pedagogy. Whichever approach is taken, there is a need for skill and expertise in applying the pedagogy of both fields, in practice.

Contextuallizing learning within a dramatic fiction

According to Kao and O'Neill, 'Drama sustains interactions between students within the target language creating a world of social roles and relations in which the learner is an active participant. . . . The language that arises is fluent, purposeful and generative because it is embedded in context' (Kao and O'Neill 1998, p. 4). This statement is borne out by our studies. When the students were deeply involved in the dramatic context they were, themselves, often surprised by their own language capability.

As an example, the final drama in Project A was based in the myth of Bukit Merah (Red Hill) in Singapore. In the story, the Sultan (driven by a jealous rage) had threatened to murder the young boy who had saved the island from ongoing attacks by swordfish. The participants (in role as families in the village, each with one young son) carefully constructed arguments to persuade the Sultan not to carry out his threat. During this lesson the participants were deeply engaged in this activity and were passionately involved in crafting strong arguments they felt would be sure to convince the Sultan. The group commitment to the task and the context was apparent in the seriousness with which the participants worked so truthfully in role. The combination of these components allowed them to access their mental dictionaries to draw on vocabulary and grammatical structures they would not use in everyday conversation. As one participant declared during reflection time, 'I used words I didn't know I knew.'

In this lesson the students were deeply immersed in the dramatic context. The process of working in role, their belief in the experience, and the tension of the drama drove them to forget for the moment that they were students in a classroom. For a time they *were* a group of people prepared to stand up against the powerful oppressor of their community.

Drama experiences like these afford a 'safe space' for learning because the students agree to enter into an 'imaginative elsewhere' for the period of the drama. The process of working in roles allows emotional distance for the participants ('this is happening to them, not me') and they are comforted by knowing that they are working as an 'other' and not themselves. This safe space of the drama permits them to try out ideas and communication strategies and minimizes the risks of failure (Maley and Duff 2005). They come to know that, if you make a mistake, drama allows you to rewind and fix it. Participants are able to construct and reconstruct a text by rephrasing and reshaping as they craft a spoken, written or embodied text in an attempt to communicate meaning or, in the case above, to persuade the Sultan to act morally. All this leads to the enhancement of confidence and the ability to take more risks in language use (Wagner 1998).

Manipulation of dramatic form and agency in the target language

In this section, we draw on Project C to suggest that, through the manipulation of form, process drama can activate *agency* in the AL learner. In the *Buongiorno* process drama, the main theme was 'mental illness and intercultural perception'. The complete sequence of this drama has been documented elsewhere (Piazzoli 2012); here, we just refer to a specific moment in one role-play. Earlier in the drama, the group had discussed the issue of mental illness and how, according to a family's cultural values, this may tend to be hidden from the community,

Table 15.2 Extract of classroom interaction from Project C

Turn	Utterance
1	Teacher in role: do we have any other question?
2	Hiru/psychologist: yes. Ehm . . . have there been instances of mental disorder in your family?
3	Olga/sister: no [shaking head]
4	Sabina/psychologist: not even Yourself?[3]
5	Olga/sister: [giggling]. No –no! 100% . . . normal
6	Everyone: [echoing, sceptical] normal . . .
7	Everyone [echoing]: very normal!
8	[Pause]
9	Olga/sister: yes [nods]
10	Teacher in role: when . . . we notified You of Your brother's conditions . . . were you surprised?
11	Olga/sister: yes ehm . . . I was surprised . . . very big! I don't know because . . . always, everything was good, normal . . . I think that . . . there's been some mistake, I don't know . . . I think that . . . this can't be . . . real . . .
12	[General whispers]

or openly exposed. In the dramatic frame, the participants took on the role of psychologists, trying to help an Italian patient in a state of shock. In the extract, in Table 15.2, above the psychologists are interviewing the patient's *sister*. All participants (including the teacher) are in role as psychologists, except for one student (Olga), in role as 'sister'.

In the discussion, we focus on the way the *dramatic elements* are manipulated to activate *agency* in the learners. First, the choice of *role* was crucial to experience the language register of a particular sub-culture: professional psychologists interviewing a young woman. Such a strategy reverses the traditional hierarchy of *status* within the participants, contributing to a more authentic context for learning. *Focus* is also important: the interview occurred just after the patient's catatonic crisis. This creates a sense of urgency in the communication. The extract can be also read in terms of *dramatic tension*: for example, in Turn 6, the 'sceptical echoing' is filled with tension, as the psychologists realize that the sister is protecting him. The participants here play an active role in reinforcing this tension. Similarly, the 'whispering' in Turn 12 is a charged moment, where the learners contribute to the growth of tension. The manipulation of these elements contributes to create a favourable condition for self-expression, and a willingness to take initiative in the target language. As Olga (in role as sister) states in the interview: 'this moment was the highlight of the class for me because it had to . . . speak myself'. Later in the interview, Olga reflects that she enjoyed learning Italian (her fourth language) through drama, because 'here, you choose the direction yourself'. These comments point to Olga's sense of *agency* as an AL/process drama learner. We argue that such agency was activated by the subtle manipulation of the elements of drama, both by the teacher and by the participants.

Metacognition and dual scaffolding: Language and drama

From a Vygotskyan perspective, learning refers to speakers becoming agents of their own actions. In order to *activate* learning, the teacher can empower learners to create their own scaffolding, both in the language, and in the drama. To illustrate this point, we draw on Project D, with attention to the strategies that supported this dual scaffolding. In this vignette, all participants are in role as psychologists, except for Jun, in role as the *mother* of a bipolar patient.

> Jun enters the space, playing the mother of the man who refuses to speak. Her classmates, in role as psychologists, are under the assumption that the mother would be familiar with her son's condition, and willing to collaborate. As the mother sits down, she mutters anxiously: "What are you doing with my son?" An awkward silence follows. The psychologists are taken aback. How can they tactfully tell her the truth? She wants her son back, while they have just interned him. The doctors attempt to ask their questions without upsetting her. The situation intensifies. Could she take her son home, she wonders?

The role-play continued intensely for 5 minutes, during which the participants were able to sustain a complex improvisation autonomously. We argue that the teacher's function was crucial to support this interaction, empowering the learners to create their own dual scaffolding, in the language and in the drama. Below, we illustrate *how* this happened.

Before the role-play, the teacher identified two sub-groups, with different needs: (a) Jun, who volunteered to play the mother; and (b) the rest of the students, in role as psychologists. Jun was at a low-intermediate level of Italian, and had very limited experience of drama. She had, for example, never worked in role before. The teacher's concern was to support her to work in role *and* to sustain the improvisation. This was especially complicated as she would not understand the language being used. As a result, the teacher worked with Jun privately, and asked her to think of a *catch-phrase* she could use as an anchor, in case she did not understand a question. The teacher also asked her to think of a *gesture* that she could repeat, and embody, as she played the mother. Jun worked independently on her catch-phrase and gesture. The teacher also encouraged her to think of her role attitudes, and to choose a prop for her role. In this way, Jun was empowered to create her dual scaffolding to manage the interview, both in terms of the language and the drama.

Meanwhile, the teacher set up a writing task for the other students (b), in role as psychologists. They prepared five questions for the mother, as a template for the interview. Through this task, they also were empowered to *create their own dual scaffolding* to support their interaction in the role-play. Participants worked independently for 15 minutes to draft these questions. Throughout, the teacher offered language assistance when needed. The role-play followed, with participants able to sustain the lengthy improvisation autonomously.

One of the teachers observing the role-play noted that this interview created high engagement, and that language was "flowing spontaneously" (Linda, p. 7). This is also confirmed by the learners' experience: in the self-evaluation about this moment, Jun scored her engagement with the language at the highest rate (10/10). In the interview, Jun, who spoke Italian as third language, reflects: 'it's easier to communicate eh . . . more naturally to communicate in Italian during the process drama'.[4] She continues:

> [During process drama] when I speak Italian it's not processed because I didn't know what I was going to be asked. So it was more . . . interaction. (Jun, p. 4)

These comments echo other participants, who also indicated that they were able to engage in a kind of communication that was more dialogic, autonomous and spontaneous. We believe that the strategies outlined above were crucial to empower participants to create their own dual scaffolding, thus becoming the agents of their own learning.

One of the means by which students became more conscious of their own learning processes (metacognition) and how they managed strategies such as dual scaffolding was the inclusion of a reflective phase in the drama/language lessons. Bolton (1979) considers reflection as an important component of dramatic form. In his words, 'experience in itself is neither productive nor unproductive; it is how one *reflects* on it that makes it significant, resulting in "heightened self-awareness"' (p. 111). Each of the lessons undertaken in the studies above built in a reflective phase towards the end of the allocated time. This reflective phase proved to offer a vital step for the students to recognize their learning in drama and in language. In these phases of the lesson, the students often commented on both the drama learning and the language learning they had experienced (see Table 15.3). Some noted the importance of choice of vocabulary and register so that the drama was 'real':

Table 15.3 Extract from student focus group interview from Project B

S3	Ok. For the captain we are supposed to speak in proper English because for the captain's sake, of course he wouldn't speak in Singlish because he's not in Singapore, of course, and we have to speak in proper English so that we are in the real drama.
I	So the captain was not a Singapore captain?
S3	He was from England.
I	From England?
S4	To be more realistic?

Others demonstrated that they were conscious that 'we were combining each other's ideas to make one big good idea' (Study A); and '[we found it] easy to communicate with each other [when in role]' (Study B). As Kao and O'Neill highlight, a comprehensive language review at the end of each drama session is integral for participant identification of their language learning: 'Reflection is a way of making students' aware of the learning that has taken place and demonstrating the significance of their achievements, both socially and linguistically' (1998, p. 32).

Liu (2002) reinforces this point, arguing that reflection is a key strategy to reinforce and explain linguistic expressions emerging through the drama. Similarly, our various research projects suggest that a language review phase at or towards the end of each lesson contributes significantly to the explicit identification of language learning where participants may recognize and consolidate their learning.

Conclusion

In this chapter, we have drawn on existing studies, as well as our own research, to highlight the vital importance of the dual proficiency of the teacher as teacher of drama-the-art-form and teacher-of-language; how working within role within a dramatic context can enhance learning; how dramatic form can promote agency within and beyond the drama/language classroom; and the importance of reflection for metacognition and dual scaffolding in language and drama.

We propose that learning in drama and in language is enhanced when teachers are proficient in the pedagogy of both fields and, thus, are able to manage learning processes and outcomes for *both* drama and language. In this way they are able to create the best possible learning opportunities for AL learning *through* drama.

We align with Kao and O'Neill (1998), who have discussed in detail the affordances of the dramatic context for language learning. In particular we note the importance of working in role and with a level of deep engagement. The imaginative act of identification with roles within a dramatic context provides purpose and motivation for language use. Since process drama requires participants to collaborate and the flexible structure supports contributions from all participants, students are enabled to become agentic both within the drama and in their own learning. Finally, we suggest that the reflective phase within drama work is an important component in the recognition and consolidation of learning in both fields of endeavour.

In this growing field we suggest that there is a need for more research, particularly into the reflective practice of both teachers and learners. And in conclusion we would like to encourage more drama teachers to learn the episteme, the skills and the practices of language teachers, and more language teachers to embrace opportunities similarly to learn about and through drama.

Notes

1　A review of recent international TESOL conferences shows a growing number of presentations about the use of drama, particularly process drama, in second language teaching. In 2011, *RIDE: the journal of Applied Theatre and Performance* dedicated a special edition to research in drama and second language learning and the e-journal *Scenario*, http://www.ucc.ie/en/scenario/, established in 2007, publishes, exclusively, articles focusing on drama and second or additional language acquisition.

2　See, in particular, Alexander, R. J. (2005), *Towards Dialogic Teaching: Rethinking Classroom Talk*, 2nd edn. United Kingdom: Dialogos.

3　The capital Y denotes the use of the formal register in the Italian language.

4　This interview was conducted in English, which was Jun's Second Language. We have kept her original statements, without editing grammar or vocabulary.

References

Araki Metcalfe, N. (2008), 'Introducing creative language learning in Japan through educational drama'. *NJ*, 31, (2), 45–57.

Bolton, G. (1979), *Towards a Theory of Drama in Education*. England: Longman.

Bournot-Trites, M., Belliveau, G., Spiliotopoulos, V., and Séror, J. (2007), 'The role of drama on cultural sensitivity, motivation and literacy in a second language context'. *Journal for Learning through the Arts: A Research Journal on Arts Integration in Schools and Communities*, 3, (1), 1–33.

Bowell, P. and Heap, B. (2005), 'Drama on the run: A prelude to mapping the practice of process drama'. *Journal of Aesthetic Education*, 39, (4), 59–69.

Donato, R. (1994), 'Collective scaffolding in Second Language learning', in J. P. Lantolf and G. Appel (eds), *Vygotskian Approaches to Second Language Research*. Norwood, NJ: Ablex, pp. 33–56.

Dunn, J. and Stinson, M. (2011), 'Not without the art!! The importance of teacher artistry when applying drama as pedagogy for additional language learning'. *RIDE: The Journal of Applied Theatre and Performance*, 16, (4), 617–34.

Eisner, E. W. (1994), *The Educational Imagination: On the Design and Evaluation of School Programs*, 2nd edn. New York: Macmillan.

Haught, J. R. and McCafferty, S. G. (2008), 'Embodied language performance: Drama and the ZPD in the second language classroom', in J. P. Lantolf and M. Poehner (eds), *Sociocultural Theory and the Teaching of Second Languages*, vol. 23. Portland: Equinox Publishing Limited, pp. 139–62.

Kao, S-M. (1995), 'From script to impromptu: Learning a Second Language through process drama', in P. Taylor and C. Hoepper (eds), *Selected Readings in Drama and Theatre Education: The IDEA '95 Papers (2nd, Brisbane, Australia, July 1995). NADIE Research Monograph Series, 3*. Brisbane: IDEA Publications.

Kao, S-M. and O'Neill, C. (1998), *Words into Worlds: Learning a Second Language through Process Drama*. Stanford: Ablex Publishing.

Kao, S-M., Carkin, G., and Hsu, L-F. (2011), 'Questioning techniques for promoting language learning with students of limited L2 oral proficiency in a drama-oriented language classroom'. *Research in Drama Education*, 16, (4), 489.

Krashen, S. (1985), *The Input Hypothesis: Issues and Implications*. New York: Longman.

Lantolf, J. P. (1994), 'Sociocultural theory and Second Language learning: Introduction to the special issue'. *The Modern Language Journal*, 78, (4), 418–20.

—(ed.) (2000), *Sociocultural Theory and Second Language Learning*. Oxford: Oxford University Press.

Liu, J. (2002), 'Process drama in second language and foreign language classrooms', in G. Braure (ed.), *Body and language: Intercultural Learning Through Drama*. Westport: Ablex Publishing.

Maley, A. and Duff, A. (2005), *Drama Techniques: A Resource Book of Communication Activities for Language Teachers*, 3rd edn. Cambridge, UK: Cambridge University Press.

McCafferty, S. G. and Stam, G. (2008), *Gesture: Second Language Acquisition and Classroom Research*. New York: Routledge.

Miccoli, L. (2003), 'English through drama for oral skills development'. *ELT Journal*, 57, (2), 122–9.

Morita, N. (2000), 'Discourse socialization through oral classroom activities in a TESL graduate program'. *TESOL Quarterly*, 34, (2), 279–311.

Neelands, J. (2009), 'The art of togetherness: Reflections on some essential artistic and pedagogic qualities of drama curricula'. *NJ (The Drama Australia Journal)*, 33, (1), 9–18.

Ntelioglou, B. Y. (2011), '"But Why Do I Have to Take This Class?" The mandatory drama-ESL class and multiliteracies pedagogy'. *Research in Drama Education*, 16, (4), 595–615.

O'Mara, J. (2006), 'Capturing the ephemeral: Reflection-in-action as research'. *NJ Drama Australia Journal*, 30, (2), 41–50.

O'Neill, C. (1995), *Drama Worlds: A Framework for Process Drama*. Portsmouth: Heinemann.

O'Toole, J. (1992), *The Process of Drama: Negotiating Art and Meaning*. London: Reutledge.

Piazzoli, E. (2011), 'Process drama: The use of affective space to reduce language anxiety in the additional language learning classroom'. *RIDE: The Journal of Applied Theatre and Performance*, 16, (4), 557–74. doi: 10.1080/13569783.2011.616395

—(2012), 'Film and drama aesthetics for Additional Language teaching', in J. Winston (ed.), *Second Language Learning through Drama: Practical Techniques and Applications*. London: Routeledge.

Pica, T. (1994), 'Research on negotiation: What does it reveal about Second-Language learning conditions, processes, and outcomes?'. *Language Learning*, 44, (3), 493–527.

Prino, M. (2005), *Buongiorno*. Bêkafilms: Milano.

Rothwell, J. (2011), 'Bodies and language: Process drama and intercultural language learning in a beginner language classroom'. *Research in Drama Education*, 16, (4), 575–94.

Stinson, M. (2008), 'Drama, process drama, and TESOL', in M. Anderson, J. Hughes and J. Manuel (eds), *Drama in English Teaching: Imagination, Action and Engagement*. Melbourne, VIC: Oxford University Press, pp. 193–212.

—(2009), 'Drama is like reversing everything: Intervention research as teacher professional development'. *RIDE: The Journal of Applied Theatre and Performance*, 14, (2), 223–41.

Stinson, M. and Freebody, K. (2006), 'The DOL project: An investigation into the contribution of process drama to improved results in English oral communication'. *Youth Theatre Journal*, 20, 27–41.

—(2009), 'The contribution of process drama to improved results in English oral communication', in R. Silver, C. Goh and L. Alsagoff (eds), *Acquisition and Development in New English Contexts: Evidence from Singapore*. London: Continuum, pp. 147–65.

Swain, M. (2000), 'The output hypothesis and beyond: Mediating acquisition through collaborative dialogue', in J. P. Lantolf (ed.), *Sociocultural Theory and Second Language Learning*. Oxford: Oxford University Press, pp. 97–114.

To, L. D., Chan, Y. P., Lam, Y. K., and Tsang, S. Y. (2011), 'Reflections on a primary school teacher professional development programme on learning english through process drama'. *Research in Drama Education*, 16, (4), 517–39.

Van Lier, L. (2008), 'Agency in the classroom', in J. P. Lantolf and M. E. Poehner (eds), *Sociocultural Theory and the Teaching of Second Languages*. London: Equinox.

Vygotsky, L. (1978), *Mind in Society: The Development of Higher Psychological Processes*. Cambridge, MA: Harvard University Press.

Wagner, B. J. (1998), *Educational Drama and Language Arts: What Research Shows*. Portsmouth, NH: Heinemann.

Yaman Ntelioglou, B. (2011), 'Drama and English language learners', in S. Shonmann (ed.), *Key Concepts in Theatre/Drama Education*. Rotterdam: Sense Publishers.

16

Drama and Learning Technologies: To Affinity Spaces and Beyond

Michael Anderson and David Cameron

Drama and technology: Activating learning through mutual affordances

We have often heard teachers say that there is an inherent contradiction between enactment in live drama classrooms and interaction with the screen-based virtual spaces of digital media. In 2002, John Carroll reported that drama teachers' widespread ambivalence towards technology manifested itself in this binary view and possibly reflected a wider 'lingering tension' in the educational system (p. 130). In other places, we (Carroll et al. 2006; Anderson et al. 2009) have urged educators to move beyond these oppositional positions to explore drama as a way to activate learning *with* technology.

As a field we have covered a lot of ground since 2002. Perhaps because a new, more 'digitally native' group of drama educators and an increasing number of researchers interested in the performative and dramatic nature of digital culture are making a difference. Alternatively, we may simply be experiencing the processes by which initially disruptive innovations are eventually diffused through society over time (Rogers 1962). In the drama context, these processes may have been accelerated because educational drama pioneers such as John Carroll and Dorothy Heathcote were able to see synergies in the innately malleable and pliable qualities of both the ancient art form of drama and modern forms of media. Dorothy Heathcote (2006, p. xi) highlighted these synergies when she noted:

> I had the good fortune recently to be involved in a close encounter of symbiosis between literature, theatre and technology which convinces me that the basic

elements of drama – ancient and proven shape shifter as it is – naturally can embrace close encounter with the technological advances in communication systems which will have changed and modified in the time it is taking me to write these ideas on the paper. Technology is the symbiotic shape shifter of our age.

Heathcote's 'close encounter' was a stage production of *Dracula* (1899). In Bram Stoker's novel media technologies of the day such as phonograph recordings and newspaper clippings are crucial narrative devices in the hunt for the elusive vampire. Heathcote was struck by how a theatre production had seamlessly updated those technologies with contemporary equivalents more familiar to a modern audience without rejecting the nineteenth-century aesthetic of the original text. Media philosopher Friedrich Kittler (1982) also noted that the plot of *Dracula* marshaled these nineteenth-century data storage and transmission forms so effectively that it avoids being dated by gothic horror tropes to remain a 'story about media machines and the technologies of writing' (Partington 2006, p. 53) that can still thrill modern audiences. In their different ways, both Heathcote and Kittler recognized *Dracula* as an early example of the rich dramatic opportunities that emerge from a hybrid approach to artistic conventions and the affordances of technology.

Much of the work of the past decade at the intersection of drama, education and technology has explored ways to manage, accommodate or appropriate the advance of technologies on existing curricula and practices. In this chapter, we consider suggestions that we are now entering a new wave of practice and research in education in which we must consider digital media and online interactions:

> . . . not for how we should manage them or necessarily accommodate them within existing educational structures, but for what they tell us about the forms of learning and literacy that are *already* instantiated within the use of these media (Duncan and Hayes 2012, p. 3).

Among these emerging forms of learning and literacy are elements that will make sense to drama educators such as play, performance and simulation (Jenkins et al. 2009, p. 4). This chapter therefore investigates how we might usefully blend the affordances of drama and technology by studying how applied learning is already occurring beyond formal settings in the new spaces in which young people learn about themselves and their world through play, enactment of identity, creative production, re-mixing, sharing and connecting. We will consider the shape-shifting nature of the symbiotic mix of drama and technology as opportunities for learning – not just in terms of formal curricula, but around the passions and interests driving a resurgence of a 'making' culture. This matters for teachers, schools and ultimately our students because there are significant affordances in both drama and technology that can support and extend learning in both drama and technology and beyond. The chapter begins with a brief discussion around the intersection between drama and technology and then provides a case study that blends drama and technology to explore a model for replicating at least some of the affordances of an 'affinity space' that could potentially change the way we think about the blending of the two domains.

Understanding affordances

Let us first define what we mean by 'affordances'. Broadly speaking, an affordance is a quality of an object or space that allows an individual to perform an action. Psychologist James Gibson initially defined affordances as the 'action possibilities' in an environment available to individual actors in that space (1977). Designer Donald Norman appropriated the term to specifically describe those action possibilities readily suggested by the design of an object:

> Affordances provide strong clues to the operations of things. Plates are for pushing. Knobs are for turning. Slots are for inserting things into. Balls are for throwing or bouncing. When affordances are taken advantage of, the user knows what to do just by looking (1988, p. 9).

It is often this sense of an affordance that is meant when talking about human–technology interaction. We believe that it is this concept of the action possibilities embedded in the design of an object or space – the affordances that immediately present themselves to an individual or an 'actor' – that suggests why drama and technology can be blended effectively to activate learning. Well-designed technologies require very little explanation or instruction to allow a user to get started with simple tasks or an exploration of more complex applications. Affordances activate learning *though* action by immediately presenting clear opportunities *for* action. In the same way, many forms of drama use a range of conventions to generate and present possibilities of action to participants that will lead smoothly to richer engagement with a problem, theme or topic.

Affinity spaces

Let us now consider another key term that we feel highlights the need to see the mix of drama and technology not as a contradiction but as an opportunity to activate learning. In 2006 we envisaged classroom spaces where the distribution of knowledge enabled by networked technology could combine with situated role-based learning. This might allow students and teachers to engage with real expertise, in the commission of real-world tasks, 'as if' they were members of a professional community:

> Imagine a classroom that is not bounded by the limits of the 'knowledge' of the teachers and students within it. Imagine a space where the collective knowledge of humankind could be accessed to enrich learning. Imagine in this space a group of young people busily engaged in a complex professional task. Engaged with their bodies and their minds, describing in the language of the profession, be it engineers, journalists, or marine archaeologists how they might fulfil a commission they have been set or solve a pressing social problem (Carroll et al. 2006, p. 87).

We were inspired firstly by the informal frameworks for learning identified by Lave and Wenger in the concept known as 'communities as practice' (1991). This seemed a good fit with some of the role-based forms of drama we were exploring, and the dramatic conventions that allowed learners to engage 'as if' a member of a professional community, albeit often at a novice or apprentice level. We were also seeing promising parallels in the technology field of 'serious' or non-entertainment video games, particularly the work of David Shaffer and others around using 'epistemic games' (2006).

Lave and Wenger's work pre-dated the explosive growth of online communities enabled by networked digital technology. Researchers became interested in the learning frameworks that exist in these fluid social organizations, particularly in the sites used by young people to engage in the fan culture around popular cultural forms like video games. Access to a space in which to share a passion or interest seemed more important than perceived membership of a homogeneous group. Rather than assuming a common bond of membership in a community, attention turned to the spaces (real, virtual or blended) where these people interact and the affordances that activate learning within them.

James Paul Gee (2004) defined these sites as 'affinity spaces' to emphasize that the activities within the space are formed around a shared interest or 'affinity'. The individuals moving in and out of a space do not necessarily see themselves as part of a community of practice, but rather find that the space affords a number of learning, social and cultural practices around a shared interest. Some of the features of these contemporary affinity spaces are:

- a common endeavour is primary;
- participation is self-directed, multifaceted and dynamic;
- participation and production of creative content is often multimodal in online spaces;
- they afford a passionate, public audience for content;
- socializing plays an important part in participation;
- leadership roles vary within and among spaces;
- knowledge is distributed across the space;
- many place a high value on cataloguing and documenting content and practices; and
- they encompass a variety of media-specific and social networking portals (Lammers et al. 2012, pp. 48–50).

The focus on the space(s) where passionate interests are turned into a shared endeavour, rather than on membership of the group or community itself, is an important distinction for drama educators. This implies that greater attention should be placed on the spaces in which young people engage with the cultural practices surrounding performance, play, drama, role and identity. Early research in this emerging area focused on the cultural and literacy practices of online video game fans (Hayes and Duncan 2012). Carroll noted a decade ago that interactive digital media such as video games were increasingly becoming one of the first spaces in which young people begin to explore the possibilities of role-based play, and that drama educators were well-placed to understand the emerging performance conventions and build upon students' 'undeveloped' engagement with these practices (2002, p. 141).

Drama and digital technology: Complementarity for learning

Dorothy Heathcote's acknowledgement of the emerging relationship between the 'ancient and proven shape shifter' that is drama, and 'the symbiotic shape shifter of our age' that is today's communication technology (2006, p. xi) uncovered a powerful possibility in the combination of two fundamentally flexible approaches to learning and teaching. As a society we are becoming increasingly aware of the shape shifting and 'mutagenic' nature of what we can broadly call digital media technology. If drama is a plastic art form, digital media is an equally dynamic means through which story, performance, role and creativity can be enacted. Ironically, technology is both an agent for change and a means for playfully exploring the impact of that change.

Digital technology also exhibits a protean capacity to both rapidly shape shift and to connect or 'mashup' (Cameron 2009), thus transforming practice at fundamental levels. This symbiotic relationship between drama and digital technology has already been observed in terms of the performative poetics underlying interactive media such as video games (Laurel 1991; Murray 1997). More recent appraisals of this emerging digital-networked culture have identified two significant features that emphasize the shape-shifting nature of technology: first there is remediation, a remixing of old and new media (Bolter and Grusin 2000), and second, there is the process of 'bricolage' which exists 'in terms of the highly personalized, continuous and more or less autonomous assembly, disassembly, and reassembly of mediated reality' (Deuze 2006). As noted by Deuze:

> The manifold scrambled, manipulated, and converged ways in which we produce and consume information worldwide are gradually changing the way people interact and give meaning to their lives. The emergence of a fragmented, edited, yet connected and networked worldview in itself is part of digital culture'. (2006)

The affordances of these inherently flexible approaches have been accompanied by the rise in accessibility of these technologies for young people and the blurring of the roles of consumer and producer.

Making the future: Production/consumption to making/performing

The rethinking about production and consumption made possible by digital media activates new opportunities for learning. The use of film and animation provides performance makers and educators the opportunity to create performance by remixing and remediating the past and present. Participants can increasingly exhibit more choice and agency in becoming active in the meaning-making processes of mediated popular culture, through these twin processes of remediation and bricolage.

Awareness of the value of creative production in educational contexts, and in youth cultures more generally, is beginning to coalesce around a new 'Maker Movement', born in part from the impact of technology on the world of cottage industries, crafts, passions and hobbies. Chris Anderson argues that we 'are all Makers. We are born Makers', and that:

> Projects shared online become inspiration for others and opportunities for collaboration. Individual Makers, globally connected this way, become a movement. Millions of DIYers, once working alone, suddenly start working together (C. Anderson 2012, p. 13).

Gauntlett also argues that 'making is connecting', as creative processes often have a social dimension, and this aspect is amplified in a Web culture grounded in messages of making, sharing and collaboration. He hopes that this might transfer to broader contexts, moving people beyond the 'sit back and be told' model of traditional schooling towards a 'making and doing' culture capable of tackling real social problems (2011, p. 8). Thomas and Seely Brown make a similar case for 'making' as twenty-first-century literacy that enables young people to explore both the content and context of creativity, either through a reshaping of the old or an exploration of the new:

> The process of making and remaking context is, in itself, an act of imaginative play (what we might call the "how" of information). Understanding that process and being able to participate in it also forms the basis for evaluation and judgment in the twenty-first century. By participating in the making of meaning, we also learn how to judge and evaluate it, giving special sensitivity to the ways information can be shaped, positively as well as negatively (2001, p. 96).

This recognition of the hands-on, creative and playful aspects of engagement in digital media presents an opportunity for drama educators to utilize their existing expertise to help young people cope with a world in which change is the norm. Considerations of the future of education and the impacts on and influences of dominant youth cultures have evolved into a broader movement around so-called 'participatory culture'. Jenkins et al's 2009 paper *Confronting the challenges: media education for the 21st century* defines this as a mediated culture with:

> Relatively low barriers to artistic expression and civic engagement, strong support for creating and sharing creations with others, some type of informal mentorship whereby what is known by the most experienced is passed along to novices, members who believe that their contributions matter, and members who feel some

degree of social connection with one another (at least, they care what other people think about what they have created). (2009, pp. 5–6)

Significantly, the paper sets out to identify a set of skills or 'new media literacies' for educators to consider. These skills are identified as play, performance, simulation, appropriation, multitasking, distributed cognition, collective intelligence, judgement, transmedia navigation, networking and negotiation (Jenkins et al. 2009, p. 4). Drama practitioners and educators will easily recognize resources that echo well-established dramatic and educational conventions that not only pre-date the influence of technology, but provide an already existing but as yet largely under-utilized body of knowledge and experience that can be brought to bear on learning in drama.

For example, Jenkins et al. define performance as 'the ability to adopt alternative identities for the purpose of improvisation and discovery' (2009, p. xiv). Drama practitioners like Paul Sutton, Creative Director of UK educational drama company C&T (www.candt.org), observe that this 'construction of new identities on the Internet is an accepted convention and that this could be regarded as another form of being 'in-role' (in Shaughnessy 2005, p. 206). In the digital world, identity play one is often 'projecting a version of self that is inherently theatrical' (Nakamura 2000, p. 713). The formation of social identity is also a central issue in affinity spaces, as the social learning that occurs is related to ways in which people express themselves in relation to the common endeavour irrespective of other social factors such as age, gender or geographical location. A focus on identity in terms of membership, as with the communities of practice framework, obscures the aspects of the identity work that participants perform in an affinity space (DeVane 2012, p. 182).

As a discipline well-versed in the constraints and possibilities of working with concepts of time and space, drama education is now provided with an opportunity to reconsider the nature of where and when learning occurs. More critically, the dramatic enactment of learning provides an opportunity to explore where knowledge is formed, stored and shared, 'In a world where context is always shifting and being rearranged, the stability of the *what* dimension of knowledge also comes into question. Only by understanding the *where* of a piece of information can we understand its meaning' (Thomas and Seely Brown 2011, p. 93). The interest in *where* young people are exploring cultural and creative practices, often formed around their personal passions and interests and the desire to participate as 'makers', is leading to more research into 'affinity spaces' (Gee 2004). While Lave and Wenger identified informal frameworks for learning in the concept that became known as 'communities as practice', Gee and others have noted the limitations of assuming a common bond of membership in a community. Focusing on the affordances and constraints of the shared environment in which participation occurs, rather than on membership in a 'community', Gee suggests a focus on the spaces (real, virtual or a blend) in which people might gather for common purpose or around a common interest, such that 'we can then go on and ask to what extent the people interacting within a space, or some sub-group of them, do or do not actually form a community' (Gee 2004, p. 89). For drama educators, this implies that greater attention should be placed on the spaces (real, virtual or blended) in which young people engage with the cultural practices surrounding performance, play, drama, role and identity. Carroll notes that interactive digital media such as video games are increasingly becoming one of the first spaces in which young people begin to explore the possibilities of role-based play, and that drama educators are well-placed to understand the emerging performance conventions and build upon students' 'undeveloped' engagement with these practices (2002, p. 14)

Reflections on practice and literature: How drama and technology activate learning

A small and committed group of teachers and researchers has been testing out the relationship between drama and technology over the last 15–20 years. Several prominent drama educators have been making the point that there are substantial synergies between drama and technology. In 2004, Brad Haseman nominated hybridity, interactivity, the input of new forms of cultural production and multi-platform delivery as features for drama education's sustainable future (Haseman 2004). John O'Toole and Julie Dunn have also found that students understand and appreciate the mutual affordances of drama and 'appreciate the complementarity of these approaches' (2008, p. 90). Inspired by the complementary affordances of drama and technology with their open and flexible opportunities for learning, this group has been exploring the exciting possibilities that open up when these two areas work together in partnership. We do not intend here to give a blow-by-blow discussion of the history of drama and technology. Rather, we would like to outline some of the ways that drama and technology have been used together to support learning.

One of the most accessible approaches to drama and learning combines the (now) everyday technology of the video and the PowerPoint presentation and the development of a dramatized (often documentary style) narrative. This allows young people to lower the barriers of access and become Makers (C. Anderson 2012) using the combined affordances of drama and technology.

Digital storytelling and digital narratives

One of the emergent intersections of drama and technology is the development of digital storytelling approaches with young people. The increased availability of tools such as digital cameras for recording still and moving images and the software for editing, sharing and publishing these stories represent a clear example of the participatory media forms now powered by ubiquitous mobile devices and Web-based media. The mass popularity of media-sharing services such as *Youtube* and *Instagram* is enabled by their simple point-shoot-click interfaces that afford recording, post-producing and publishing content. Digital storytelling in educational drama settings often involves the development of a 2- to 3-minute multimedia movie narrated in the first person by the creator and inspired by a significant event in their lives. The projects are developed through a series of process drama techniques including enactment of the expert and tableaux (McGeoch and Hughes 2009). Commenting on a project aimed at developing intercultural understanding McGeoch and Hughes observe that digital storytelling can '. . . activate both thinking and feeling by engaging participants through movement, visualization, imagination, creative problem solving and shared oral and written activities' (2009, p. 126). In recent work in Singapore, Prue Wales suggests that this approach encourages young people to engage with personal, aesthetic and technological learning. She comments

> Once they invested in telling the kinds of stories they wanted to tell, youth from the informal settings began to explore different types of programmes and technologies they could use for their story constructions. Their interest and skill in the aesthetic experience of digital storytelling rose as their confidence and ability with the technology developed. Not surprisingly as their aesthetic and technological skills improved so did their storytelling . . . These initial findings, revealing the interrelationship between agency, engagement, confidence, skill-set and the ability to communicate a story, are something we would like to see flow back into formal school settings (2012, p. 545).

In addition to these multimedia approaches to digital storytelling, drama educators are also engaging more closely with the narrative potential of other media forms such as virtual worlds (Flintoff 2009; Nicholls and Philip 2012) and video games (O'Mara 2012). The use of game software to produce animated movies in a process known as 'machinima' is another example of how the affordances of role-based performance and game technology have been blended to produce new narrative forms (Cameron and Carroll 2011). These approaches have brought educational drama conventions to media production processes to explore digital storytelling forms. Another method has been to adopt and adapt the affordances of technology to the well-known and effective drama convention of pretext, to produce hybrid rich media entry-points for educational role-based drama.

Digital pretexts and drama networks

The use of digital pretexts was first advocated by John Carroll around the turn of the last century (2002). He saw the possibility of taking the richness of the dramatic pretext (O'Neill 1995, p. 20) and developing it further using the affordances of technology. In essence '... the pervasiveness of digital technologies within school classrooms means that the use of a computer constructed pretext may provide new avenues for the development of dramatic role performance conventions' (Carroll, Anderson and Cameron 2006). Since that time we have seen the approach applied to emergent technologies such as twitter (Wotzko 2012), web-based pretexts (Davis 2009, 2012) and dedicated systems for generating digital pretexts (Bossomaier et al. 2010). Work by companies such as C&T has pursued this further with the concept of 'Networked Theatre'. Sutton describes this approach as 'a collision of pedagogy, technology, aesthetics, drama practice and business' (2012, p. 65). Networked theatre has the following aspirations:

- To build an online collaborative community of applied theatre practice that mirrors the best aspects of process drama methodologies.
- To build an online community for the long-term development and benefit of partner schools, not for the needs of short term, one-off projects.
- To use the capacity of the internet to reach out to a diversity of partners, building an inclusive, glocalized community of practice (Sutton 2012).

The networked theatre approach embeds digital pretexts within a broader drama and technology ecosystem in the same way drama has always embedded pretexts within a process drama pedagogy. The inclusion of digital pretexts into broader strategies provides some sense of where drama pedagogy might interact more fully with online gaming where the online and offline interact as one large game/simulation/drama. In essence large-scale video games are designed to be flexible and immersive worlds with multiple possible outcomes. A skillfully designed game that interacts with live drama could offer some of the same opportunities as digital pretexts but in a blended manner, providing the liveness and interactive qualities of the live drama experience with the ability to create cinematic and immersive worlds through the online space. In the ongoing quest for 'immersive' or 'flow' learning experiences drama has also blended online and offline learning.

Role-based and epistemic games

Jenkins et al. argue that a more sophisticated use of role-play as one of the media skills developed in participatory culture 'enables us to envision and collaboratively theorize about manipulating entirely new worlds . . . [that] invites a reimagining of self and world' (2009, p. 52). As a tool for exploring the future, role-play can be seen as a key component of the 'universal joint' of drama that starts to connect role-based drama and applied theatre techniques and conventions and digital technology, particularly when viewed in the light of educational applications of digital game forms. One specific form is that of the 'epistemic game' (Shaffer 2006) that seemingly unconsciously shares much from the educational drama field:

> In an epistemic game, the game world is designed to simulate the social context of a profession and by working through realistic but simulated problems, players learn the ways of acting, interacting and interpreting that are necessary for participating in the professional community. In effect rather than memorising facts or formulas, through performances of being an urban planner, lawyer, doctor, engineer, carpenter, historian, teacher or physicist, the player learns these professions' particular ways of thinking (Jenkins et al. 2009, p. 54).

Jenkins suggests that 'role play, in particular, should be seen as a fundamental skill used across multiple academic domains' (2009, p. 52). The similarities between Shaffer's epistemic games and forms of drama such as Heathcote's Mantle of the Expert have been identified (Carroll and Cameron 2007, 2009; Cameron et al. 2011). Both Epistemic Games and Mantle of the Expert share similar frameworks for the use of role and identity. Both fields apply sociologist Erving Goffman's (1974) concept of frames for better understanding the adoption of identities. As approaches to education, both create a performance frame that enables participants to act in professional roles with role protection and role distance (Carroll and Cameron 2005). At the simplest level, participants are protected as their roles are 'as if' in the real world, allowing 'risks where real-world consequences are lowered' (Gee 2003, p. 62), encouraging a playful and protected approach to problem-solving and learning through exploration.

When talking about the development of educational drama resources based around video game conventions, we are aware that the cultural reference points most familiar to many educators or practitioners are big-budget commercial game products. The financing, time, resources and skills to produce this type and scale of product make it an unfeasible approach for most educators. However, it is also important to note that it is precisely these types of products that tend to generate a large base of enthusiastic fans who display the requisite shared passion to support emergent affinity spaces. Is it feasible (or even possible) to build an affinity space for game-like drama-based education from scratch? Are there options for making use of existing affinity spaces generated 'in the wild', and borrowing them for educational purposes? The affinity spaces approach is one attempt to find out.

Case study: Towards affinity spaces and drama education

As with 'communities of practice' there is a danger that attempts by institutions and organizations to operationalize the concept of 'affinity spaces' will detach it from its foundational framework. DeVane observes that although Lave and Wenger made a clear distinction of their descriptive work on communities of practice from any prescriptive pedagogical or instructional framework, it was nonetheless used a prescriptive device for good teaching practice in the educational research literature (2012, p. 165).

However, we have already outlined that affinity spaces provide an opportunity to learn about the social learning processes that can occur around a shared endeavour. Rather than being a pedagogical framework, they are a location to be observed, recorded and analysed for clues as to how we might reproduce some of the affordances of these spaces that seem to prompt and facilitate the sharing of beliefs, literacies, values, actions, knowledge, practices and social interactions around a particular domain. At the same time the forms of identity work, play, performance, simulation and production typically occurring in these spaces should be of great interest to all educators, especially to drama educators. These are core areas for continued engagement with young people in the cultures they inhabit.

This case study describes some first steps towards a prototype for combining some affordances of digital media and virtual spaces with the conventions of drama to produce a hybrid form of drama/technology for learning. Drama and game conventions such as role protection, role distance, pretext, simulation and epistemic framing were considered as key design features in the first steps towards a system for gathering learners in a blended (real-time distributed) space to engage them in a shared endeavour. Although clearly not an organic affinity space in the sense of those emergent forms found 'in the wild', this project provides some early experiences in the process of working from a hybrid drama/ technology model.

From 2007 to 2010 a joint project between Charles Sturt University and the Australian Defence Force (ADF) explored ways in which a blended space for learning might be built, based on a combination of dramatic and technological conventions. Funded by an Australian Research Council linkage project, one aim of the project was to prototype an online role-based scenario management system. The ADF interest as a partner in the work was focused on the potential use of simulation tools by military public affairs personnel to explore, analyse and enhance crisis communication management.

A prototype application called Communications and Applied Drama Game Engine (CADGE) was developed for piloting with the ADF public affairs personnel (Bossomaier et al. 2010). Another element of the project was the definition of a scenario development language, dubbed Communication Representation and Specification Language (CRASL). The aim of CRASL is to provide a non-technical scenario creation language, modelling a typical lesson plan that a teacher might create for a drama session, and therefore accessible to domain experts with absolutely no computer programming experience.

Drawing on the conventions of role-based drama, the CADGE/CRASL system was designed to allocate participants into attitudinal roles, for example, 'journalist' or 'media officer' and provide them with a short pretext for the dramatic scenario. In the prototype, the pretext took the form of a small text-based narrative to position the participant in the world of the scenario, though the system also allowed for a range of media types such as images, movies and sounds to be used. The system was designed to operate in a distributed model, with participants interacting via networked computers rather than necessarily being in the same physical space. Students could *communicate* with each other via a simple text chat system, and share files via an online document repository.

Central to the design of the prototype was the concept of providing a shared virtual space that afforded opportunities for the teacher to participate in the online drama either in or out of role. The teacher could manipulate the scenario in real-time by triggering the playing of media files, or by engaging in chat with the participants. The system design also allowed for the use of pre-programmed 'triggers' based on a timer or in response to participant actions, for example, a media clip representing an urgent telephone call might appear shortly after the session commences to introduce tension into the scenario.

Although the prototype scenario was not formally classified as high security, the ADF requested that access be restricted. The project team therefore worked on a more open scenario for wider use, and in May 2011 CADGE was used to deliver a pilot scenario to a class of undergraduate media students studying the role of social media in crisis communication. The students logged into the scenario through a browser-based Flash client, and were again allocated one of two roles: a journalist working for a local media outlet or a public relations officer working for a local government organization. The participants worked through a dynamic scenario in an attempt to unravel a complex and dramatic unfolding narrative around a natural disaster. Participants generally found the experience an engaging and active approach to learning about the topic, and there is clearly more knowledge to be gained by future experiments with these types of mediated learning communities.

One of the difficulties confronted by the project team was that of being able to keep pace with developments in technology and digital culture during the long period of time required to design and implement the technological framework for this more committed type of drama/technology hybrid. Moving away from readily available 'everyday' technology and into custom-built platforms proved a costly and lengthy process. However, the process did offer glimpses of the new powerful forms of engagement, participation and creativity that might emerge in a focused blend of drama conventions and online technology, using scenarios to explore the world through the 'what if?' opportunities both drama and technology offer.

Conclusions and ways forward

We have moved on from that moment in education (if indeed it ever existed) where teachers had a choice between engaging with technology and teaching without it. Our lives and critically the lives of our students are saturated with various technologies that have strong potential when blended with drama pedagogy. Beyond the school and the home, young people are engaging with technology to create and recreate who they are and what they do. In these places, there is a distinct opportunity for drama to make an impact. Technology and drama allow for a playful reinterpretation of time, space and presence (physical or virtual). If drama educators reconceptualize learning as a process that, when pushed beyond school, can occur in many places and at many times, then we may begin to rejuvenate what's possible, not just for drama learning but for learning more generally. Although speculative and experimental, the affinity spaces case study presented here provides a distinctly new way of blending technology and drama to maximize their combined affordances. Rather than the two areas sitting in tension, the common ground the two offer learning requires exploration and imaginative examination from teachers and researchers who understand that the combination of drama and technology could activate learning in novel and exciting ways.

Obviously these partially imagined and unimagined synergies are the stuff of future research and practice. The combined affordances of the live, embodied, affective realm of drama education and the networked mediated world offer some stunning opportunities. In our view we have not yet even begun to realize the full potential of this learning opportunity. Approaches that embrace hybridity such as affinity spaces, combining technology and drama, do not cancel each other out, rather they provide the possibility of future learning that goes beyond what we know is possible now using drama or technology. There is very real promise in the combining of both that we can create a powerful new approach to learning.

References

Anderson, C. (2012), *Makers: The New Industrial Revolution*. New York: Random House.

Anderson, M., Carroll, J., and Cameron, D. (2009), *Drama Education with Digital Technology*. London: Continuum.

Bolter, J. D. and Grusin, D. (2000), *Remediation: Understanding New Media*. Cambridge, MA: MIT Press.

Bossomaier, T., Tulip, J., Carroll, J., and Cameron, D. (2010), *SCCRASL and CADGE: Crisis Representation and Simulation in Serious Games*. Paper presented at the The International Workshop on Applied Modelling and Simulation, Rio de Janeiro, Brazil.

Cameron, D. (2009), 'Mashup: Digital media and drama conventions', in M. Anderson, J. Carroll and D. Cameron (eds), *Drama Education with Digital Technology*. London: Continuum, pp. 52–66.

Cameron, D. J. and Carroll, J. (2011), 'Encoding liveness: Performance and real-time rendering in machinima', in H. Lowood and M. Nitsche (eds), *The Machinima Reader*. Cambridge, MA: The MIT Press, pp. 127–42.

Cameron, D., Carroll, J., and Wotzko, R. (2011), *Epistemic Games and Applied Drama: Converging Conventions for Serious Play*. Paper presented at the Digital Games Research Association, Hilversum, Netherlands.

Carroll, J. (2002), 'Digital drama: A snapshot of evolving forms'. *Melbourne Studies in Education*, 43, (2), 130–41.

Carroll, J., Anderson, M., and Cameron, D. (2006), *Real Players? Drama, Technology and Education*. Stoke-On-Trent: Trentham.

Carroll, J. and Cameron, D. (2005), 'Playing the game: Role distance and digital performance'. *Applied Theatre Researcher*, 6.

—(2007), *Epistemic Video Games and Mantle of the Expert: A Communities of Practice Approach IDEA Conference*. Hong Kong, China.

—(2009), 'Drama, digital pre-text, and social media'. *Research in Drama Education: The Journal of Applied Theatre and Performance*, 14, (2), 295–312.

Davis, S. (2009), 'Interactive drama using cyberspaces', in M. Anderson, J. Carroll and D. Cameron (eds), *Drama Education with Digital Technology*. London: Continuum, pp. 149–67.

—(2012), 'Liveness, mediation and immediacy – innovative technology use in process and performance'. *Research in Drama Education: The Journal of Applied Theatre and Performance*, 17, (4), 501–16.

Deuze, M. (2006), 'Participation, remediation, bricolage: Considering principal components of a digital culture'. *Information Society*, 22, (2), 63–75.

DeVane, B. (2012), 'Whither membership? *Identity and social learning in affinity spaces*', in E. R. Hayes and S. C. Duncan (eds), *Learning in Video Game Affinity Spaces*. New York: Peter Lang Publishing, pp. 162–85.

Duncan, S. C. and Hayes, E. R. (2012), 'Expanding the affinity space: An introduction', in E. R. Hayes and S. C. Duncan (eds), *Learning in Video Game Affinity Spaces*. New York: Peter Lang, pp. 1–22.

Flintoff, K. (2009), 'Second life/simulation: Online sites for generative play', in M. Anderson, J. Carroll and D. Cameron (eds), *Drama Education with Digital Technology*. London: Continuum, pp. 201–21.

Gauntlett, D. (2011), *Making is Connected*. Cambridge: Polity Press.

Gee, J. P. (2003), *What Video Games have to Teach Us about Learning and Literacy*. New York: Palgrave.

—(2004), *Situated Language and Learning: A Critique of Traditional Schooling*. New York: Routledge.

Gibson, J. J. (1977), 'The theory of affordances', in R. Shaw and J. Bransford (eds), *Perceiving, Acting and Knowing*. Hillsdale, NJ: Erlbaum.

Goffman, E. (1974), *Frame Analysis: An Essay on the Organization of Experience*. New York: Harper and Row.

Haseman, B. (2004), 'Cooking and drama education in the global kitchen'. *Drama Australia Journal*, 28, (2), 15–24.

Hayes, E. R. and Duncan, S. C. (eds) (2012), *Learning in Video Game Affinity Spaces*. New York: Peter Lang.

Heathcote, D. (2006), 'Foreword', in J. Carroll, M. Anderson and D. Cameron (eds), *Real Players? Drama, Technology and Education*. Stoke-On-Trent: Trentham, pp. ix–xix.

Jenkins, H., Clinton, K., Purushotma, R., Robinson, A. J., and Weigel, M. (2009), *Confronting the Challenges of Participatory Culture: Media Education for the 21st Century*. MacArthur Foundation.

Kittler, F. (1982), 'Dracula's legacy', in J. Johnston (ed.), *Literature, Media, Information Systems*, trans. W. S. Davis. Amsterdam: G+B Arts, 1997, pp. 28–49.

Laurel, B. (1991), *Computers as Theatre*. Menlo Park: Addison Wesley.

Lammers, J. C., Curwood, J. S., and Magnifico, A. M. (2012), 'Toward an affinity space methodology: Considerations for literacy research'. *English Teaching: Practice and Critique*, 11, (2), 44–58.

Lave, J. and Wenger, E. (1991), *Situated Learning: Legitimate Peripheral Participation*. Cambridge: Cambridge University Press.

McGeoch, K. and Hughes, J. (2009), 'Digital storytelling and drama: Language, image and empathy', in M. Anderson, J. Carroll and D. Cameron (eds), *Drama Education with Digital Technology*. London: Continuum, pp. 113–28.

Murray, J. (1997), *Hamlet on the Holodeck: The Future of Narrative in Cyberspace*. New York: The Free Press.

Nakamura, L. (2000), 'Race in/for cyberspace: Identity tourism and racial passing on the Internet', in D. Bell and B. M. Kennedy (eds), *The Cybercultures Reader*. London: Routledge.

Norman, D. A. (1988), *The Design of Everyday Things*. New York: Doubleday.

O'Neill, C. (1995), *Drama Worlds: A Framework for Process Drama*. Portsmouth: Heinemann.

O'Toole, J. and Dunn, J. (2008), 'Learning in dramatic and virtual worlds: What do students say about complementarity and future directions?'. *Journal of Aesthetic Education*, 42, (4), 89–104.

Partington, G. (2006), 'Friedrich Kittler's "Aufschreibsystem"'. *Science Fiction Studies*, 33, (1), 53–67.

Rogers, E. M. (1962), *Diffusion of Innovations*. New York: Free Press.

Shaffer, D. W. (2006), *How Computer Games Help Children Learn*. New York: Palgrave Macmillan.

Shaughnessy, N. (2005), 'Truths and lies: Exploring the ethics of performance applications. Research in Drama Education'. *The Journal of Applied Theatre and Performance*, 10, 201–12.

Sutton, P. (2012), 'Shaping Networked Theatre: Experience architectures, behaviours and creative pedagogies'. *Research in Drama Education: The Journal of Applied Theatre and Performance*, 17, (4), 603–16.

Thomas, D. and Seely Brown, J. (2011), *A New Culture of Learning: Cultivating the Imagination for a World of Constant Change*. Lexington, KY: CreateSpace.

Wotzko, R. (2012), 'Newspaper Twitter: Applied drama and microblogging'. *Research in Drama Education: The Journal of Applied Theatre and Performance*, 17, (4), 569–81.

17

Drama and Writing: 'Overcoming the Hurdle of the Blank Page'

Julie Dunn, Annette Harden and Sarah Marino

Introduction

Most educators, across their careers, have faced the challenge of the reluctant writer. With cries of, 'I can't think of anything to write!', these students are generally not struggling with the technical demands of writing, such as spelling, grammar and punctuation, but rather, with their inability to generate ideas worth communicating. Neelands, Booth and Zeigler (1993, p. 13) aptly refer to this experience as the 'hurdle of the blank page', suggesting that dramatic structures such as role provide a useful means of supporting these children and young people 'to take the risk of putting pen to paper'.

The positive impact that drama can have on children's writing has been the focus of a good deal of literature, especially within recent Australian publications (Ewing 2009, 2010; Gibson 2012), with both anecdotal and research-based evidence being offered to support claims of its positive effects. Within this chapter, this evidence will be summarized and extended upon by drawing on the findings of three research projects. Spanning both New Zealand and Australian school contexts, with students ranging in age from 4 to 10 years, each project had its own particular goals and areas of focus. However, what these projects shared was an interest in the connections between drama and the writing process. By examining these studies and their findings, the chapter aims to summarize the benefits that drama pedagogies afforded in terms of supporting children's writing in these contexts, while also identifying the particular features of drama and dramatic play that enabled these benefits. In other words, we aim to articulate how drama activated writing for these children.

Benefits and features – the key literature

One of the most comprehensive and useful lists of the benefits of linking drama and writing has been offered by Joe Winston (2004). Drawing on teacher feedback from a range of projects undertaken in classroom situations, he suggests that the positive effects of drama on writing include improved motivation to write; providing children with substantial ideas and experiences that can be used in their writing; the ability to respond as individuals; increased output of writing in a shorter period of time; richer vocabulary and sentence structures; a stronger sense of audience; and improved empathy for the characters being written about (p. 26).

Recent work by Cremin, Goouch et al. (2006) offers a useful summary in respect to the second area of focus for this chapter – the features of drama that support these benefits. They outline a comprehensive list, built upon understandings developed across two key studies. The first of these studies was a pilot that explored the idea of 'seizing the moment' to write. In this work, they were interested in differences between the quality of children's writing where the genre of the written work was predetermined in advance and set by the teacher, compared to the quality achieved when the participants were given free rein to spontaneously respond to the drama context by selecting their own genres.

As a result, the researchers determined that the participants were more engaged and that the quality of their writing was higher when they were given free choice. Later, during their main study where the 'seize the moment' approach was applied, the team explored the features of drama that seemed to be influencing this enhanced engagement and more effective writing outcomes. This second study revealed that these were: the presence of tension; the degree of engagement; time for incubation which the extended imaginative experiences in the drama and writing allowed; and the strong sense of stance and purpose, gained in part through role adoption, which helped to provide audience and purpose for the writing (pp. 8–15).

Similar benefits and features have been noted by other authors, extending back to Carole Tarlington's work in 1985. She noted that drama provides a meaningful context in which writing can take place (p. 199), with these contexts offering a range of purposes and registers. These include formal and public registers, as well as reflective and personal ones that allow for the affective aspect of learning to be explored. Significantly, she also recognized the importance of what she called 'pressure' in providing the impetus, urgency and motivation for writing to occur, while noting as well that these tensions provide opportunities for strong engagement with the affective domain.

This link between emotion, tension and children's writing has recently been explored by Dunn and Stinson (2012) who argue that it is the intentional provocation of emotion which sets drama work apart from other approaches used in educational contexts. They draw on the work of Courtney (cited in Booth and Martin-Smith 1988), who suggests that it is the link between imagination and emotion that is critical. He claims (p. 71) that 'imagination, by relating emotion and knowledge, brings about an affective – cognitive synthesis; our imagination enables us to both know and feel about dramatic events and to unify these to a new species of knowledge'. In the context of activating children's writing, this affective-cognitive synthesis can be very powerful, generating a range of emotions. These emotions, when coupled with the rich visualizations conjured by the imagination during engagement within dramatic worlds, can be a powerful motivating force, leading to the creation of detailed and high-quality written texts.

Miller and Saxton (2004) have also discussed motivation, describing in their work the responses of a student who continued to write in role even after going home. In response to questions about why he made this choice, he noted that it was drama 'that made me want to write more' (p. 9). Similar commitment has been noted by Macy (2003) who suggests that this occurs because through drama children have a direct and personal experience with what needs to be written (p. 1).

Greenwood (2010) too sees drama as being a 'strong motivator', but notes as well its role as a 'powerful reinforcer'. She believes that as students go through the process of dealing with writing and other tasks within role, the idea that they are actually capable of doing similar tasks in real life is reinforced (p. 127). This notion, which echoes that of 'mantle of the expert', was first flagged by Heathcote (1981) and later by Heathcote and Bolton (1995).

The value of drama as a planning activity in preparation for writing has been investigated by Moore and Caldwell (1993), with their conclusion being that drama gives the writer the chance to 'test out, evaluate, revise and integrate ideas before writing begins', offering a 'more complete form of rehearsal than discussion' (p. 10). Importantly however, Crumpler (2005) reminds us of the dangers of seeing drama work merely as a prewriting activity, arguing instead that the writing should be viewed as 'a component of the drama work and not separate from it' (p. 359).

As noted earlier, Neelands et al. (1993) have considered the relationship between drama and writing, and in particular, the importance of role which takes children 'inside their own stories' (p. 13). McNaughton (1997) suggests that this insider view helps writers develop the personal voice of their character and the ability to 'identify with him/her on an affective as well as a cognitive level', demonstrating a greater use of dialogue, giving variety and interest to the written text and helping 'to give the reader a sense of being witness to the story' (p. 76).

The idea that drama provides authentic situations for writing to occur, despite the imaginary nature of the contexts generated, was investigated by Jasinski Schneider and Jackson (2000), who claim that writing in role gives students the ability to think in a different way and from a range of perspectives about both the forms and the content of their writing. This is supported by the cross-study analysis of children's writing from five classrooms performed by Crumpler and Jasinski Schneider (2002), who found that when students are 'engaged in the reading, writing , thinking, responding process – their *whole being* is engaged' (p. 78).

In the literature examining the relationship between dramatic play and writing, perhaps the most celebrated study has been that of Hall and Robinson (2003) who examined the impact of introducing literacy events around the topic of a garage, provoking children to write for a variety of purposes as part of that play. The findings of this study suggest that this authentic play situation was effective in creating opportunities for written responses, while also providing a strong sense of audience and purpose for children's writing. As with studies on drama and writing, they discovered that across the period of the garage play, a world was created which unified the children in their focus, and facilitated the creation of written texts that were deemed by the participating children to be useful and indeed necessary for their purposes.

In the Scandinavian context, Lindqvist's (1995) pioneering work in developing contexts to promote both play and subsequently writing has also been significant. In this work, adults introduce the children to characters, settings and plots of key stories through the creation of brief interactive performances and play episodes that are designed to stimulate rich, imaginative dramatic play sequences that develop over extended periods and involve children and adults as co-players. Since this work was first published, extensive research has been conducted internationally to explore the possibilities which the creation of these playworlds offer (Marjanovic-Shane, Ferholt et al. 2011), including in relation to the development of young children's emerging literacy. For example, Baumer, Ferholt and Lecusay (2005) found that following participation in a 'playworld' that involved adult/child joint pretence, children aged 5–7 years showed significant improvements in narrative length, coherence and comprehension, although not in linguistic complexity.

Taken together, these studies indicate that one of the major benefits of dramatic structuring by adults is the role it plays in building children's narrative competence, which Feagans and Appelbaum (1986) contend 'is the single most important language ability for success in school' (p. 359). It has two aspects: narrative comprehension (understanding story events and actions as temporally sequenced and causally motivated) and narrative production (the ability to produce longer, more coherent, and more linguistically complex stories) (Baumer et al. 2005; Groth and Darling 2001). Children therefore need to have opportunities to engage with narratives as both producers and consumers, with a range of modes of production and consumption being important as well. Drama and play both offer children and young people the chance to experience narratives in a non-textual form that provides the foundation for later production in written modes.

Set against the background this brief review of the key literature has presented, what do the three studies at the centre of this chapter have to offer in terms of advancing our understanding of the benefits of drama and dramatic play, and the specific features of these forms that facilitate these benefits?

The informing studies

As noted above, three studies inform this discussion. The first of these involved 4- and 5-year-old children in their first year of formal schooling. Here, play, drama and puppetry experiences were facilitated or supported by their classroom teacher who was also the researcher (Harden 2012). These experiences included the modelling of cultural purposes for literacy, the enactment of and innovation on stories, the development of phonemic awareness, drama games, small group improvisations, process drama and child-structured play. The overall goal of this approach was to charge the learning experiences with dramatic elements in order to generate learning where the systematic and explicit introduction of elements of early literacy (such as phonemic awareness) was balanced with dramatic pedagogies. The methodology employed by the teacher/researcher saw her developing a reflective study of her own pedagogical journey and four case studies mapping in detail the progress of individual children across the full school year.

Analysis of the data revealed that this approach was highly effective in supporting these children into early literacy practices. Across the period of the project, they developed as confident, competent, engaged, motivated and productive writers, achieving useful understanding of narrative, role and audience. Alongside these outcomes, their oral confidence and competence improved noticeably, while their skills as dramatists also grew markedly. They became players in worlds which were complex, shared and sustained and in which literacy activities of many types were naturally embedded by them as favoured play pursuits.

The written texts they created included signs to assert their power and ownership, to warn cheeky monkeys about crocodiles in the river and to distract snakes searching for bunnies in burrows. They co-created petitions to a forester begging him not to chop down trees which were the homes of their favourite puppets, they read messages in bottles and letters from trapped friends. They created offices and wrote programs, tickets, shop signs, letters of greeting, friendship and apology, and instruction booklets for fire and safety. Writing was something they wanted to do all the time. In summary, a combination of play and drama generated in them a disposition to write, with this disposition being made possible through a process described as the mediation of expertise – a dynamic process that saw the positioning of the children as expert writers within the dramatic context flow on to all of the literacy contexts they engaged in. Here the contexts created in the drama and play sequences became the conduit not only of literary practices, but also of the dispositions integral to the roles which accompany that practice.

Friendships were also vital in this process of mediation of literacy, with friends being 'significant others' (McNaughton 2003) in the play world, guiding their peers in the creation of written artefacts and keeping the play world alive through their skills as 'master-dramatists' (Creaser 1989).

The second study was conducted in a New Zealand middle primary classroom and involved 9- and 10-year olds (Marino 2012). The site of the research was a school focused on raising student achievement in writing, while the researcher was one of the children's teachers. Implemented across a full school term, the process drama and writing sessions were based around the text '*How to cheat a dragon's curse by Hiccup Horrendous Haddock the Third*' (Cowell 2006). Across the lesson series, the students and teacher worked in a variety of different roles, drawn from the book and developed as part of the drama context. Many of the student roles required them to act as experts – for example, as expert bards and storytellers, while the teacher roles were often ones which required assistance from these experts.

The sessions were video recorded, while journal observations were made by the teacher/researcher and written artefacts were collected. These included samples of writing created by the students in response to and within the drama work. In addition, the students wrote their own reflective journals detailing their thoughts about the drama and writing processes.

The findings of this study confirm and build strongly on the existing literature, but in particular, the work of Cremin et al. (2006). Once again the importance of key elements of drama including role and tension was noted, with the work done by the teacher in managing these elements being crucial. In particular, the study revealed that tension raised the stakes and gave the students a sense that their writing was important, useful and in some cases, essential for those they were writing for.

Allied to this sense of the writing being important was the finding that, irrespective of ability, all children engaged more fully when they understood the purpose of the texts. Interview data from both students and another of their teachers revealed that many of the children had been switched off by the current emphasis on genre-based or 'formulaic' approaches to writing. Instead, they wanted to be able to use a more creative and imaginative approach that drew on their prior knowledge, where their interest and emotions were sparked, and where they felt that what they were writing about mattered and would be important to the person reading it. Drama, they all seemed to agree, offered these kinds of opportunities.

Other findings included the view that drama enhanced motivation, gave the children an emotional involvement with the characters and built on oral language as an essential component of the writing process. In a reciprocal relationship, oral language was enhanced by the drama work while also acting to enhance the written result, with the heightened language used during the in-role frames serving to reinforce the children's status as experts.

Finally, the third study (Dunn and Stinson 2012) involved year one children attending a school in an urban edge Queensland school. The form of the work here consisted only of teacher-structured process drama, unlike study one which also involved young children and included play and puppetry opportunities.

Focused on an original narrative where a selfish young girl captures a 'little person' to keep in a jar as a 'pet', the sequence of drama lessons in focus here was implemented by one visiting researcher while the other documented the action and recorded reflective observations.

Across five extended sessions conducted daily during one school week, the children participated within a dramatic world intentionally infused with a series of teacher-initiated tensions introduced in order to provoke a range of emotional responses. Based on the premise that drama work characterized by deep engagement and high levels of identification with roles or situations is more likely to generate emotion (Dunn et al. 2012), the drama was structured to be as engaging as possible, while providing plenty of opportunities for the children to identify closely with the community of 'little people' and the difficult situation that confronted them. To this end, enrolled as members of the 'council of little people' (a title provided by 1 of the 6-year-old children) the children were required to negotiate the release of their 'kidnapped' citizen. Later in the drama they would also be called upon to use critical and thoughtful reasoning skills to achieve democratic consensus about how best to respond to the 'ransom' request –the granting of a wish.

Analysis of the data emerging from this study revealed that the drama generated strong emotions including concern, determination, frustration, and even anger, with the resultant written texts being reflective of these. In addition, the rich oral language 'rehearsed' within the drama work ensured that the children not only had plenty of ideas for their writing, but also had a good vocabulary to express these ideas. Finally, a clear sense of audience and purpose was apparent in the texts created, with the children drawing on their emotional engagement to produce written materials that clearly expressed their concerns and calls to action.

Benefits and features summarized

When considered together, the findings of the three studies described above serve to reinforce many of the existing claims about the impact of drama pedagogies on the writing process, while also providing some useful additional insights. These findings have been summarized in Tables 17.1 and 17.2, with the first of these (Table 17.1) outlining the benefits of drama and dramatic play as revealed across the three projects. Table 17.2 unpacks the specific features of these forms that were found to be most significant in activating these outcomes. Importantly,

Table 17.1 Summary of benefits

Summary of benefits
Enhanced motivation to write
Greater quality in terms of cohesiveness, narrative structure, vocabulary, and character development
Quantity of writing increased, especially among reluctant writers
More diverse and more complex registers used
Keener identification with the characters and a stronger sense of empathy revealed

Table 17.2 Summary of features of drama that achieve these benefits

Summary of the features of drama that achieve these benefits
The narrative structure of drama work, including its use of roles, setting, time and place has a significant effect on the development of children's narrative competence which in turn, positively influences writing.
Through the adoption of multiple roles, children are able to identify with individual characters while also gaining an enhanced appreciation of multiple perspectives.
Again through role, the teacher is able to model both language and register, supporting children's ability to apply these in their writing.
Role provides children with the chance to try out the status of the expert writer. This experience flows back into their out of role writing, giving them greater confidence even when writing is not associated with drama.
Through the careful management of tension, the teacher is able to provoke the emotions of the children – emotions that motivate writing.
The dramatic contexts generated by drama create audience and purpose for the written texts children create.
The imaginations of the participants are stimulated and a sense of 'realness' is generated. This sense of realness makes the task of writing easier – especially in creating descriptions.
Drama creates a rehearsal for writing, with the oral language preceding the writing process being critical to most aspects of the written task.
The open-ended nature of drama work means that diverse genres can be stimulated from one experience.
Peer support and group collaboration, essential for play and drama, carries over to the writing process meaning that children often scaffold the success of others.

these summaries align very closely with those previously outlined in an earlier section of this chapter.

The limitations of this chapter mean that there is insufficient space to explore in detail key data from across the three studies that underpins these findings. However, in the section below, examples drawn from the three data sets are offered as support. Including extracts from interviews with the children, teacher and student reflective journals, and of course, written artefacts created during and in response to the drama work, these materials will focus mainly on the findings shown in the second table, relating to how drama and play activate learning.

The features revealed by the three projects

Study one, involving the youngest children across these three research projects, provides useful examples relating to the last of the features noted in Table 17.2 – how drama encourages collaboration and peer support. In this case, the children's collaborations supported the development of emergent written literacy, with more confident players and writers supporting and scaffolding the work of peers. For example, within one of the play sessions described in this preparatory year study, James guided Martin in creating hand icons and then dotted out the outline to his name so that his play partner could create an ownership sign for their shared police office play space. In another, Lucy kept a play sequence about a magic garden alive by reliving a moment of tension from the teacher facilitated drama. Her goal in doing this was to draw others back to a climactic moment of that sequence. In response, James came into the dramatic world she had re-established and became a co-constructor of a hotel for teddies visiting the magic garden. During the play, Lucy needed a sign for her hotel and so as she composed it, James wrote it. Together with Lucy's message of 'Hotel is open', James included the hand icon Martin had helped him with in a previous play session – to warn others not to destroy their building. Later he added a 'pool' sign as the hotel was extended into the magic garden.

In another session, Sally, a competent and imaginative player, assisted Edward's awareness of print by creating a message in a bottle as they played together in an underwater world. He recognized the initial sound of her name and began to realize that individual words in print had meaning. This enabled him to connect reading with writing. The guided drama stimulus had included teacher-generated messages between a fish trapped in a bottle and his friend Ollie the Octopus.

This early years study also highlights the importance of role taking. In one example, the teacher/researcher showed the children how to add 'Don't touch' signs to their carefully constructed play spaces, but Edward, as police officer, wanted a stronger message so enlisted the teacher/researcher's help to make a sign saying $100 fine. The next day in the play, James joined Edward in his role as a high ranking official of the law. From within this role James worked on his own to create a sign which read '$100 to the judge' (spelt gag). Here the combination of role and teacher scaffolding had given these children a context to write within, a purpose for the writing and perhaps most importantly the willingness to take a risk.

Role-taking continued to be a powerful incentive for Edward's writing as the year progressed, with this young boy constantly adopting roles as powerful rescuers. In one particular session some 6 months later, after the dramatic rescue of a cat, performed by children in role as fire officers, Edward would write: 'A cat is stuck up in the tree. A fireman comes to rescue the cat. A ladder comes up to the cat. The little cat is safe.'

The importance of the play time as a space for children to try out new competencies was illustrated again and again. From within these, Lucy would write 'sorry' notes to the three bears as Goldilocks, James would create police 'details' after a day of police 'duties', Martin would practice signs for animal cages in the zoo he and James constructed, while he, James, Lucy and others would label fossil remains at a museum after a day spent in role as archaeologists within a teacher facilitated drama.

The older children from the second study offer different perspectives on how drama supports writing, with their interviews providing some of the most revealing insights. For example, one student notes that writing in role is not the same as when you are doing *'normal writing'*, suggesting that this is because in drama *'whatever thing you think can be real in your mind'*.

Others from this New Zealand study expressed views about how drama empowered them to write more effectively by elevating their status, positioning them as someone who is an expert writer. Lydia, for example, claimed: *'I love writing in role 'cause it kind of makes me feel different, 'cause you kind of get so into character that you feel like you're that person'*. She then went on to explain that she doesn't normally like writing, but when she writes in role, *'it's kind of like you're creating this new person that likes writing'*.

An awareness of audience and purpose generated as a result of tension in the drama work is also explicitly identified by these older children. Xavier, for example, reported:

> When I write in role it's more fun than other writing because it's fun to have a reason to do the writing. The reason we had to write a recipe was because whoever got stung by the Venomous Vorpent would die and I was under pressure so I knew I had

to write the recipe down quickly or else the person who got stung by the Venomous
Vorpent would die.

Brendan's writing progress, built upon his work in role, is also of interest. In his first attempt at creating a diary entry for the character called Fishlegs, he wrote:

Hi, my name is Fishlegs. One day I went Berserk on Mount Villany. I attacked the Hysterics

After his work in role, however, he was able to offer a much more expanded entry:

Dear diary,
   Why did I attack the Hysterics today, with Gobber the Belch on the Pirate training group? There I was with my friend Hiccup and Toothless on Mount Villany. It was scary because I was attacking Norbert the Nutjob. I don't normally attack Norbert the Nutjob. I should of (sic) hide away from him . . .

This second draft, like those of the students in McNaughton (1997) and Jasinski Schneider and Jackson's (2000) research, has a stronger emotional pull to it, providing a sense of how the character felt about the situation that he had been in.

Finally, the writing samples created by the year one children in the third research project offer different insights. In the first of these, one child's repeated use of the words 'we will' seem to be an intentional device aimed at emphasizing his defiance as a 'little person' towards the threat of further 'kidnapping' attempts by the child intent on collecting 'pets'. Here role, identification and emotion seem to have combined to support the development of a written text that effectively presents his views about whether or not the community of 'little people' should continue with the tradition of parading:

we will do the prayed tmorrow. We will bett them. We will be ok tmorrow.
   (We will do the parade tomorrow. We will beat them. We will be ok tomorrow).

Later in the drama, another child's writing offers support for the notion that the oral language used in drama provides opportunities to rehearse the vocabulary necessary for written texts. Here he draws upon the keen understanding of letter-sound relationships that his classroom teacher has created through a systematic programme of phonic awareness, to create a rescue plan that includes complex words such as reinforcement, royal and parade that had previously been used repeatedly during a heated meeting of the little people.

Tmoro we wil hava plan Salee had a plan the litl pep had a plan too the ledr macs reaformis for rool grds

(Tomorrow we will have a plan. Sally had a plan. The little people had a plan too. The leader makes reinforcement for royal guards).

Finally, the intentional provocation of emotion within the drama appears to have had an impact on the 5 year old author of the extract below that seems to suggest strong identification with and empathy for the plight of the victim of the 'kidnapping'. Her plea is an urgent one:

Dear sally cen we plis have our litll girl bac as she is a put of our kmati and we love her and we wot hir bac.

(Dear Sally, Can we please have out little girl back as she is part of our community and we love her so and we want her back.)

Conclusion

Further research into the power of drama to activate writing is needed. This chapter has drawn together some of what is already known, while offering a brief summary of the findings from three studies to extend on this knowledge; however, given the current international emphasis on the measurement of and benchmarking in written literacy, researchers within the field of drama interested in children's literacy need to do more. For example, collaborative, large scale, international studies are needed to determine if the results generated by the relatively small scale, local studies presented here and in the literature, might be replicated in the larger ones. Such studies need to be longitudinal in design, for as Annette Harden has discovered through the research reported in this chapter, the impact of play and drama on children's writing can be significant when the approach is continued across one full year.

In the meantime, the studies described here have suggested that the 'hurdle of the blank page' need not be an obstacle to children's success as writers, for the structures, strategies and elements of drama, when carefully managed, seem to provide the 'leg up' many children need to build their confidence and commitment. Even if, like Lydia, some of these children are initially just pretending to be people who like to write, the hope is that eventually this pretence will become a reality.

References

Baumer, S., Ferholt, B., and Lecusay, R. (2005), 'Promoting Narrative Competence through adult-child joint pretense: Lessons from the Scandinavian Educational Practice of Playworld'. *Cognitive Development*, 20, (4), 576–90.

Booth, D. and Martin-Smith, A. (eds) (1988), *Re-cognizing Richard Courtney: Selected Writings on Drama and Education*. Ontario: Pembroke.

Booth, D. and Neelands, J. (eds) (1998), *Writing in Role: Classroom Projects Connecting Writing and Drama*. Hamilton, ON, Canada: Caliburn Enterprises.

Cowell, C. (2006), *How to Cheat a Dragon's Curse by Hiccup Horrendous Haddock III*, translated from the Old Norse by Cressida Cowell. London, England: Hodder's Children's Books.

Creaser, B. (1989), 'An examination of the four-year-old master dramatist'. *International Journal of Early Childhood Education*, 21, 55–68.

Cremin, T., Goouch, K., Blakemore, L., Goff, E., and Macdonald, R. (2006), 'Connecting drama and writing: Seizing the moment to write'. *Research in Drama Education*, 11, (3), 273–91. doi: 10.1080/13569780600900636.

Crumpler, T. P. (2005), 'The role of educational drama in the composing processes of young writers'. *Research in Drama Education: The Journal of Applied Theatre and Performance*, 10, (3), 357–63. doi: 10.1080/13569780500276103.

Crumpler, T. and Jasinski Schneider, J. (2002), 'Writing with their whole being: A cross study analysis of children's writing from five classrooms using process drama'. *Research in Drama Education: The Journal of Applied Theatre and Performance*, 7, (1), 61–79. doi: 10.1080/13569780120113148.

Dunn, J., Bundy, P., and Stinson, P. (2012), *Exploring Emotion in Process Drama*. Paper presented at the 7th International Drama in Education Research Institute, Limerick, Ireland, 10–15 July.

Dunn, J. and Stinson, M. (2012), 'Learning through emotion: Moving the affective in from the margins'. *International Journal of Early Childhood*, 44, (2), 203–18.

Ewing, R. (2009), 'Creating imaginative possibilities in K-6 English', in J. Manuel, P. Brock, D. Carter and W. Sawyer (eds), *Imagination, Innovation, Creativity: Revisioning English Education*. Sydney: Phoenix.

—(2010), *The Arts and Australian Education: Realising Potential*. Camberwell, Victoria: Australian Council for Educational Research.

Feagans, L. and Applebaum, M. (1986), 'Validation of language subtypes in learning disabled children'. *Journal of Experimental Psychology*, 78, 358–64.

Gibson, R. (2012), *Evaluation of School Drama 2010*. Sydney: University of Sydney.

Greenwood, J. (2010), 'Playing with text', in J. Fletcher, F. Parkhill and G. Gillon (eds), *Motivating Literacy Learners in Today's World*. Wellington, New Zealand: NZCER Press, pp. 121–31.

Groth, L. and Darling, L. (2001), 'Playing "inside" stories', in A. Göncü and E. Klein (eds), *Children in Play, Story and School*. New York: Guildford Press, pp. 220–37.

Hall, N. and Robinson, A. (2003), *Exploring Writing and Play in the Early Years*, 2nd edn. London: David Fulton.

Harden, A. (2012), *Children Down-Under Play with Literacy: A Dramatic Story*. Paper presented at the 7th International Drama in Education Research Institute, Limerick, Ireland, 10–15 July.

Heathcote, D. (1981), 'Drama as education', in N. McCaslin (ed.), *Children and Drama*, 2nd edn. New York, NY: Longman, pp. 78–90.

Heathcote, D. and Bolton, G. (1995), *Drama for Learning: Dorothy Heathcote's Mantle of the Expert Approach to Education*. Portsmouth, NH: Heinemann.

Jasinski Schneider, J. and Jackson, S. A. W. (2000), 'Process drama: A special space and place for writing'. *The Reading Teacher*, 54, (1), 38–51.

Lindqvist, G. (1995), *The Aesthetics of Play: A Didactic Study of Play and Culture in Preschools*. Uppsala Studies in Education, Uppsala University.

Macy, L. (2003), 'Drama and writing: Complementary meaning making processes'. *Language & Literacy*, 5, (2). Retrieved from http://www.langandlit.ualberta.ca/Fall2003/macy.html

Marino, S. (2012), *"It's easy to imagine . . . because you've been there!" – A Case Study of Drama as a Pedagogy for Writing in One New Zealand Classroom*. Unpublished Masters thesis, Griffith University, Brisbane.

Marjanovic-Shane, A., Ferholt, B., Miyazaki, K., Nilsson, M., Rainio, A., Hakkarainen, P., Pesic, M., and Beljanski-Ristic, L. (2011), 'Playwords – an art of development', in C. Lobman and B. O'Neill (eds), *Play and Performance. Play & Culture Series*, vol. 11. Lanham, Maryland: University Press of America, pp. 3–32.

McNaughton, M. J. (1997), 'Drama and children's writing: A study of the influence of drama on the imaginative writing of primary school children'. *Research in Drama Education: The Journal of Applied Theatre and Performance*, 2, (1), 55–86. doi: 10.1080/1356978970020105.

McNaughton, S. (2003), *Meeting of Minds*. New Zealand: Learning Media.

Miller, C. and Saxton, J. (2004), *Into the Story – Language in Action through Drama*. Portsmouth, NH: Heinemann.

Moore, B. H. and Caldwell, H. (1993), 'Drama and drawing for narrative writing in primary grades'. *The Journal of Educational Research*, 87, (2), 100–10. Retrieved from http://www.jstor.org/stable/27541905

Neelands, J., Booth, D., and Ziegler, S. (1993), *Writing in Imagined Contexts: Research into Drama-influenced Writing*. ERIC Document Reproduction Service No. ED 255 576.

Tarlington, C. (1985), '"Dear Mr Piper . . .": Using drama to create context for children's writing'. *Theory into Practice*, 24, (3), 199–204. doi:10.1080/00405848509543173.

Winston, J. (2004), *Drama and English at the Heart of the Curriculum: Primary and Middle Years*. London, England: David Fulton.

18

Drama and Science: An Unlikely Partnership for Inquiry

Christine D. Warner

Introduction

Educators often make assumptions that all children and young adults entering the classroom know the meaning of the word *science* and the reasons they study it in school. Many teachers discover, though, that teaching scientific inquiry for novice students can be both intimidating and difficult. This is especially true for children and/or young adults who come to school having had little exposure to science. Many educators and scholars will agree that for student inquiry to be authentic, it must be meaningful, in that learners feel a personal connection with the purpose, content and processes of the inquiry (Warner and Andersen 2004).

Both U.S. national as well as international standards and recent calls for reform in science education reflect remarkable consistency in what it means *to do* science (American Association for the Advancement of Science 2006). Learning *to do* science and to write like a scientist is central to learning the processes of mainstream science inquiry in the science classroom (Halliday and Martin 1993; Lee 1999; Lemke 1990). Since the National Research Council (NRC) reaffirmed inquiry as the guiding theme for science education reform in the past decade (National Research Council (NRC) 2006, 2010), research has continually revealed that science teachers face many dilemmas in this pursuit (Anderson 2002, 2007). In fact, teacher and student roles and work change as they engage in classroom inquiry. As part of these changes, teachers must modify how they interact with their students because inquiry teaching requires non-traditional interactions. Typically, in guided inquiry the students are the ones directing the science investigation, while the teacher simply facilitates the area of research. Unfortunately, much research indicates that many teachers simply do not have the knowledge, skills or theoretical framework to interact with students in ways that promote rather than prevent inquiry in the classroom (Anderson 2007). Often, teachers do not have a clear understanding of the new roles required of them (Davis et al. 2006; Simmons et al. 1999). Furthermore, teachers are uncertain about how to appropriately respond to students' questions and facilitate science inquiry (Furtak 2006).

In response to these dilemmas, primary and secondary educators have begun to look for research-based methodologies that establish 'suitable situations for inquiry' (Anderson 2007; Renk 1993). By using process drama as a method of teaching and learning, students are involved in fictionalized, unscripted and spontaneous dramatic scenes while also engaging in the actual and authentic process of scientific inquiry. This method of teaching promotes constructivist, contextual learning that structures an inquiry-based learning experience. By recasting students in the role of 'expert inquirers' committed to group construction of knowledge, the drama method provides a context that keenly engages students in the inquiry process.

Previous studies focusing on drama in education demonstrate that the process of student engagement in learning involves a participant going beyond causal association with an event or inquiry (see Morgan and Saxton 1991; Warner 1997, 2004). The process of engaging is not merely acquiring content knowledge, but also making an investment in formulating personal questions that lead to more meaningful knowledge. This chapter will focus on how drama aligns itself to science through the processes of inquiry.

Scientific inquiry

Scientific inquiry refers to the ways in which scientists study the natural world (NRC 2006, 2010). When children and young adults inquire, they investigate either a question or problem deemed worthy of study by either themselves or someone else, usually the teacher. They use the processes of scientific inquiry to conduct their investigations. The end result of an inquiry is some sort of a conclusion. Any kind of inquiry involves seeking information, which is not the same as seeking the 'right' answer.

Science education standards and research literature use inquiry in two senses. The first views inquiry in the classroom as an investigative process. The elements that are common to most views of student inquiry include:

- Asking meaningful questions
- Designing the investigation
- Obtaining the evidence
- Deciphering from fact and theory in order to draw conclusions.

If students are engaged in asking questions and pursuing investigations to address those questions, then inquiry takes place (Warner and Andersen 2004).

This view of inquiry forms the basis for the second category of inquiry – formal scientific method. Formal scientific method, with its hypotheses and types of variables and statistical interpretations of data, can be intimidating to the novice. The discourse around the scientific method is odd and stilted to the uninitiated because it represents the limits the method places on unrestricted inquiry in the interest of systematic, replicable observations.

The scientific process begins with a question and then proceeds to a hypothesis which is kind of a story. These types of stories have been told since the beginning of human civilization in the form of myths, religious beliefs and cultural tales. Ancient humans wanted to know what causes rain and how the stars appear in the sky. They observed the world around them and created stories to account for what they saw and experienced. Scientific process consists of a careful choosing of a story and then testing it by predicting certain points that could only happen if the story were true and then observing successive events. While a hypothesis might not sound like a story, as it is often a simple statement, the statement represents the series of events that give rise to it.

Narrative inquiry

Narrative inquiry is a form of inquiry associated with qualitative research practices but was additionally developed for the field of cognition and knowledge management. This type of inquiry focuses on the organization of human knowledge as more than merely the collection and processing of data (Lave 1988). It also implies that knowledge itself is valuable and noteworthy, even if known by only one person. Narrative inquiry is a powerful tool in the transfer or sharing of knowledge; a tool that is bound to cognitive issues of memory, both constructed and perceived (Rogoff 1990). The narrative inquiry approach captures the emotion of the moment described, rendering the event active rather than passive and infused with the latent meaning being communicated by the teller. The narrative-inquiry method accepts the idea that knowledge can be held in stories that can be relayed, stored and retrieved.

Research has always made a distinction between scientific inquiry and narrative inquiry, and though each area does have distinct differences, narrative inquiry and scientific inquiry share at least four major stages, as Table 18.1 shows:

Table 18.1 Shared processes between narrative inquiry and scientific inquiry

	Narrative inquiry	Scientific inquiry
Process 1 Questioning	Asking questions about the prospective narrative.	Asking personally and scientifically meaningful questions
	Suggested process:	Suggested process:
	Questioning personal story; Questioning the narrative to be constructed; Research (from classroom/ reading experiences and other narrative sources, e.g. the library)	Library research
Process 2 Designing	Narrative construction	Designing the investigation
	Suggested process:	Suggested process:
	Isolating parts of the narrative; Anticipating what will happen	Isolating variables
Process 3 Collecting	Collecting narrative	Obtaining evidence
	Suggested process:	Suggested process:
	Describe and collect pieces of the narrative	Laboratory technique
Process 4 Interpreting	Selecting episodes of the narrative	Interpreting the evidence
	Suggested process:	Suggested process:
	Constructing and reconstructing narrative episodes for the purpose of constructing a meaningful narrative	Separating theory from evidence

It is important to note that the inquiry process, whether scientific or narrative, does not take place linearly; it is a process that constantly regenerates throughout the investigation (Warner and Andersen 2004).

Process drama and inquiry

At first glance, drama seems antithetical to science learning that appears initially to focus on retaining facts. Yet today's science teachers want students to understand by doing so they can construct their knowledge using logical processes, rather than simply memorizing a collection of facts (Warner and Erchick 2006). Process drama methodologies offer important alternate avenues for learning through inquiry and these have been explored by key theorists and practitioners from the field (Heathcote and Bolton 1995; O'Neill 1995; Wilhelm and Edmiston 2000; Warner and Erchick 2006). They have noted that the process allows for broad flexibility in its application, with key defining elements that make it appropriate for creating 'suitable' situations for inquiry. First, the frame of drama embeds knowledge into the relationship between context and personal experience. Second, students can never be mere receivers who are told about inquiry and knowledge. Instead, participants have a responsibility to be engaged with the drama. This responsibility is not to knowledge itself, although that is what the students are indirectly acquiring, but rather to the endeavour they have undertaken (Heathcote and Bolton 1995). Third several pieces of information emerges from the context iguidelines; regulations; theories; formulas; pre-existing findings and artefacts, all of which are to be questioned. This is an active, urgent and purposeful view of learning, in which knowledge is operated on, not merely taken in. Fourth, the process of drama facilitates students' pursuits of their own research agendas by creating investigative (thinking) environments where they can ask their own questions, thereby engaging students in authentic inquiry and learning (Heathcote and Bolton 1995).

Structuring drama for science inquiry

As a means to better understand the new roles required of science teachers who are enacting inquiry, researchers have examined the practice of expert teachers who have successfully enacted self-designed inquiry curricula (e.g. Crawford 2000; Crawford et al. 1999; Roth 1994; Roth and Bowen 1995). These studies are useful because they provide insights into the new roles that teachers and students must assume in the inquiry classroom. However, none of these studies incorporated a process of drama approach that contextualized 'roles.' Instead, some of these studies utilized 'role-play' as simply an opportunity to pretend and dialogue as 'experts' in the field of science.

What separates process drama from these other approaches is that it constructs a frame around the lesson that also allows the teacher to assume an alternative role. This role has the potential to place the student in the position of being 'the one who has some information that is enough to inquire about more' or the 'expert.' The power of the communication of knowledge is invested within the class; the teacher does not assume the role of the main communicant. Instead, the traditional role of the teacher as giver of information is relinquished in favour of becoming a member of the learning community and sharing in the group construction of knowledge. The role of the teacher switches from the 'giver' of knowledge to the 'enabler' of knowledge acquisition.

In developing process dramas for learning, teachers create a series of *frames* or scenarios that contextualize the role-play in order to engage in the act of inquiry. Each frame has a possible group of expert roles for students, a teacher role and some kind of problem, conflict or inquiry, which students will agree to solve. The teacher is not limited to staying within a single frame, but can string together a series of episodic scenarios that can incorporate the different stages of the shared inquiry for the purpose of a shared learning experience. In her book *Drama Worlds*, Cecily O'Neill (1995) described the episodic organization of process drama; it instantly entails structure because it implies a more complex relationship between parts of the work than do the linear connections of sequence or narrative where the segments of the work are strung together like beads on a string rather than part of a web of meaning.

Additionally, innovator Dorothy Heathcote identified the *mantle of the expert* as a dramatic investigative method of teaching that embodies experts committed to an enterprise. Not only does the mantle of the expert support student engagement through drama, but it is also essential to the learning that takes place through the process of doing drama. The mantle of the expert is based on the belief that children and young adults learn best if they feel more like an expert in a particular field rather than a pupil, empowering them through purposeful dramatic frames. It gives students of all ages the opportunity to learn together to find solutions to problems, discuss how they will proceed and create their own path through learning. As experts, children take on the role of someone who has a degree of knowledge and understanding in an area, but who needs to work on the problem with peers to develop the additional skills required to solve this particular problem.

The idea of students seeing themselves as experts in their roles influences their learning in positive ways. Cognitive psychologists have characterized the components of *expertise thinking* for many years. According to Bereiter and Scardamalia (1993), expertise thinking is a venture beyond natural abilities. A universal characteristic of expertise thinkers is a knack for defying ordinary rules of reasoning. In young children and young adults, studies suggest that the use of deep-planning, multitask strategies in classroom problem solving facilitates expertise thinking and learning rather than having students find a best-fit strategy to solve an area of inquiry (Rogoff 1990).

The inquiring 'role'

When used as a method for inquiry-based lessons, the mantle of the expert empowers students to take themselves seriously and learn effectively within that role. An example of this is a second-grade science class of students transitioning into expert scientists in the context of a zoo. The drama facilitator begins the inquiry-based drama by explaining the subject of the inquiry. The teacher then transitions into the role of Zookeeper, and in doing so, begins to build belief in the roles and frame of the drama.

> Zookeeper (teacher-in-role): I want to thank all of you here for leaving the other important research projects you have to be here with us to help and guide us with this latest challenge we have had here at the zoo. And maybe this isn't a problem . . . I mean . . . well, you tell us. We have an exciting opportunity here at the zoo. A very generous benefactor has donated an enormous number of snails. Since we have never had snails here at the zoo, we are wondering if we have enough knowledge to care for them.
> Tom (second grader): Excuse me, but have you ever taken care of snails before?
> Zookeeper: No and I am sorry, what is your name? You are Professor . . .?
> Tom: [pause] uh Professor Tom.
> Zookeeper: Thank you, Professor Tom.
> Esther (second grader): Do you know anything about snails?
> Zookeeper: You are Professor . . . ?
> Professor Esther: Professor Esther
> Zookeeper: Thank you, Professor Esther. Nothing, we know nothing about snails. Since you [referring to 2nd graders] are all expert zoologists, we are hoping that you could give some help to us [other role-playing zookeepers] to learn

about the snails. I realize that you have other research projects, but you do have the means and the method to conduct scientific investigations that will yield information that we will find useful (The teacher in role is the motivator, learner, and guide).

Professor Esther: I have some experience with snails. It is my science experiment right now.

Professor Tom: I do, too. I think you have a problem [referring to the Zookeeper]. Don't you think they have a problem [refers to 2nd grade classmates and 2nd grade students agree]?

Zookeeper: What do you think our problem is?

Professor Anna: You don't know how to take care of snails. They can all die and then children can't see them at the zoo. That's a problem.

Zookeeper: Can you, as experts in your field, advise us about these snails? (learner, guide)

Professor Tanya: Yes we can, but we have to test them.

Professor Tom: The question is, what do you need to know so that you can take care of the snails?

Not only is the teacher-in-role shifting between teaching roles, but also the students were beginning to initiate their own direction and means of the scientific inquiry. D.W. Smithenry (2009), in an important study in which he examined the interaction of a role-playing teacher in a scientific inquiry-based lesson with elementary school children, noted that the teacher initiated 39 per cent of the interactions while the students initiated 61 per cent of them. Clearly, the example of the drama dialogue demonstrates that not only are the interactions of the teacher different than a typical classroom lesson but the students initiate more than half of the interactions.

Framed expertise: A case study

Recently, I completed a year-long study involving 19 seventh-grade students and a team of teachers who were using a process drama as an inquiry approach within integrated learning. This cross-disciplinary work was based on the young adult book by Lois Lowry entitled *The Giver*. *The Giver* is a novel in which a boy inhabits a seemingly ideal world that is void of conflict, poverty, unemployment, divorce, injustice, racial tension and inequality. To promote pure justice, virtually all differences have been wiped out. This society's existence depends on 'sameness.' Since The Giver incorporates with in its story, science and mathematical concepts such as the control of DNA in order to produce all 'brown-eyed children' as well as the mathematical concept of probability, in order to examine the probability of genetics. The teaching team agreed to use *The Giver* as the year-long premise as it could easily encompass many classroom objectives across the curriculum, including the integration of mathematical probability along with genetics and ethics in science.

Narrative inquiry is commonly associated with the use of a process drama, and drama often takes on narrative form. However, a finding of this study suggested that by constructing a different frame of the drama to incorporate scientific inquiry components, certain aspects of drama can facilitate both types of inquiries adequately. This finding suggests that when one inquiry-based drama frame within a structured process drama was strategically placed, it enabled and supported full and authentic inquiry. The identified frame is labelled *frame expertise* (Warner 2004), where the 'frame' is exclusively structured to encompass both narrative and scientific inquiry. Furthermore, students, while engaged in the inquiry-based frame, exhibited characteristics similar to those of expertize thinkers. It is important to note that expertise thinking is not knowledge based. Instead, when expertise thinkers agree on an inquiry, they are able to solve multiple problems using highly diverse problem-solving strategies. Frame expertise seems to enhance this type of thinking in participants and is successful in whatever inquiry-based context the teacher chooses to construct.

Several different sets of structured process drama were designed and utilized; specifically, the frame expertise was constructed so that the students took on the role of inquirers examining a recently discovered artefact from a community that no longer exists. Prior to this lesson, students were asked to read the book, and engage in various drama experiences in their Language Arts class. Concurrently, the mathematics and science educators each conducted separate classroom experiences both with and without drama, in which students learned the nature of scientific inquiry and the properties of probability. Table 18.2 shows a sample of the frame expertise dramas that took place during the series of integrated classroom experiences. The table highlights how frame expertise supports the four characteristics of narrative enquiry and scientific inquiry.

Since the above lesson is not a scripted scenario, the hypothesis, laboratory technique and outcomes are all student directed. The teacher-in-role is only acting as a facilitator who is keeping the process of the inquiry focused. However, this learning experience empowered the students to take responsibility for their learning, to use a variety of thinking processes to gather information from diverse

Table 18.2 Scientific enquiry and narrative inquiry process through drama

Episodes	Drama/Frame expertise elements
Process 1 – Questioning	**Process 1**
The teacher takes on the role of an archaeological site supervisor and informs the students that a recently discovered artefact from the archaeological site they have been working on has been found.	This frame is set immediately, and this moves the students from a schoolroom world to an as-if virtual world.
Teacher-in-Role (Archaeological Site Supervisor): 'Good afternoon. Thank you so much for agreeing to meet with me to discuss your recent findings and progress on this important archaeological site.'	While the teacher-in-role is talking to the students and building belief in the virtual world, the students are invited to take on the role of anthropologists engaged in researching a society that at one time flourished but no longer exists.
Processes 1 and 2 – Questioning and Designing	**Processes 1 and 2**
The role-playing teacher asks the now role-playing archaeologist students their impressions of the work they have done on the site so far. A discussion unfolds with the role-playing students verbalizing their impressions and particular findings of the site. Many role-playing students describe artefacts they have found that were directly discussed in the book *The Giver*.	This enables the role-playing anthropologists to access from previous experience and knowledge acquired in previous drama/reading experiences. A part of this prior knowledge involves recalling and reviewing the events and details that were included in the novel *The Giver*. Research
For example:	
'It seems to me that all the children wore the same clothing. I have found numerous pieces of clothing that look all the same. Color, style, etc.'	Through this discussion the teacher-in-role is signalling to the students-in-role that they are the experts and only they can obtain the knowledge. This is isolating variables and parts of the narrative.
'Similar to what my colleague has found, I, too, have found many bicycles that are the same style and color.'	
The teacher responds in an interested and positive way to each contribution, often seeking more information to further the discussion.	

Table 18.2 (Continued)

Episodes	Drama/Frame expertise elements
The Artefact	
Teacher-in-Role (Archaeological Site Supervisor):	
'Many of you were invited to this site because each of you brings your own research expertise to this significant archaeological site. I now must ask for you to collaborate and combine your skills with others in this field of study which is an archeological scientific area of interest.'	At this point the teacher has turned over the potential for inquiry over to the students. (This is isolating variables and narrative continues.)
'Recently, another artifact has been brought to us by a source outside our established research team. *I don't know anything about the person who brought this artifact to our attention or about the artifact itself. I am not even sure this artifact belongs to this site or not.*' 'This is for you to decide. Are you ready to see the artifact?'	The teacher-in-role is introducing the tension into the frame expertise and, as a result, is opening the door to inquiry. Students must agree that this is a problem and an inquiry they choose to explore.
Process 2 – Designing	**Process 2**
The artefact is presented in the form of incomplete documents that represent 50 years of recorded civilization of this particular archaeological community. The documents contain detailed population data in addition to notes on rituals and terms with no definitions.	Tension is the result of contrast and, in order to make the tension work, it must be left to chance. The tension is fuelled by the inquiry.
These documents provide insight into birthrate, gender, eye, hair and skin colour, cultural effects and environmental conditions.	The role-playing students identify two points of inquiry.
Through classroom discussion, the collective problem with the artefacts is identified by the role-playing students. The problems they choose to address are: • Based on previous knowledge about this site, does this artefact belong to this archaeological site?	With the identification of the inquiry, students are agreeing on the problem and begin to focus on their inquiry.

Table 18.2 (Continued)

Episodes	Drama/Frame expertise elements
• Each year an even number of children were born: 50 boys and 50 girls. • For every three brown-eyed children born, there was one blue-eyed child.	The role-playing expert students are presented with the documents and begin to discuss in small groups the methods of inquiry or scientific tools needed to obtain the knowledge.
Process 2 – Designing	**Process 2**
After the questions and problem are defined and agreed upon, the teacher in teacher-in-role asks students what they think the answers to these questions might be: 'At this point can you tell me what you think might be the most important finding in these documents? Of course, because your inquiry is just beginning, I understand your perception might be superficial.'	The teacher-in-role is asking the students to develop a hypothesis.
Process 3 – Collecting	**Process 3**
Through careful questioning and discussion, the students identify areas of inquiry and develop the questions: • What is the probability that if there are births that the community is keeping with the 50/50 ratio boys and girls? • Based on class findings, how is this colony making the numbers work to show that there is a 50/50 ratio of boys and girls in this community?	The role-playing students generate the inquiry questions. By generating the questions, the role-playing students begin to discuss and decide scientific tools (e.g. laboratory technique, collecting pieces of narrative) that will help them answer their inquiry.
Process 3 – Collecting	**Process 3**
While in groups, anthropologists decide how to represent their work as they begin to collect the data.	The necessary information needs to be recorded and the role-playing students decide how they will remember the data they will collect.
Process 3 – Collecting	**Process 3**
Anthropologists decide that these comprise the information and tools they need to further their inquiry: • Document analysis • Probability • DNA genetic script	Role-playing anthropologists begin to discuss and list inquiry tools they will employ. Obtaining and collecting the evidence

Table 18.2 (Continued)

Episodes	Drama/Frame expertise elements
Processes 2 and 3 – Designing/ Collecting	**Processes 2 and 3**
Once the role-playing anthropologists decide which tools they will use, they begin to collect data from the artefact and represent it. Several suggest using tools they have used in past, successful inquiry projects.	The finding and recording process is carried out on a large sheet of paper or blackboard. One group suggests using the probability test used in a previous class.
Process 4 – Interpreting	**Process 4**
Anthropologists separate theory and evidence according to the research method chosen. The class agrees that the best forum to present these findings is at an international research forum for anthropologists. As a result of the forum, implications for further inquiry are developed. Example: How did this society change the genetic stripping, and what effect did it have on the society?	To authenticate their findings, the role-playing students will share the information with the rest of the class. At this point, the students test, reject the illogical and verify the logic of their findings. Each group will defend its findings. Those students who are not presenting their findings will act as fellow anthropologists who question the validity and authenticity of the conclusions each group presents.
Process 4 – Interpreting Conclusion	**Process 4**
The historian site supervisor/teacher will remind the anthropologists that their findings will reflect history.	The role-playing students sequenced their data, separated the data into what is factual and what may only be theory, which is based on their findings from the probability tests, information developed through the inquiry and what they know and remember from the text. The role-playing students decide how they will represent their work in a way that history can make sense of it. In this version the students chose to continue their role play by planning a 'conference' in order to present their findings.
Process 4 – Interpretation and Reflection	**Process 4**
This is the last episode and a crucial part of the lesson. New frame: Gathering 30 years later, the role-playing anthropologists look back on their work and discuss how it influenced others' work and how society has reacted to it.	This activity focuses on the past and the conclusions of the anthropologists' work. Through discussion, the previous inquiry is analyzed, and the role-playing students engage in 'thinking about their thinking' (Andersen 2002, p. 17).

Table 18.2 (Continued)

Episodes	Drama/Frame expertise elements
Process 1 – Questioning: New Inquiry	**Process 1: New Inquiry**
Both teacher and students come out of role.	Through questioning by the teacher, the students reflect on their inquiry, findings and the ethical issues surrounding the lesson and negotiate what inquiry should be explored next. The students decide that they need to look at the ethical considerations of genetic manipulation.

Note: The action of the frame expertise is taking place 100 years after the events of the book, *The Giver*, took place.

resources and to make sense of that information in relation to the content of the study. It is important to note that the students were placed in the role of experts, but it was only through careful negotiation and the developmental process of inquiry that the students chose to think as experts involved in a community that agreed to the research paradigm. So what did drama teach these students about science? The expertise-like thinking that was involved in the inquiry-based drama is not guaranteed when students are positioned as experts, but rather when they negotiate the inquiry as a group of inquirers committed to a question. Participants in the drama are framed as inquirers committed to asking questions of the problem to develop their own inquiry. Thus, through their investigation process, they solve the puzzle. As a result of the learning experiences in this particular set of frames, the students were empowered to generate their own inquiry, take responsibility for their inquiry, and use a variety of thinking strategies to gather information from diverse resources. Ultimately, they had to make sense of that information in relation to the content of their mathematics and science classes to answer scientific questions. Making sense of that content includes discovering concepts and the interrelationships among concepts that form important ideas. Making sense of the process requires learners to talk about thinking and, more importantly, think critically about their own thinking.

What does drama teach us about science?

Though drama fosters the use of academic skills and content found in traditional classrooms, drama-based inquiry can also be used to create frames where students can think, learn and inquire within scientifically meaningful contexts that support situated cognition (Brown et al. 1989). A unique feature of the process drama approach to education is that the aspect of looking at a part of a subject in terms of the whole is built into the method. Any one subject or learning area is interconnected with a broad spectrum of knowledge. Even more importantly, it is understood by the diversity of individualized 'thinking' processes used by the diverse learners, while also being connected within the community of the inquiring classroom or laboratory (Warner and Erchick 2006).

The goal of childhood and young adult science education is to enable children to investigate phenomena so they can construct their own valid conceptualizations about science. The process-oriented inquiry method of teaching science is a constructivist way of making this possible. The use of drama in the classroom is simply another possibility for a methodology that not only supports and encompasses scientific inquiry within the community of learners, but also specifically promotes and uses inquiry. Furthermore, it stimulates high-order thinking at all levels of the educational classroom.

However, further research and development of inquiry-based methodologies are essential in the development of learning pedagogy with built-in possibilities for dialogue. Furthermore, joint opportunities between teachers and actual scientific researchers are needed in order to continue to design authentic 'frames' or scenarios for drama in the classroom that will also incorporate teachers and students working along the side of scientists and engaging in authentic scientific projects. In order 'to do' science there should be multiple opportunities to collaborate with actual scientists and teachers over a sustained period of time. Such experiencs will not only provide 'real' contexts for the *drama* of science, but will also contribute to shared experiences and evaluations about the processes used in examining scientific questions.

The idea that inquiry-based drama can be used as a tool in the classroom holds a manifold of promises. First, as a construct, the use of drama offers the possibility of building bridges between humanities professionals and math/science professionals. Further, the students are able to address their own understanding of science concepts as experts within the inquiry. They are also able, within the inquiry and subsequent discussion in the teacher led classroom, to confront and address those factors that, in the world outside this inquiry, are barriers to their expert status in science. Those factors might be social factors such as race, class and gender or they might be issues of understanding and the teaching and learning the interns have experienced to date. Finally, the students can gain a new vision of their role as lifelong inquirers, for within an inquiry-based drama lesson, students are freed from looking to authorities for answers and instead are able to guide, assist and wonder with the teacher, who becomes a co-inquirer free to ask questions and join in an exploration with students.

Using inquiry-based drama can harness the imagination to open up new vistas of unexpected connections with people across time and space. These areas of inquiry change perspectives, question content, and discover and question new visions of the future. As Maxine Greene stresses, when the imagination is released, 'no accounting, disciplinary or otherwise, can ever be complete. There is always more. There is always possibility' (Greene 1988, p. 7).

References

American Association for the Advancement of Science (2006), *Summary Comparison of Content between National Science Education Standards, Benchmarks for Science Literacy, and Science for All Americans.* Washington, DC: Author. http://www. project2061.org/publications/rsl/online/COMPARE/NRC/SUMMTOC.HTM

Andersen, R. D. (2002), 'Reforming science teaching: What research says about inquiry'. *Journal of Elementary Science Education*, 13, (1), 1–12.

—(2007), 'Inquiry as an organizing theme for science curricula', in S. K. Abell and N. G. Lederman (eds), *Handbook of Research on Science Education*. Mahwah, NJ: Lawrence Erlbaum Associates, pp. 36–72.

Bereiter, C. and Scardamalia, M. (1993), *Surpassing Ourselves: An Inquiry into the Nature and Implications of Expertise.* La Salle, IL: Open Court.

Brown, J., Collins, A., and Duguid, P. (1989), 'Situated cognition and the culture of learning'. *Educational Researcher*, 18, (1), 32–42.

Crawford, B. A. (2000), 'Embracing the essence of inquiry: New roles for science teachers'. *Journal of Research in Science Teaching*, 37, (9), 916–37.

Crawford, B. A., Krajcik, J. S., and Marx, R. W. (1999), 'Elements of a community of learners in a middle school science classroom'. *Science Education*, 83, (6), 701–23.

Davis, E. A., Petish, D., and Smithey, J. (2006), 'Challenges new science teachers face'. *Review of Educational Research*, 76, (4), 607–51.

Furtak, E. M. (2006), 'The problem with answers: An exploration of guided scientific inquiry teaching'. *Science Education*, 90, (3), 453–67.

Greene, M. (1988), *The Dialect of Freedom*. New York City: Teachers College Press.

Halliday, M. A. K. and Martin, J. R. (1993), *Writing Science: Literacy and Discursive Power.* Pittsburgh, PA: University of Pittsburg Press.

Heathcote, D. and Bolton, G. (1995), *Drama for Learning: Dorothy Heathcote's Mantle of the Expert Approach to Education.* Portsmouth, NH: Heinemann.

Lave, J. (1988), *Cognition in Practice.* New York: Cambridge University Press.

Lee, O. (1999), 'Equity implications based on the conceptions of science achievement in major reform documents'. *Review of Educational Research,* 69, 83–115.

Lemke, J. L. (1990), *Talking Science: Language, Learning and Values.* Norwood, NJ: Ablex.

Morgan, N. and Saxton, J. (1991), *Teaching, Question and Learning.* City: Routledge

National Research Council (NRC) (2006, 2010), *National Science Education Standards.* Washington, DC: National Academy Press.

O'Neill, C. (1995), *Drama Worlds: A Framework for Process Drama.* Portsmouth, New Hampshire, USA: Heinemann Publishers.

Renk, H. (1993), *The Work of Dorothy Heathcote and the New Paradigm of Constructivism.* Paper presented at the International Conference on the Work and Influence of Dorothy Heathcote, Lancaster, England.

Rogoff, B. (1990), *Apprenticeship in Thinking: Cognitive Development in Social Context.* New York: Oxford University Press.

Roth, W.-M. (1994), 'Experimenting in a constructivist high school physics laboratory'. *Journal of Research in Science Teaching,* 31, (2), 197–223.

Roth, W.-M. and Bowen, G. M. (1995), 'Knowing and interacting: A study of culture, practices, and resources in a grade 8 open-inquiry science classroom guided by a cognitive apprenticeship metaphor'. *Cognition and Instruction,* 13, (1), 73–128.

Simmons, P. E., Emory, A., Carter, T., Coker, T., Finnegan, B., and Crockett, D., et al. (1999), 'Beginning teachers: Beliefs and classroom actions'. *Journal of Research in Science Teaching,* 36, (8), 930–54.

Smithenry, D. W. and Gallagher-Bolos, J. A. (2009), *Whole-Class Inquiry in the Science Classroom.* NSTA Press.

Warner, C. D. (1997), 'The edging in of engagement: Exploring the nature of engagement in drama'. *Research in Drama Education,* 2, (1), 21–42.

Warner, C. D. and Andersen, C. (2004), 'Snails are science: Creating context for science inquiry and writing through process drama'. *Youth Theatre Journal,* 15, (1), 14–22.

Warner, C. D. and Erchick, D. (2006), 'On beyond word problems: Using inquiry-based framed expertise to create a context for integrating mathematics and science'. *Education International,* 2, (2), 7–10.

Warner, C. D. (manuscript submitted), 'The Theory of Frame Expertise'. Manuscript submitted to *Research in Drama in Education,* eds.

Wilhelm, J. and Edmiston, B. (2000), *Imagining to Learn: Inquiry, Ethics, and Integration through Drama.* Portsmouth, NH: Heinemann.

19

Drama and Literature:
Masks and Love Potions

George Belliveau and Monica Prendergast

The best in this kind are but shadows;
and the worst are no worse,
if imagination amend them.

Theseus, Act 1, Scene i, *A Midsummer Night's Dream*

Introduction and literature review

This chapter presents two case studies that look at how drama strategies can activate the learning of literature. We begin with a succinct literature review that locates a number of ways drama educators/scholars have used drama pedagogy to engage students with literature, in this case specifically with dramatic literature. There are many sources available that focus on drama and other forms of literature, such as story drama structures (Booth 2005; Miller and Saxton 2004) in elementary and middle school grades (ages: 5–13), or on how drama works in language arts curricula (Andersonet al. 2008; Byron 1986; Moss 2003; Smith 2013; Struthers 2005). In addition, many drama education textbooks include lesson plans connected to a story, poem or novel (for a sampling, see Ackroyd and Boulton 2001; Baldwin 2008; Hulson 2006; Neelands 2005; O'Neill 1995; O'Neill and Lambert 1982; Swartz 2002; Swartz and Nyman 2010). Rather than reproducing a well-established and documented body of literature on that topic, our intention is to offer a perspective that values the use of drama strategies in relation to the study of plays as literature. To show specific examples as to ways literature can be activated through drama, we present two case studies using Shakespeare's *A Midsummer Night's Dream* with school-aged students (ages: 5–18). The drama-based strategies discussed in both studies could be readily adapted to other literature, applied as preparation for students to see live theatre or to view dramatic films.

Somers (2008) developed various drama approaches in facilitating his Applied Theatre research projects, one being *compound stimulus* (p. 67). Compound stimulus engages participants through the use of artefacts, usually objects, images or letters, all set within an appropriate container that suits the story, and the flow of the story 'is given significance by the careful juxtaposition of its contents – the relationships between them – and how the detail of the objects suggest human motivation and action' (p. 68). Somers goes on to suggest that when 'the relationship is just right, the participants generate visceral hypotheses which beg to be explored' (p. 68). This drama-based strategy has proven to deepen the experience for participants and further their understanding about motivations and rapports between characters and specific artefacts as they prepare to engage with a given work (Somers 2008). Building on his theory of multiple intelligences, Gardner (2000) proposes *entry points* to introduce learners to complex and challenging topics and/or works. He notes the benefits of using 'narrative, hands-on, and aesthetic [e.g. dramatic] entry points' to stimulate students to approach new work, encouraging curiosity and anticipation, as well as appealing to diverse learners (p. 199).

Drawing on Gardner's entry points and Somers' compound stimulus, we now take a look at published lesson plans and units that bring drama strategies and dramatic literature together as an effective way to invite students into the world of a play (Fuchs 2004). Two well-known sources for drama-based lesson plans connecting to dramatic literature are *Key Shakespeare 1 & 2* (Ackroyd et al. 1998a, 1998b). In one example of a role drama from these texts, students studying *Twelfth Night* put Malvolio's bullies on trial for character defamation, even cruelty, with the teacher-in-role as Clerk of the Court overseeing the trial proceedings enacted by students who are also in-role (1998a, pp. 42–56). O'Neill and Lambert (1982) offer a structure built around *Macbeth* that also invites students to carry out a post-mortem tribunal, as requested by Lady Macbeth's imaginary sister, that will determine her guilt or innocence (p. 221). In another example of how drama-based strategies prepare students to read, see or perform a given playtext, Bolton (2000) invites students to consider what superstition means to them, and then asks them to stick pins in a rag doll as a way to dramatically connect students with the world of Miller's *The Crucible*.

Other drama structures use playtext as part of larger dramatic investigations. Eriksson (2004) creates a hard hitting sociopolitical drama structure about resistance and sacrifice that draws together a tragic Greek heroine and a tragic contemporary one in the intertwining tales of *Antigone* and Rachel Corrie, the American student activist killed in 2003 by an Israeli bulldozer operator in Palestine. Hulson's (2006) drama schemes include a number connected to literature, particularly Greek mythology. She also offers senior level (ages 16 to 18) schemes built around two contemporary British plays, *Saved* by Bond and *Mountain Language* by Pinter (pp. 84–91). These sets of lesson plans invite students to role-play similar situations to those presented in Bond and Pinter's challenging and controversial plays that deal unflinchingly with youth violence and political oppression. One role-play involves teacher-in-role as an irate parent who does not wish this class to study the Bond play, the challenge being for students to defend the play and its educational and artistic value for them (pp. 86–87). In *Lessons for the Living* (Clark et al. 1997), the titular lesson plan uses quotations from the stage version of *The Diary of Anne Frank* in a role drama that challenges students to confront racism and anti-Semitism in the contemporary world. Another drama structure, called 'Star-Cross'd Lovers', draws a powerful parallel between *Romeo and Juliet* and the true story of a young mixed-marriage couple killed in the Serbo-Croatian civil war in former Yugoslavia. A third structure, 'Eating Peas, Nothing But Peas', uses extracts from Buchner's 1837 play *Woyzeck* as source for a role drama that investigates moral issues surrounding cloning and genetic engineering.

Building on drama education research, particularly in process drama (Bowell and Heap 2001; O'Toole 1992; O'Neill 1995), Prendergast developed initiating activities for students in preparation to view live theatre through her audience education research and practice (2002a, 2002b, 2003, 2006, 2008). Prendergast's drama-based audience education curriculum includes using catalysts such as the theatre production poster and programme, props, set design, synopses and lines pulled from the script to have student audience members improvise and devise short scenes through collaborative creation. This work is not about performing scenes or monologues from a play; instead the initiating activities are focused on discovering central themes, conflicts and dramatic actions, responding to Heathcote's (in Wagner 1976) notion of 'Dropping to the Universal' (pp. 76–96) to help prepare students prior to seeing a play. Creatively engaging with these objects and concepts allows students to predict and make connections with the play they are about to see, and Prendergast's research (2002b, 2006) demonstrates that these approaches have a positive impact on students' level of engagement.

Belliveau (2012, 2009) has carried out investigations on the effects of using process drama strategies with elementary students prior to their staging/studying of adapted Shakespeare productions. This 5-year drama-based research project gathered data from four multi-grade classrooms of elementary students, their teacher, family members and other members of the school community. In each of the 5 years of the study, teachers led their students for a period of 4 months in a variety of drama-based approaches connected to a Shakespeare play and then through a rehearsal process the respective classes staged in-class productions. The findings of this study, a component of which will be analyzed in the first case study below, strongly suggest that the drama-based integrated curricular process had positive effects for students in various areas: comprehension; writing; speaking; socioemotional learning; arts appreciation; motivation; artistic development, to name a few (Belliveau 2012; Shira and Belliveau 2012; Mackenzie et al. 2011).

To conclude this concise overview of our work and that of a number of other drama educator/scholars, there is convincing evidence that employing drama-based pedagogical strategies is an effective way to build integrated and engaging curricula in language arts classrooms. However, as Anderson (2012) urges us, "more research is required to confirm the hunches" we have about drama's positive impact on learning (p. 95). The two case studies we share below are informed by recent scholarship on how drama can be brought into the study of literature of all kinds, with an intentional focus on dramatic literature, or plays in performance or on film. As former English/Drama teachers in Toronto and Victoria, we have led and integrated a variety of pre-reading or pre-performance approaches in our teaching, and many of our pre-service and in-service teachers have successfully been using and adapting our drama-based work to teach literature.

Case study 1: Entering *A Midsummer Night's Dream* through mask and image

In this first case study we describe a component of Belliveau's ongoing research on Shakespeare and young learners. Prior to engaging with the given literary playtext, in this case *A Midsummer Night's Dream* (*AMND*), primary teachers in Belliveau's study invite their students to participate in a variety of drama-based activities, to gradually ease their comfort with drama and understanding of Shakespeare. One of the early activities, prior to reading the play, centres on mask and image work where students explore key characters, relationships and objects/props from the given play. In the next few paragraphs, I (George) will focus on one primary class's (ages: 6–9) experience of undertaking this mask-based activity (see Figure 19.1), highlighting findings and observations based on my analysis.

I spent a week in the spring of 2010 observing the progression of this particular activity in one of the primary classrooms within my research. Additional data consists of an interview with the teacher, student journal reflections, the actual mask students created, and a focus group with eight randomly selected students 2 years later. There was a vivid sense of curiosity, discovery and intuitiveness among the young students reported throughout the research data. The curiosity began immediately after the teacher had written the character names from *AMND* along with brief descriptions on the white board (e.g. *Titania* – Queen of the Fairies, in a battle with Oberon over the

Figure 19.1 *AMND* character masks.

Indian child; *Francis Flute* – a bellows mender, workman, nervously performing Thisbe, female hero in a play). The children looked at the various Shakespearean names: trying to pronounce them, *De-me-tri-us*; deciphering if the character was a boy or a girl, *I'm sure Peaseblossom is a girl, I want to be her, and be a fairy*; playing with names such as *Puck, Bottom, Helena*; recognizing warriors such as *Theseus, I read about him fighting the minotaur*; sharing how one of their relatives once visited Athens; had an aunt named Helena; and who would ever have a name like *Ly-san-der* (field notes). A number of early connections were made with *AMND* as the children tried to make sense of the characters and descriptions, with the teacher intersecting and providing some background to the play: *Yes Tara, there is a play within the play, where the workmen, Flute, Bottom and friends will perform at the Duke's palace for a wedding celebration* (field notes).

Questions, predictions and debates continued as each student created a mask on oval cardboard pieces using available pencil crayons, scissors, sparkles, stickers, and glue to depict through images one of the characters, *I did hart-shaped eyes for Hermia wih an X on one eye cuz she was hrt* (student journal). As they worked on their masks in groups of 3–4 at each table, the informal conversations had them repeatedly saying various character names, predicting their attitudes and relationships in a playful manner, *I want to be Titania, Queen of the Fairies* (field notes).

Once the masks were created, the teacher created four groups to establish the worlds within the play: (1) fairies, (2) lovers, (3) workman and (4) court. With their masks in hand, *we glooed stiks on our mask so we cud old them* (student journal), the respective worlds created tableaux to depict a moment within the play: *Our group did a frozen image of the wedding at the end of the play* (focus group). Key objects or props were also introduced and then inserted within the tableau work. This was done as the teacher narrated small sections of the plot and the children, with the help of their masks and props, pantomimed brief scenes: *Can I wear the ears and be the donkey-guy?* (field notes). Puck's love potion created intrigue, as did the lion's mane, provoking the students to ask several questions. One of the final activities had students speaking a line of text from their (mask) character, *These are the forgeries of jealousy*, putting Shakespeare language in their mouths. Then, as an entire class, they worked on the final speech of the play, *If we shadows have offended*, collectively holding their masks.

The masks (with character names) and key props were placed on one of the classroom walls for display. These artefacts became visual reminders for the students as they continued their journey with the play. The various steps within the mask and image activity provided entry points into *AMND*, activating curiosity as well as insights for the students about the characters and story. The learning that emerges from this kind of deliberate and careful scaffolding of drama-based activities is well supported in drama education literature (Booth 2005; Bowell and Heap 2001; Fels and Belliveau 2008; Miller and Saxton 2004).

Case study 2: Using role-play and moral education in preparing students to see *A Midsummer Night's Dream*: A reflection on practice

Shortly after my actor training at the University of Regina, Saskatchewan, I (Monica) had the opportunity to work with Brian Way (1967, 1981) at Regina's Globe Theatre. I then moved to Toronto and was hired as an actor/teacher with Young People's Theatre [YPT]. YPT is one of the largest theatres for young audiences companies in Canada and the 1980s were its heydays. I worked with two other actor/teachers in what was called the Outreach Project, in which we were 'living study guides' visiting schools both before and after students were to attend a YPT show. Our focus was to offer professional development to teachers through drama-based strategies to make the theatre experience more enriched and educationally valuable. One of the many shows we worked with over the five seasons I was at YPT was a touring production of *AMND*.

Much time has passed since this pre-show workshop took place, nearly 30 years ago. Yet as fate would have it, just recently the role play cards I used to create the drama structure fell out of my bookcase, hidden between some books I had pulled out. The workshop we planned centred on pulling out a key dramatic action from the play, in this case the use of a love potion, and using it as the basis of a role drama. Students were informed that a love potion capable of making anyone fall in love with the next person they saw had been developed by a group of medical scientist/researchers. They were then divided into groups to carry out a number of interrelated tasks:

SCIENTISTS/RESEARCHERS

- Create formula for potion, correct dosage, antidote and write group statement in favour or against marketing the potion

DOCTORS/PSYCHIATRISTS

• Write patient profiles, go to doctors for potion, and write effects on patients, use of antidote, medical opinion of benefits/drawbacks

THE MEDIA

• Create news report on potion, get interviews from other groups in addition to man-on-the-street interviews, put together and present news report

ADVERTISING

• Create marketing package for potion (name, slogan, package design, cost, profit) and a television advertisement

CONCERNED CITIZENS

• Organize to express your concerns about the potion (by going to other groups) and create a television public service announcement airing your views

My memories of how this role drama played out in classrooms are that students were engaged and busy carrying out the assigned group tasks, which were then shared as presentations for the rest of the class. The idea of a love potion – especially with the use of a small bottle containing a coloured liquid as the only necessary prop to carry out this structure – was an excellent compound stimulus and entry point. The work appeared relevant to the middle-school students (age: 11–13) as it was set in the present and appealed to their stage of development in terms of dealing with sexual attraction and potential manipulation of this with the use of a potion. It also heightened their engagement with the play they were to see, in that they now knew to look out closely for how a love potion was an integral aspect of Shakespeare's magical plot.

In reflection, I see how Dorothy Heathcote's Mantle of the Expert approach informs this structure (Heathcote and Bolton 1995), as does moral (also known as character or values) education incorporating drama (Winston 1998), although these books were to appear some time in the future. Students were given adult roles and invited to wrestle with an alluring dilemma, to market or destroy a drug that can make people fall in love against their will. I also see how an interest in audience education, which became my chosen research topic in graduate studies (see Prendergast in References), started at this early stage of my career. Mostly, what resonates with me in writing this narrative is gratitude at having had the privilege of working with Brian Way, the first of a number of important mentors who have guided my development as a drama/theatre educator. No doubt it was in part my training with him that led me to co-create this preparatory role drama, as he knew how much young people wished to be offered adult-level challenges, 'to practice living' (Way 1967, p. 6) and also to be invited to 'release their imaginations' (Greene 1995).

Discussion

These two reflective case studies are meant to highlight ways that facilitators have led students into the world of the play, and at the same time encourage them to predict and make initial connections. The use of drama-based approaches to initiate the study of literature supports the work of literacy and drama scholars who suggest that predicting and finding connections increases students' ability and willingness to read and comprehend (Baldwin and Fleming 2003; Booth 2005; Smith and Herring 2001; Wilhelm 2002). Drama-based pre-texts (Bowell and Heap 2001) invite students to imagine the world of the literature to be encountered, offering entry points and building confidence prior to studying the literary work. In *Exploring Curriculum: Performative inquiry, role drama, and learning* (2008), Fels and Belliveau ground their research in complexity and learning theories (pp. 24–30) and share how drama becomes a critical way to explore various content areas of the curriculum. More specifically, in Chapter 4 on literature and Chapter 5 on poetry they illustrate drama-based approaches that can be used to begin or end a literature unit. Pre-reading drama strategies invite students to experientially enter the literary texts, using body and/or voice to explore the context, conflicts and characters of the fictional or non-fictional world encountered within the text (Fels and Belliveau 2008, p. 13).

Future considerations

To build on the work observed in the two case studies and literature in the field, it is important to consider how drama-based strategies can also become stimuli for post-reading, allowing students to reflect on their learning experience. Using, for example, the hot seat strategy where students can question characters or one another through role playing, asking how they feel, what they think, about certain decisions and outcomes (e.g. At the end of the play, has Egeus changed his outlook regarding his daughter's decision to marry? Have Oberon and Titania settled their differences?) Other post-reading strategies could include dramatizing sections of the piece of literature being studied. Creating videos is another popular choice with students. A technique that Prendergast's audience education curriculum model (2002b, 2006, 2008) employs is to invite students to create original dramatic stories in responsive dialogue with the literary source. In other words, small groups of students studying *AMND* could consider what aspects of the play intrigued them most and consider what situations or scenarios could be explored, through improvisation or tableaux or other drama strategies, and shared with the rest of the class. Offering key themes as catalysts or generating them with students gives good starting points for their own drama-making activities. 'Unrequited Love' is a key theme in *AMND*, as is 'When Worlds Collide' (the human and magical worlds of the play), and 'Play-Within-A-Play'. Any of these three themes is universal enough for students to create their own dramas (or written stories, artworks etc.) in a dialogical process that is centred on using the arts to respond to the arts. Selected one-line quotations from a given text also make great catalysts for new stories that begin (or end) with Shakespeare lines such as, 'The course of true love never did run smooth', 'Lord, what fools these mortals be!' and 'I have had a most rare vision?'

As well, the drama-based activities within the reflective studies we share above could be revisited for post-discussion. For instance, in relation to the mask and image activity, what could be added to the *AMND* masks after studying the play? What other layers have been discovered? Do these Shakespearean characters resemble other literary characters encountered in class or outside of class? What new levels could be added to the initial tableaux (created during the pre-reading) among the characters and objects? And, with the role-play and moral education lesson plan, what connections can students make between their preparatory work and what happens in the play? What advice could they offer the young lovers in the play (which could be hot-seated in class with volunteer students in-role)? What would they have to say to Puck about his use of the love potion? What might the young lovers have to say to the medical researchers who have decided to either market or not market their love potion? Revisiting the initial pre-reading drama work helps students recognize the journey they took, reviewing where they began and how far they have come, essentially marking the path of their learning.

Assessment

Using body and voice through drama strategies allows students to illustrate aspects of their learning that may not otherwise have been shared through reading, writing and/or discussion, offering teachers another lens to assess student learning. 'A question of Evaluation' (Fels and Belliveau 2008, pp. 205–19) provides a full discussion on the often complicated journey of evaluating and assessing drama-based work. Written reflections are always good assessment opportunities in a language arts class, and Prendergast (2006, 2008) developed a set of post-performance (or, in this case, post-reading) reflective questions. They are adapted here for a language arts curriculum context:

- What did I recognize in the play (or poem, story or novel)? What surprised me?
- How was the play relevant to my life and experience?
- How did the play stimulate my creativity and imagination?
- What puzzled me or confused me?
- What was illustrated/represented by the play?
- What were the social, political and cultural contexts of the play?
- What perspectives were given by the play? How valuable were these perspectives?
- What new questions has this play generated in me?

These questions do not look like the kind of standard English questions, which traditionally are more focused on literary elements and on students working towards a 'correct' (often teacher-led) interpretation. Much has changed since we were students in English classes like this, and mostly for the better. However, in our admittedly biased view as drama and English educators, language arts include reading, writing, speaking and listening. Engagement with literature of all kinds should offer multiple opportunities for students to creatively practice all four of these key areas of literacy development. Drama-based teaching strategies offer many options for teachers who see literature as part of a process that moves from page to stage, and from the past into the present and towards a future vision that – like the dreamers in Shakespeare's magical romantic comedy – will challenge us to better know ourselves (and perhaps each other) by the time the curtain comes down.

If we shadows have offended,
Think but this, and all is mended,
That you have but slumber'd here
While these visions did appear.
And this weak and idle theme,
No more yielding, but a dream . . .

Puck, Act V, Scene ii, *A Midsummer Night's Dream*

References

Ackroyd, J. and Boulton, J. (2001), *Drama Lessons for Five to Eleven-year-olds*. London: David Fulton.

Ackroyd, J., Neelands, J., Supple, M., and Trowsdale, J. (1998a), *Key Shakespeare 1: English and Drama Activities for Teaching Shakespeare to 10-14 Year Olds*. Abingdon, UK: Hodder & Stoughton.

—(1998b), *Key Shakespeare 2: English and Drama Activities for Teaching Shakespeare to 14-16 Year Olds*. Abingdon, UK: Hodder & Stoughton.

Anderson, M. (2012), *MasterClass in Drama Education: Transforming Teaching and Learning*. London: Continuum.

Anderson, M., Hughes, J., and Manuel, J. (2008), *Drama and English Teaching: Imagination, Action and Engagement*. Melbourne: Oxford University Press.

Baldwin, P. (2008), *The Primary Drama Handbook*. London: Sage.

Baldwin, P. and Fleming, K. (2003), *Teaching Literacy through Drama: Creative Approaches*. London: Routledge/Falmer.

Belliveau, G. (2009), 'Elementary students and Shakespeare: Inspiring community and learning'. *International Journal of the Arts in Society*, 4, (2), 1–8.

—(2012), 'Shakespeare and Literacy: A Case Study in a Primary Classroom'. *Journal of Social Sciences*, 8, (2), 170–7.

Bolton, G. (2000), 'A lesson devised originally for adolescents: Preparing to study *The Crucible* by Arthur Miller'. *Contemporary Theatre Review*, 10, (2), 11–15.

Booth, D. (2005), *Story Drama: Creating Stories through Role Playing, Improvising, and Reading Aloud*, 2nd edn. Markham, ON: Pembroke Publishers.

Bowell, P. and Heap, B. (2001), *Planning Process Drama*. London: David Fulton.

Byron, K. (1986), *Drama in the English Classroom*. London: Methuen.

Clark, J., Dobson, W., Goode, T., and Neelands, J. (1997), *Lessons for the Living: Drama and the Integrated Curriculum*. Newmarket, ON: Mayfair Cornerstone.

Eriksson, S. (2004), 'The voices of two female activists – Rachel Corrie (2003) and Antigone (442 BC)'. Workshop given at triennial *International Drama Education Association* (IDEA) conference, 2–7 July, Ottawa, Ontario, Canada.

Fels, L. and Belliveau, G. (2008), *Exploring Curriculum: Performative Inquiry, Role Drama, and Learning*. Vancouver, BC: Pacific Education Press.

Fuchs, E. (2004), 'EF's visit to a small planet: Some questions to ask a play'. *Theater*, 34, (2), 4–9.

Gardner, H. (2000), *The Disciplined Mind*. New York: Penguin.

Greene, M. (1995), *Releasing the Imagination: Essays on Education, the Arts and Social Change*. San Francisco, CA: Jossey-Bass.

Heathcote, D. and Bolton, G. (1995), *Drama for Learning: Dorothy Heathcote's Mantle of the Expert Approach to Education*. Portsmouth, NH: Heinemann.

Hulson, M. (2006), *Schemes for Classroom Drama*. Stoke on Trent, UK: Trentham.

MacKenzie, D., Belliveau, G., Beck, J., Lea, G. W. and Wager, A. (2011), 'Naming the Shadows: Theatre as research'. *Canadian Journal of Practice-based Research in Theatre*, 3, (1): http://cjprt.uwinnipeg.ca/index.php/cjprt/article/viewFile/29/18

Miller, C. and Saxton, J. (2004), *Into the Story: Language in Action through Drama*. Portsmouth, NH: Heinemann.

Moss, J. (2003), 'Drama', in J. Davison and J. Dowson (eds), *Learning to Teach English in the Secondary School: A Companion to School Experience*. London: RoutledgeFalmer, pp. 199–219.

Neelands, J. (2005), *Beginning Drama 11-14*, 2nd edn. London: Routledge.

O'Neill, C. (1995), *Drama Worlds: A Framework for Process Drama*. Portsmouth, NH: Heinemann.

O'Neill, C. and Lambert, A. (1982), *Drama Structures: A Practical Handbook for Teachers*. Portsmouth, NH: Heinemann.

O'Toole, J. (1992), *The Process of Drama: Negotiating Art and Meaning*. London: Routledge.

Prendergast, M. (2002a), 'Belfry 101: Audience education in professional theatre'. *STAGE of the Art*, 34, (2), 4–8.

—(2002b), *"Imaginative complicity": Audience education in professional theatre*. Unpublished Master's thesis, University of Victoria, Victoria, BC.

—(2003), 'I, me, mine: Soliloquizing as reflective practice'. *International Journal of Education and the Arts*, 4, (1). Available: http://ijea.asu.edu/v4nl

—(2006), *Audience in Performance: A Poetics and Pedagogy of Spectatorship*. Unpublished doctoral dissertation, University of Victoria, BC.

—(2008), *Teaching Spectatorship: Poems and Essays on Audience in Performance*. Amherst, NY: Cambria.

Shira, A. and Belliveau, G. (2012), 'Discovering the role(s) of a drama researcher: Outsider, bystander, mysterious observer'. *Youth Theatre Journal*, 26, (1), 73–87.

Smith, R. (2013), 'Drama in English', in A. Green (ed.), *A Practical Guide to Teaching English in the Secondary School*. Abingdon, UK: Routledge, pp. 30–6.

Smith, J. L. and Herring, D. J. (2001), *Dramatic Literacy: Using Drama and Literature to Teach Middle-level Content*. Portsmouth, NH: Heinemann.

Somers, J. (2008), 'Interactive theatre: Drama as social intervention'. *Music & Arts in Action*, 1, (1), 61–86.

Struthers, J. (2005), 'The role of drama', in A. Goodwyn and J. Branson (eds), *Teaching English: A Handbook for Primary and Secondary School Teachers*. London: Methuen, pp. 81–102.

Swartz, L. (2002), *The New Dramathemes*, 3rd edn. Markham, ON: Pembroke.

Swartz, L. and Nyman, D. (2010), *Drama Schemes, Themes and Dreams*. Markham, ON: Pembroke.

Wagner, B. J. (1976), *Dorothy Heathcote: Drama as a Learning Medium*. London: Hutchinson.

Way, B. (1967), *Development through Drama*. London: Longmans.

—(1981), *Audience Participation: Theatre for Young People*. Boston, MA: W. H. Baker.

Wilhelm, J. (2002), *Action Strategies for Deepening Comprehension*. Toronto: Scholastic Professional.

Winston, J. (1998), *Drama, Narrative and Moral Education*. London: Falmer Press.

Part Five

Conclusion

20

Drama and the Future: Activating New Possibilities

Julie Dunn and Michael Anderson

Introduction

The case studies and exemplars of work shared within this book reveal that in this second decade of the twenty-first century, drama has become an adaptable and energizing human enterprise that can span and expand the compartmentalized, discipline-based learning approaches that characterize so much of contemporary education. With participants ranging from children in their first year of schooling through to adults operating as drama advisors, across these pages a range of dramatic forms have been put to work in classrooms, community spaces and theatres to achieve learning outcomes that are aesthetic, personal, social, political, and broadly educational. Not narrowly confined or limited by prescribed curriculum documents, rules or philosophies, it seems instead that contemporary drama and applied theatre practitioners freely select forms and styles that suit the needs of their participants, the outcomes they hope to achieve and the contexts in which they operate. This eclecticism is refreshing and highlights the distance the field has travelled in recent years, leaving behind binary notions of process/product to embrace a more comprehensive view of drama as a complex and diverse art form capable of continually reshaping itself according to its context, purposes and participants. However, as O'Toole and Stinson (2009, p. 193) have asked previously, 'What shapes might it assume in the future and why?'

Within this chapter, this question will be considered along with an exploration of the roles drama might play in supporting young people's engagement with the future. Here Freire's (1998) notion of the future as 'something constructed by people engaged together in life', something not pre-determined but 'always in the process of becoming' (p. 72), is foundational. In addition, Neelands' (2009) view of the drama classroom as a laboratory for this 'becoming', where profound realizations about possible futures can take place and grow, is also critical.

First, however, an overview or mapping of contemporary drama, as revealed through the research and practice outlined in the previous pages, will be offered. This overview is of course partial and unbalanced, reflective only of the (mostly) Western views held by the authors we invited to contribute. In turn, these views have been shaped and influenced by the specific social, political, educational and artistic environments these researchers, educators and artists work within. Nevertheless, we believe that it reveals some interesting insights into the nature of drama, supporting readers to appreciate not only how it activates learning, but also the types of learning it is capable of generating, together with the specific conditions it both creates and requires.

In Chapter 1, we provided a view of the global educational landscape drama inhabits. This landscape, as noted there, can be hostile, imposing barriers and narrowing opportunities for learners. However, there are also sites within this landscape where opportunities exist and at times these sites of welcome can be positioned deep within territory that might otherwise appear to be hostile. Indeed, across the chapters of this book there are many examples of drama practitioners engaging young people in contexts that many other fields may see as too difficult or too alien. In offering a mapping of contemporary drama for learning, our aim is to determine how drama might be understood across all these varied landscapes.

First, though, a couple of further caveats, beginning with one that relates to our readers. Here we want to note that just as landscapes differ from one region to another, so too do the experiences of our readers, and as such, the contours and characteristics of drama identified below may not match with their understanding of it. For example, actors or directors in professional theatre may find our mapping confusing as so little of what has been revealed here relates to the formal presentation of scripted texts for a public audience. This is not to say that this work is not part of contemporary drama's geography, but rather, that it is simply not the focus of the work explored here. Similarly, for readers who operate in contexts where political views are constrained or where pedagogical approaches are highly structured and averse to playfulness, dialogue and collaboration, the overview of practice offered here may seem misleading or misguided, suggesting purposes and approaches that may be unhelpful in their particular landscapes.

Next, colleagues working in the multiple disciplines that intersect with drama and highlighted across the various sections of this book may view our mapping process as a form of 'colonisation', an attempt to inhabit spaces already occupied by their existing pedagogies and approaches. This is not our purpose. Instead, our goal is to support the ongoing work of all educators by offering a summary of the claims made by drama practitioner/researchers about what drama is capable of achieving, how it works and the conditions it requires for success. In doing this, we hope to provide clarity and support in contexts where this art form and its purposes are not well understood.

Finally, in attempting this mapping exercise, we will undoubtedly fail to do the work of the various authors, or indeed the art form itself justice, running the risk of simplifying the complexity of ideas that have been shared. We therefore encourage all readers to engage critically with the individual chapters so that this highly distilled overview can be read for what it is – just one mapping of a very complex form.

Activating communities

In mapping the features of drama in the context of communities, the most immediate observation is that this is a political geography, for as Neelands and Nelson note in their chapter, drama provides the opportunity to 'introduce politicized curriculum which directly addresses questions of power and agency'. They suggest too that, 'Acts of theatre, socially made and shared as lived experience, offer a paradigm for engaging youth in explorations of power, agency and the distribution of economic and cultural capital'. Other political goals are also evident in this section, including those relating to race, cultural identity, voice, emancipation and sustainability, suggesting that a key part of what drama generates within communities and through communities is a form of personal and social activism. In these spaces where community is both a focus and a vehicle, the pedagogies of drama seem to be effective in both promoting and providing opportunities for learners to engage in active citizenship in a world where marginalization and unequal power relations dominate.

However, just as contexts for drama work and the forms that are applied in these contexts vary markedly, so too do the claims in relation to learning. Of immediate interest, is the limited attention given to artistic achievement or learning about the art form. Perhaps these outcomes are assumed within a book about learning and drama, but across the pages devoted to activating community (and indeed in every other section as well), explicit discussion of aesthetic learning outcomes tends to be somewhat overwhelmed by exploration of a myriad of social, academic, political and personal ones. These include suggestions that drama offers its participants, audiences and makers: the chance to re-orient towards positive leadership roles (Burton); intellectual achievements such as risk-taking, creative thinking and problem solving (Neelands and Nelson); knowledge, discovery, cognition and recognition (Sinclair and Kelman); or as we have seen above, how to be active citizens who possess skills of critical thinking, reflection, empathy, collaboration and listening (Chan).

This final skill of listening is also revealed as a critical part of the process of working in drama. For example, Gallagher and Yaman Ntelioglu describe it as 'listening for critical and social dialogue', with this dialogue generated to find 'respectful ways to make others less know-able'.

How then are these outcomes achieved? What characteristics of drama create this learning? For some authors it seems that one essential ingredient for learning about community is the creation *of* communities, where trust is a feature and where social and artistic dissonance is valued. In these participatory and collaborative spaces, individuals, according to Gallagher and Yaman Ntelioglu, are 'free to hear and see in ways less bounded by the social norms and stigmas that reign all powerful' in other learning contexts. Opportunities for critical thinking and deep reflection also appear to be key features that support learners, while dialogue that is both respectful and critical is essential. But are these qualities of the form or are they instead the conditions within which it can flourish – conditions that are created by effective, politically active, democratically aware educators who value participatory and critical pedagogies? Is it drama that is educating in this manner, or is it instead the philosophies and practices of those that guide and facilitate it? What is it about drama itself, as an aesthetic form that activates learning?

This is of course a difficult question to answer, partly due to the wide range of dramatic approaches that have been applied by the various researcher/practitioners including Theatre-in-Education, storytelling, devising, scripted work, public performances, workshops and process drama. However, in spite of these differences, some common qualities seem to include: the importance of achieving a simultaneous sense of deep immersion while also experiencing awareness of the dual nature of the experience (Sinclair and Kelman; Freebody and Finneran); the importance of storying, enactment, reflection and distancing

(Burton); and the use of authentic contexts where participants can achieve identification with roles and situations to create empathy (Chan).

As we move on to share the map relating to how drama activates learners, many of the purposes, pedagogical conditions and features of the form outlined here will be revisited.

Activating learners

In their chapter on drama and mind/brain compatibility, Saxton and Miller note that drama supports its learners to 're-imagine and question the templates of how we live and may best live', while O'Connor's provocative work suggests that it can assist learners to 'build resistance to discourses that offer binary notions of good and evil' through felt understanding to 'remake ourselves as human beings'. It is not then just within notions of drama for community that activism and politics are apparent, for it seems that in suggesting that each individual is supported through drama to become active in re-creating or revising themselves, notions of power, agency and voice are again critical. In a world that Cahill refers to as driven by consumerism, drama is described (by her) as a pedagogy where individuals can 'rehearse resistance skills', as they develop self-awareness, self-expression and a critical and politicized sensibility.

Significantly, others highlight quite different learner outcomes, with Winston reminding us that through engagement with drama, we can also learn about beauty, developing 'vocabularies of pleasure, hope, passion, emotion, experience and togetherness', while O'Toole and Stinson focus on those other vocabularies – the vocabularies of oracy essential for both literal and metaphoric notions of voice. Here, the active engagement of participants is clearly needed to achieve these outcomes.

Participation as an audience member at live theatre is also described as an embodied and active experience by Bundy, Ewing and Fleming who draw on Hurley's (2010) work to claim that theatre is capable of generating understanding that is multi-dimensional, including intellectual, social and emotional understanding.

In terms of the conditions that generate this rich array of learning outcomes, once again the creation of a community where risk-taking and playfulness are valued, and where a personal 'disposition to explore critically and creatively' (Saxton and Miller) is actively nurtured, emerges as significant. Here the 'risks' that may be associated with these approaches in other learning contexts seem to be ameliorated in drama through empathic facilitation, a sense of shared responsibility across all participants and perhaps most importantly of all, through the aesthetic management of form.

For O'Toole and Stinson, role and dramatic context are the core features of the form that activate learning, with role serving to reduce risk, while dramatic context offers individuals purpose and opportunity. Additional features of drama are identified by others, with O'Connor suggesting that drama activates learning by combining distancing and empathy within the same action, remaking reality through imagined worlds, while Cahill also notes that distancing is critical. For her, distancing is achieved through fictional stories and scenarios that are 'theirs and not theirs', with these stories and scenarios providing opportunities for health education participants to contest and resist dominant discourses and to 'bridge the gap between knowledge and its application within social and relational contexts'.

How drama works is expressed quite differently for Winston, however, who explores, as we have seen, its capacity for beauty, revealed through hope rather than duty, pleasure of surprise, plot reversal and shifts in energy, shifts in rhythm, tone and sensuality, and through both lavishness and austerity. Ambiguity and the activation of curiosity are additional features of drama identified by Saxton and Miller, who suggest that drama is a pedagogy 'that makes use of conditional language, metaphor and opportunities to subvert taken for granted responses'.

Another key feature of drama identified here is that learning does not just occur during periods of active participation within the art form, but also through processes of reflection. Consistently, reflection has been highlighted across these pages as being a critical feature of drama, offering opportunities for both individuals and groups to deconstruct, reconstruct and 'articulate complexity' (O'Connor). This key aspect of drama pedagogy is not immediately obvious to those who work outside the field, but it is clearly a feature of our work that is being increasingly acknowledged as central to the activation of learning.

Activating curriculum

The task of identifying how drama activates learning and what learning it generates within the school curriculum would seem to be a fairly straightforward one, for within this context learning goals are usually made explicit, recorded in both formal and informal written documents. Here important but predictable goals might include: an enhanced understanding of history; the learning of a new language; improvements in writing; a richer understanding of literature; an ability to manipulate new technologies to make or engage with media products; or the development of authentic science investigations. But is this the only or indeed the most important work that drama does?

O'Toole and Stinson (2009) draw upon the ideas of Richard Courtney (1980) to remind us that curriculum should not only be understood as a noun, but as a verb as well – as a process that teachers and students engage in together. Through collaborative 'curricking', learning outcomes far beyond those formally prescribed or planned for are made possible. For example, in the context of the history classroom, Kempe describes an approach to learning that is once again critical, moving participants beyond the purely experiential to engage them in ways that induce reflection and analysis. Here, Kempe suggests that drama's purpose is to 'galvanise perception and imagination in order to inform, enlighten, and enrich', applying approaches where emotion and empathy support learners to understand, not only historical events but perhaps more importantly, the effects of these events on people. For Dunn, Harden and Marino, as well as Belliveau and Prendergast, drama's role is not simply to create better quality written texts or an enhanced understanding of literature so that higher grades or results might be achieved, but rather, to engage and motivate learners through participatory pedagogies that are collaborative, open-ended, and empathic so that as Stinson and Piazzoli suggest, they become agentic learners.

Once again these outcomes can only be achieved through the aesthetic and skilful management of the elements, structures and affordances of dramatic form, preferably by all participants, but certainly by facilitators, directors, actors and teachers. Whether this management takes place within the affinity spaces of virtual worlds made possible by new advances in digital technology, or within traditional classrooms that more often characterize the 'live, embodied, affective realms' of drama education (Anderson and Cameron), high-quality learning will only be activated if there is careful consideration of and close attention to form.

Analysis of what the authors in this section have identified as being the most critical features of dramatic form once again reveals some common territory and hence our mapping exercise sees us revisiting some now common geographies. Emotion and empathy, the imagination, embodiment, the importance of the fictional context, identification with roles, the application of narrative, collaboration, open-endedness, juxtaposition and reflection all reappear as key features of the landscape. Added to this list though are some key ideas, such as Belliveau and Prendergast's use of the notion of the compound stimulus, Warner's reminders about mantle of the expert and the particular way this approach enhances role through investment, and the critical importance of tension as an essential feature of the fictional context (Dunn et al.; Stinson and Piazzoli).

Of these regular features, identification with roles and situations within and beyond the fictional context and the empathy this identification seems to generate, together with the key role played by reflection, seem to have emerged in this section as the most significant features of drama for learning in and across the curriculum. O'Toole and Stinson have previously (2009, p. 203) described drama as having a 'double face' that creates *both* empathy and distance, so that we not only identify with the 'other' but 'also deconstruct and interrogate the other's otherness, revealing and reengaging with it'. Here it seems then that while drama is clearly capable of generating authentic learning within the curriculum, it is simultaneously capable of producing learning that is active, reflective, critical, political and personal.

Activating future research possibilities

Having offered a geography of drama as revealed through the chapters of this book, this section now steps off into the unknown to consider its future characteristics and purposes. As noted above, we began this book by identifying the political and educational landscapes drama works within. Highlighted there were both constraints and possibilities that are *mostly* outside of our control. However, as researchers and practitioners, one powerful vehicle exists which has the potential to transport drama into new landscapes, that of research. To date and possibly even within this book, we have evidenced ourselves to be highly effective in generating and reporting research that is convincing for those who already appreciate and are able to take advantage of, the activating forces of drama. What we have not been so successful in doing, is converting this ever-increasing volume of material into an argument that convinces 'others' that drama's case for a more central pedagogical role is a strong one. In spite of our claims that drama creates agency and voice, it could be argued that our success in gaining these powers for the field itself have been at best patchy.

Set against this backdrop, we invited each authorial team to consider future research opportunities and in response, many interesting ideas were offered.

They include calls for research specific to the contexts, participants and purposes of their work. For example Neelands and Nelson call for research into 'the value of theatre and drama for exploring unequal power dynamics and facilitating student understanding of the socio-cultural obstacles they face in their lives'. Through such research, they hope that for the urban young in particular, a means for 'gaining what Freire called the vital knowledge which becomes solidarity' might be identified.

In the theatre context, Bundy, Ewing and Fleming call for further research that focuses on the 'relationship between theatre confidence, theatre literacy and how trust can enhance the transformative potential of being a spectator at a live event', while Dunn et al. suggest that the current emphasis on testing and international benchmarking of literacy means that now would be an ideal time for drama researchers to invest their energies into more longitudinal studies that examine its impact over time.

Others have suggested that future research should also look inward, that what is required is an interrogation of what it is that we already do. For example, as Gallagher and Yaman Ntelioglu ponder, 'does listening in the drama classroom simply reinforce our image of the Other?', while Chan wonders about the ongoing impact of what we do. She asks of her work in Hong Kong, 'When they step out of the drama classroom . . . how much of the impact of programs like these remain? Importantly too, how does the impact stand up against the grand narratives of social development that privilege economic growth over justice?' Winston also seeks an interrogation of what occurs in the drama classroom, but in his case, he seeks to understand in more detail the impact of our aesthetic considerations, considering and comparing the artistry of the drama educator to that of any other artist who 'works through live action performed in narrative time'. By using this approach, his aim is to bring the concept of beauty into the practice of research.

Saxton and Miller make different calls in relation to research, seeking to identify the implications for drama of the rapidly growing evidence emanating from the field of neuroscience. By considering scientific research of this kind, new and possibly critical insights into drama will almost certainly be achieved. Also critical will be the development of multi-site international studies (such as the one described here by Gallagher and Yaman Ntelioglu), where researchers in different regions of the world work collaboratively to generate findings that transcend local and national borders. In addition, large-scale, international and mixed method studies that have been collaboratively designed and similarly applied, will most surely be needed in order to generate the kind of data that education and community agencies increasingly value, for while drama practitioners should continue to generate exciting, small-scale research projects that impact positively on the participants and offer useful insights into a whole range of theoretical and practical aspects of our form, broadly based studies will also be needed in order to progress the field in the future. Is it time to collaborate and combine our energies to create research that draws upon diverse methods and approaches to create research that speaks to multiple audiences?

Another way forward, and one that is growing in popularity among drama researchers, is to ensure that participatory forms of research are privileged. In this volume, Sinclair and Kelman achieved powerful outcomes by inviting into the research process the young migrant and refugee artists and performers of one Melbourne based community theatre group. Through a process of collaborative reflective practice, these young people became metacognitive about the processes they were engaged in, using a methodological framework of formal reflection to create 'a culturally sensitive performance event where the goals transcended the immediate and personal, and pointed to a bigger picture of being and becoming'. Indeed, across many of the case studies and examples of practice outlined, invitations to engage simultaneously with the art and the researching of this art through reflection (Stinson and Piazzoli) appear to have been a key feature.

Is this the vehicle then that is capable of taking us into future territories – a pedagogy that not only engages its participants as learners, but also develops learner voice and agency through the explicit acknowledgement of reflection as and for research?

Activating the future – learning and learners

With this idea of reflective practice as being core to the future of drama, we turn now to the role drama might be able to play in supporting young people to activate their futures. In the same way that language and communication are rights, it may be that one of the most important responsibilities we share as individuals interested in drama education is to ensure that we apply this art form to imagine and enact new futures where narrowness is expanded and where an appreciation of creativity infiltrates new spaces and places. As our colleague Helen Nicholson (2011) so poetically suggests:

> In a modest way, the theatre can help imagine what the shape of [the future] might look like. If theatre is an interweaving of memory and liveness and learning is constructed in negotiation and dialogue, theatre education offers a powerful place to encounter the unexpected, to extend horizons of expectations and consider where we are positioned in the world. It is material and ephemeral, and recognizes that meaning is made not only in the symbols, metaphors and narratives of drama, but between spaces and places, in the gaps and the silences of reflection as well as in the movement of and activity of practice (p. 214).

The power to know and understand our world through theatre that Nicholson glimpses here should not be the privilege of a few. Through high-quality practice and research, where methodologies that suit the needs of our community and not just the needs of the academies are pursued, drama practitioners have the chance to re-imagine learning and in so doing, transform the educational landscape to create new spaces where young people can become active co-constructors of the future.

In these spaces, created when drama educators of all types including actors, directors, playwrights, dramaturges, workshop facilitators and teachers work together with learners positioned as participants, players, audiences, and performers, opportunities are created to access what Suzanne Langer identified so long ago as a 'virtual future'. For her, drama offers the chance for 'abstraction' as an 'act, which springs from the past, but is directed toward the future, and is always great with things to come' (Langer 1953, p. 306). By playing with ambiguity and instability, drama provides rich opportunities for individuals to re-imagine their futures. As Neelands (2010) comments:

> In acting 'differently', in acting 'as-if' the world was otherwise, students may be encouraged to discover that at personal, local, national and international levels they are free to negotiate, translate and therefore transform the problem of identities and the problem of the representation of identities.

As the participant's perceptions of themselves and their relationship to world changes, so too might the world in their imaginations. This shift in the imagining of children and young people is critical, for it is only possible to achieve change when a new reality can be imagined. For example, through drama, the student who has been bullied might be able to use the power of role to envisage herself as a hero, the popular boy can gain an understanding of what unpopularity might feel like and thus take steps to include, and the individualist may be given the chance to work authentically with a team for the first time and may thus achieve new motivation to share. These exercises in empathy are therefore opportunities to simultaneously enact and create the future. Within this work though, what must always be kept uppermost in our minds is the need to avoid singular notions of 'preferred futures'. These are at best utopian, and at worst marginalizing for they fail to take account of the multiple perspectives individuals hold on the world. As O'Connor's chapter so clearly identified, your identity as a troll or a billy-goat will greatly influence not only your views about the present, but also inevitably about the future.

Across this process of actively co-creating their multiple futures, young people will inevitably need the support and scaffolding of adults. Facer (2012) argues such support should provide them with opportunities to engage in futures discourses. Fortunately, the geography of drama seems to offer this necessary scaffolding, giving young people a means to become active 'designers of our social futures' (NLG 1996, p. 88). Where so often they are offered pedagogies of passivity and individualism, educators must find ways to support young people as they co-create the future landscapes they want to inhabit. To do this, learning environments free from personal or cultural risk, where collaboration is characterized by critical dialogue and listening, where engagement, emotion and empathy are not only valued but are also in fact key goals and purposes for learning, *and* where learning activates activism need to be applied. Is drama, capable of all of this? We think so.

References

Courtney, R. (1980), *The Dramatic Curriculum*. London: Heinemann.

Facer, K. (2012), 'Taking the 21st century seriously: Young people, education and socio-technical futures'. *Oxford Review of Education*, 38, (1): 97–113.

Freire, P. (1998), *Pedagogy of Freedom*. New York: Rowman & Littlefield.

Hurley, E. (2010), *Theatre and Feeling*. New York: Palgrave Macmillan.

Langer, S. (1953), *Feeling and Form: A Theory of Art*. New York: Scribner.

Neelands, J. (2009), 'Acting together: Ensemble as a democratic process in art and life'. *Research in Drama Education*, 14, (2): 173–89.

Neelands, J. (2010), 'Mirror, dynamo or lens? Drama, children and social change', in P. O'Connor (ed.), *Creating Democratic Citizenship through Drama Education: The Writings of Jonothan Neelands*. Stoke: Trentham Books.

New London Group (1996), 'A pedagogy of multiliteracies: Designing social futures'. *Harvard Educational Review*, 66, (1): 60–92.

Nicholson, H. (2011), *Theatre, Education and Performance*. Basingstoke, UK: Palgrave Macmillan.

O'Toole, J. and Stinson, M. (2009), 'Pasts, presents and futures: Which door next?', in J. O'Toole, M. Stinson and T. Moore (eds), *Drama and Curriculum – A Giant at the Door*. Dordrecht, Netherlands: Springer, pp. 193–208.

Index

312

Index

Lightning Source UK Ltd.
Milton Keynes UK
UKOW05n1534100214

226214UK00006B/41/P